AN A–Z OF
FAMOUS EXPRESS TRAINS

JULIAN HOLLAND

AN A–Z OF
FAMOUS EXPRESS TRAINS

JULIAN HOLLAND

AN ILLUSTRATED TRIP DOWN MEMORY LANE

D&C
David and Charles

CONTENTS

INTRODUCTION

Naming trains reached its peak in the early British Railways era during the 1950s but the practice started as early as 1848 when the all-important 'The Irish Mail' between Euston and Holyhead first received its name. The Anglo-Irish mail traffic had previously been carried by stage coach along Telford's A5 road until the opening of the Chester & Holyhead Railway in that year. Next to receive a name was the 'Special Scotch Express' between King's Cross and Edinburgh in 1862 – this train was the forerunner of the famous 'The Flying Scotsman' which received its name in 1924. The Great Western Railway named its premier express between London and Cornwall the 'Cornish Riviera Limited' in 1904, and by the outbreak of the Second World War this train was carrying slip coaches and through coaches to many West Country resorts. During the 1920s and

▲ The 1950s saw a plethora of named trains introduced by British Railways and to mark them out from the crowd headboards were attached to the front of the locomotive. The later Western Region examples were works of art in themselves – featuring the linked crests of England and Wales the locomotive headboard of the 'Cambrian Coast Express' is seen here attached to 'Manor' Class 4-6-0 No. 7803 'Barcote Manor' on 28 March 1959. Large sums of money are now paid by collectors for these rare headboards.

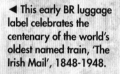

◄ This early BR luggage label celebrates the centenary of the world's oldest named train, 'The Irish Mail', 1848-1948.

1930s there was fierce rivalry, not only between the British 'Big Four' railway companies but also among railways worldwide, to lay claim to providing the fastest scheduled passenger service in the world. At the forefront was the Great Western Railway which in 1932 claimed the title of the 'World's Fastest Train' with its record-breaking 'Cheltenham Flyer' (the unofficial name for the 'Cheltenham Spa Express'). The introduction by the London & North Eastern Railway of streamlined steam locomotives in 1935 saw the debut of the non-stop 'The Silver Jubilee' between King's Cross and Newcastle. Britain's first streamlined train, this was soon followed by the London, Midland & Scottish Railway's 'The Coronation Scot' streamlined train between Euston and Glasgow in 1937.

The railways' publicity departments had a field day and graphic designers were soon turning out iconic and romantic posters advertising the new high-speed train services for businessmen and holidaymakers. Together with these posters, beautifully designed

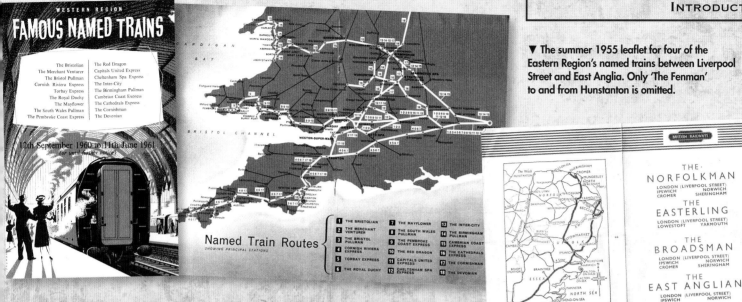

▲ The Western Region's winter 1960/61 leaflet and route map for their 18 named trains. While it includes the inter-regional 'The Devonian', it has omitted the 'Pines Express' which crossed its territory between Bath Green Park and Templecombe. Obviously the powers that be at Swindon and Paddington were desperate to hide the fact that they had completely controlled the northern half of the Somerset & Dorset Joint Railway since 1958!

luggage labels, restaurant car menus and fold-out leaflets describing the 'view from the window' all enticed travellers to travel on these opulent expresses.

The 1930s were heady days for these trains, ended only by the outbreak of the Second World War. Nationalisation of the railways in 1948 saw our run-down railways merged as one giant state-owned concern and within a few years the publicity departments of the newly created British Railways' regions were hard at work glamorising rail travel all over again by bringing back named trains. The late 1940s and early 1950s not only saw the reintroduction of some of the pre-war named trains but also the introduction of a plethora of new trains – ornate locomotive headboards,

publicity material, luggage labels, restaurant car menus and fold-out route guides were designed to lend an air of romanticism to these journeys which criss-crossed Britain into the 1960s. Sadly, this golden age of train travel was soon to end with the demise of steam haulage and the introduction of modern diesel and electric locomotives. In their early years the diesel locos still carried the all-important named train headboards but these were soon quietly forgotten as the railways entered a new age of uniformity. Today, apart from a 'Flying Scotsman' electric-hauled service between Edinburgh and King's Cross and a few names that linger on only in timetables, the golden age of named trains is just a distant memory.

THE STARS OF THE SHOW
This book would not be complete without mentioning the stars of the show – the locomotives that hauled these famous named trains also feature in all their glory. From Collett's 'Kings' and 'Castles' on the expresses to and from Paddington; Stanier's mighty 'Princess Royal' and 'Coronation' Pacifics on the West Coast Main Line; Bulleid's innovative 'Merchant Navy', 'Battle of Britain' and 'West Country' Pacifics on Southern routes; Gresley's unforgettable 'A3' and 'A4' Pacifics; Peppercorn's 'A1' Pacifics on the East Coast Main Line; to Riddles' BR Standard locos operating across the network – and, for the modern traction fan, even diesels – full details of each locomotive are given where they appear in this book.

THE ABERDONIAN

LONDON (KING'S CROSS) TO ABERDEEN

Inaugurated in 1927, 'The Aberdonian' had its origin in the famous East Coast express of 1895 that raced its West Coast rival for the fastest overnight service from London to Aberdeen. In the end the West Coast route won but not without some speedy high jinks by the two rivals up to the finishing post at Kinnaber Junction north of Montrose. Operated by the Great Northern Railway, the North Eastern Railway and the North British Railway, the lightly loaded East Coast train (weighing only 105 tons) managed to cover the 523.7 miles in 8hrs 40min on the night of 21/22 August and deposited its passengers at Aberdeen Joint station at the unearthly hour of 4.40am. By mutual agreement the racing was stopped and over the following years the evening departure from King's Cross of the Aberdeen sleeper became heavier and longer with the inclusion of additional sleeping cars to Perth, Inverness and Fort William. With the inclusion of a dining car the train was weighing in at around 500 tons by 1939 and was hauled over the winding and heavily graded section north of Edinburgh by Gresley's powerful new Class 'P2' 2-8-2 locomotives. During the summer the train ran in two sections with the Inverness and Fort William portion being named the 'Highlandman' and the main Aberdeen portion also conveying a sleeping car for Lossiemouth.

▲ The locomotive nameboard of 'The Aberdonian' featured the coats of arms of the cities of London and Aberdeen.

▶ Photographs of 'The Aberdonian' in steam days are quite rare due to the train's evening departure from King's Cross. Here the northbound express of 'blood-and-custard' coaches roars through Hadley Wood station behind Peppercorn 'A1' 4-6-2 No. 60123 'H. A. Ivatt' in the 1950s. The loco was the first of its class to be withdrawn following damage sustained in a collision at Offord on the East Coast Main Line in 1962.

During the Second World War 'The Aberdonian' was one of only four British named trains to hold on to its title, but even heavier loads and wartime conditions took their toll on the schedules, with 13½ hours being allowed for the down journey to Aberdeen. There were only slow improvements in the schedules after the war and by 1960 the down train left King's Cross at 7.30pm and arrived in Aberdeen at 7.19am the next morning; the up train fared slightly better with an 8.20pm departure from Aberdeen arriving at King's Cross at 7.47am the next morning. However, the introduction of the powerful 'Deltic' diesels in 1961 soon saw a marked improvement with nearly an hour being shaved off journey times. In the early 1970s the late evening departure from King's Cross

ABERDEEN

via
Darlington	Stonehaven
Newcastle	Edinburgh
Kirkcaldy	Dundee
Arbroath	Montrose

BR21717/31

▲ A coach window sticker for the daytime 'The Aberdonian' in the days of diesel haulage.

and Aberdeen was renamed the 'Night Aberdonian' and the title 'The Aberdonian' was bestowed on a daytime service between the two cities. While the title 'Night Aberdonian' was dropped in the autumn of 1982 the introduction of InterCity High Speed Train (HST) 125s in 1978 saw a rapid acceleration of the daytime service, in 1982 taking over the 10am departure slot from King's Cross held for years by the 'Flying Scotsman' with a journey time of just under 7½ hours for both the up and down services. The title 'The Aberdonian' was dropped in 1987. In 2012 the 10am departure from King's Cross takes just over seven hours to reach Aberdeen.

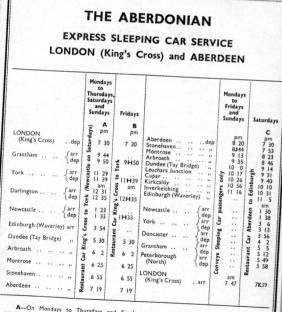

THE ABERDONIAN
EXPRESS SLEEPING CAR SERVICE
LONDON (King's Cross) and ABERDEEN

		Mondays to Thursdays, Saturdays and Sundays A pm	Fridays B pm			Mondays to Fridays and Sundays	Saturdays C pm
LONDON (King's Cross) ..dep		7 30	7 30	Aberdeen .. ..dep		8 20	7 30
				Stonehaven.. ..		8J44	7 53
				Montrose		9 13	8 23
Grantham .. { arr		9 44		Arbroath		9 35	8 46
{ dep		9 50	9H50	Dundee (Tay Bridge)		10 0	9 14
York .. .. { arr		11 29		Leuchars Junction ..		10 17	9 31
{ dep		11 39	11H39	Cupar		10 26	9 40
		am	am	Kirkcaldy		10 56	10 10
Darlington .. { arr		12 31		Inverkeithing ..		11 16	10 31
{ dep		12 35	12H35	Edinburgh (Waverley)			11 5
						am	am
Newcastle .. { arr		1 23		Newcastle .. { arr			1 30
{ dep		1 33	1H33	{ dep			1 38
				York .. .. { arr			3 6
Edinburgh (Waverley) arr		3 54		{ dep			3 13
				Doncaster .. { arr			3 56
Dundee (Tay Bridge) ..		5 30	5 30	{ dep			4 2
Arbroath		6 2	6 2	Grantham .. { arr			5 5
Montrose		6 25	6 25	{ dep			5 12
				Peterborough { arr			5 49
Stonehaven		6 55	6 55	(North) { dep			5 58
Aberdeen		7 19	7 19	LONDON (King's Cross) ..arr		am 7 47	7K39

Column notes (vertical): Restaurant Car King's Cross to York (Newcastle on Saturdays) | Restaurant Car King's Cross to York | Conveys Sleeping Car passengers only | Restaurant Car Aberdeen to Edinburgh

A—On Mondays to Thursdays and Sundays conveys Through Carriages and Sleeping accommodation King's Cross to Fort William (arr 10 12 am)
B—Conveys Through Carriage and Sleeping accommodation King's Cross to Fort William (arr 10 12 am)
C—Conveys Through Carriage and Sleeping accommodation Fort William (dep 2 56 pm) to King's Cross.
H—Calls to take up passengers only
J—Calls by request only
K—Passengers arriving London (King's Cross) in Sleeping Cars may remain in the cars until 8 0 am

Seats are reservable in advance for passengers travelling from London (King's Cross), also from Aberdeen on Saturdays only, on payment of a fee of 2s. 0d. per seat
For particulars of Sleeping Berth charges, etc., see page 35

◀ The winter 1960/61 timetable for 'The Aberdonian'.

ATLANTIC COAST EXPRESS

LONDON (WATERLOO) TO TORRINGTON, ILFRACOMBE, BUDE, PADSTOW AND PLYMOUTH

Until the Great Western Railway opened its shorter route from Paddington to Plymouth (via Westbury and Castle Cary) in 1904 there was immense competition between that company and the rival London & South Western Railway to provide the fastest service between the two cities. The latter's 11am departure from Waterloo to Plymouth was the forerunner of what became known as the 'Atlantic Coast Express', which by 1927 under Southern Railway management contained through carriages to many destinations in Devon and North Cornwall. The name was selected in a competition organised by SR among its employees, the winner being a guard from Woking.

Trains between Waterloo and Exeter had always been forced to stop at Salisbury following a serious derailment at the station in 1906. It was here that locos were usually changed but with the introduction of the 'Lord Nelson' 4-6-0s in 1927 through running became the order of the day.

However, due to the lack of water troughs on the SR, the Salisbury stop continued to be included until the end of steam to take on water and a crew change. By the outbreak of the Second World War the down 'ACE' consisted of through coaches to Sidmouth, Exmouth, Ilfracombe, Torrington, Bude, Padstow and Plymouth.

Halted by the Second World War, the 'ACE' resumed service soon after the end of the war with Bulleid's new 'Merchant Navy' Pacifics in charge of the heavily loaded train as far as Exeter. Beyond this the various portions were taken on to their destinations behind his new 'Battle of Britain/West Country' Class light Pacifics. By 1952 the train had become so

▶ Complete with acetate window, this delightful book published by the Southern Railway described the journey, as seen from the compartment window, of the 'Atlantic Coast Express' from Waterloo to North Devon and North Cornwall. It was written by the celebrated travel writer S. P. B. Mais with 'whimsical' illustrations by Anna Zinkeisen.

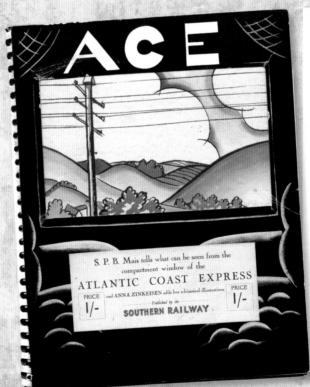

ACE

S. P. B. Mais tells what can be seen from the compartment window of the
ATLANTIC COAST EXPRESS
and ANNA ZINKEISEN adds her whimsical illustrations
PRICE 1/- PRICE 1/-
Published by the
SOUTHERN RAILWAY

A.C.E.

It has often been said by authorities on England's countryside that the best way of seeing the country is by train. This is largely because the windows of a railway carriage, except in cuttings, are higher than the fences which guard the lines. On the other hand, long stretches of the roads of England are confined by houses or high hedges in such a way as to prevent the country beyond them being seen.

Frequently the Southern Railway have been asked whether they provide books which tell the traveller what can be seen from the carriage windows.

As it was thought that there was more need for this on long journeys through the less inhabited parts of the country, a first attempt has been made for the route covered by the Southern Railway's famous train, the "Atlantic Coast Express," which journeys between Waterloo and the West of England.

Mr. S. P. B. Mais and Miss Anna Zinkeisen have therefore collaborated to tell you by word and picture some of the history of the countryside which you see from the carriage window.

You will notice that the places mentioned in this book are printed either in blue or in red. This is done for a special purpose. The names in red are of places on the down side of the line, that is the left-hand side of the train as you leave London and face the West; the names in blue are on the other side, the up side.

The chief purpose of the book is to bring to life the towns, country and counties you will pass through, but you will discover it achieves more than that. You have only to take the book out of your bookshelf, turn its pages and you will find yourself again among the green fields, farmhouses, tors and valleys or renewing an acquaintance with Sir Francis Drake, Reynolds, Cromwell or Henry VIII. Your holiday will have become more than a fleeting moment of the year: it will be always with you in a tangible and satisfying form.

On your journey by the "A.C.E." you, no doubt, often wished that you could have lingered a while to explore the country you were passing through. Mr. S. P. B. Mais did; and has recorded the result of his ramblings in a booklet entitled "Let's get out here." It contains a full description, with maps and photographs, of 26 walks that can be made from different points on the route of the "A.C.E." The price is only 6d., and it is on sale at all station bookstalls.

opular with holidaymakers that it departed rom Waterloo in two separate portions. During ts peak in the late 1950s extra relief trains, eaded by the rebuilt 'Merchant Navy' locos, vere also added to cope with the amount of traffic; even as late as the summer of 1963 here were five daily departures from Waterloo: 0.15am with through coaches to Ilfracombe nd Torrington; 10.35am with through coaches o Padstow and Bude; 10.45am to Seaton with through coaches to Lyme Regis; 11.00am with through coaches to Torrington and lfracombe; and 11.15am with through coaches

▲ 'Merchant Navy' Class 4-6-2 No. 35030 'Elder Dempster Lines' is the centre of attention for this young trainspotter at Clapham Junction as it heads through with the down 'Atlantic Coast Express' in the early 1960s. The last of its class, the loco was built at Eastleigh in 1949, rebuilt in 1958 and withdrawn in July 1967.

THE ATLANTIC COAST EXPRESS
By S. P. B. MAIS

MY object in this book is quite simple. It is to make you look out of the carriage window. You may object to this that you can't possibly read a book and look out of the window at the same time. Well, here for once, you can. This book will help you to look out of the window.

You may say that you see no point in looking out of the carriage window because you know every point of interest already.

If you're so sure about that I would ask you to spot the photographs of scenes taken from the carriage window that are included in this book and if you can accurately place them all you needn't worry to read any more.

You may say that you won't look out of the carriage window because there is nothing particular to see. May I say, Sir, that I have travelled through many countries at many seasons of the year, but I have never been more moved by the beauty of what I have seen from the carriage window than I was on that golden early morning on the last day of December when I looked down from the moor bathed in sunlight, with fields all about me white with rime, on two sinuous snake-like ribbons of white billowy mist that traced out the course of the rivers Tavy and Tamar, five hundred feet below the railway line. It was as majestic as Switzerland.

Nothing to see ?

to Plymouth, Padstow and Bude.

Timings were continually improved until 1963, when the 171¾-mile journey from Waterloo to Exeter Central was scheduled to take only 2hrs 56min – this included stops at Salisbury and Sidmouth Junction.

Although increased car ownership in the early 1960s can partly be blamed for the downfall of the 'ACE', the other contributing factor came in 1963 when all lines west of Salisbury came under Western Region control. Anxious to stamp their authority on their erstwhile competitors, the end was swift and painful. The last 'ACE' ran on 5 September 1964, and, soon, downgraded 'Warship' diesel hydraulics took over services on what would now become a secondary route: much of the line west of Salisbury was singled and branch lines to seaside destinations in Devon and North Cornwall, the latter much loved by the poet John Betjeman, were all closed.

BELFAST BOAT EXPRESS

MANCHESTER VICTORIA TO HEYSHAM

Originally introduced by the London Midland & Scottish Railway, the 'Belfast Boat Express' has the dubious honour of being the last steam-hauled named train on British Railways. Connecting with steamers to and from Belfast at Heysham Harbour, the last down steam-hauled train left Manchester Victoria at 8.55pm on 4 May 1968 behind Carnforth shed's Stanier 'Black 5' 4-6-0 No. 45342 – the next day the last steam-hauled up train left Heysham at 6.15am behind sister engine No. 45025. The train continued to run with diesel haulage until the withdrawal of the ferry service in April 1975.

► The headboard of the down 'Belfast Boat Express' is attached to Stanier 'Black 5' 4-6-0 No. 45342 at Manchester Victoria on 4 May 1968. This was the very last working of the steam-hauled down train.

▼ The end of an era – Stanier 'Black 5' 4-6-0 No. 45025 heads out of Preston on 5 May 1968 with the very last up 'Belfast Boat Express' for Manchester Victoria.

BLUE PULLMANS (WESTERN REGION)

LONDON (PADDINGTON) TO BIRMINGHAM AND WOLVERHAMPTON (LOW LEVEL)

LONDON (PADDINGTON) TO BRISTOL

LONDON (PADDINGTON) TO CARDIFF AND SWANSEA

LONDON (PADDINGTON) TO OXFORD

Apart from the steam-hauled 'South Wales Pullman' which was introduced in 1955, there were no other Pullman car trains on the Western Region of British Railways until 1960 when new streamlined diesel-electric Pullman trains were introduced between Paddington and Bristol, and also Paddington and Wolverhampton (Low Level).

Back in 1954 the British Transport Commission had become the proud owners of the British Pullman Car Company and a year later the British Railways Modernisation Programme was published – one of its main objectives was the replacement of steam by diesel power. A committee was soon set up to look into the introduction of diesel-hauled express passenger trains and in 1957 it was announced that the Metropolitan-Cammell Carriage & Wagon Company

▲ The down Paddington to Wolverhampton (Low Level) 'Blue Pullman' speeds through the Oxfordshire countryside near the site of the closed Blackthorn station in August 1965.

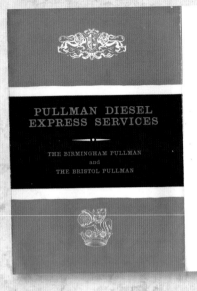

PULLMAN DIESEL EXPRESS SERVICES

THE BIRMINGHAM PULLMAN
and
THE BRISTOL PULLMAN

PULLMAN DIESEL EXPRESS SERVICES

THE BRITISH TRANSPORT COMMISSION, as part of the Modernisation Plan, has decided to introduce de-luxe Pullman Diesel trains between important business centres.

On the Western Region, commencing 12th September, 1960, new trains, catering for First and Second Class passengers, will run between Wolverhampton (Low Level), Birmingham (Snow Hill), Solihull and Leamington Spa (General) and London (Paddington), also between Bristol (Temple Meads) and Bath Spa and Paddington. As far as practicable, their schedules have been designed to meet the travel requirements of the business executive.

Built at the Birmingham Works of the Metropolitan-Cammell Carriage & Wagon Company, Ltd., on the multiple-unit principle with diesel-electric traction, these new Pullman trains are of an entirely new design, incorporating air-conditioning and many recent technical developments in vehicle and bogie construction.

The vehicles are of the saloon, centre vestibule type, and special consideration has been given to the exterior styling and to the interior décor.

Meals and refreshments will be served throughout the trains, to the traditional high Pullman standards.

THE BIRMINGHAM PULLMAN

MONDAYS TO FRIDAYS ONLY

WOLVERHAMPTON & BIRMINGHAM TO LONDON

Wolverhampton	(Low Level)	dep.	7. 0 a.m.	
Birmingham	(Snow Hill)		7.30 a.m.	2.30 p.m.
Solihull			7.40 a.m.	
Leamington Spa	(General)		8. 0 a.m.	2.55 p.m.
London	(Paddington)	arr.	9.35 a.m.	4.25 p.m.

LONDON TO BIRMINGHAM & WOLVERHAMPTON

London	(Paddington)	dep.	12.10 p.m.	4.50 p.m.
Leamington Spa	(General)	arr.	1.34 p.m.	6.19 p.m.
Solihull				6.44 p.m.
Birmingham	(Snow Hill)		2. 5 p.m.	6.55 p.m.
Wolverhampton	(Low Level)			7.20 p.m.

THE BRISTOL PULLMAN

MONDAYS TO FRIDAYS ONLY

BRISTOL TO LONDON

Bristol	(Temple Meads)	dep.	7.45 a.m.	12.30 p.m.
Bath Spa			*	12.45 p.m.
London	(Paddington)	arr.	9.35 a.m.	2.25 p.m.

LONDON TO BRISTOL

London	(Paddington)	dep.	10. 5 a.m.	4.55 p.m.
Bath Spa		arr.	11.40 a.m.	*
Bristol	(Temple Meads)	..	12. 0 noon	6.45 p.m.

*Via Badminton

LIMITED ACCOMMODATION
AIR CONDITIONED · SOUND INSULATED
MEALS & REFRESHMENTS SERVED AT EVERY SEAT

of Birmingham would build five high-speed diesel multiple-unit (DMU) sets to be introduced in 1958 on the London Midland Region between London St Pancras and Manchester Central, and on the Western Region between London Paddington and Bristol and Birmingham.

At that time the design of these luxurious trains was fairly ground-breaking – the classic Pullman livery of brown and cream was replaced by blue (known as 'Nanking blue') and white with a grey roof; the passenger coaches were fitted with double glazing, air conditioning and sumptuous seating, and passengers were served at their tables by staff dressed in matching blue uniforms. Sporting the Pullman Car Company's crest on the

▲ The down 'Birmingham Blue Pullman' halts at Birmingham Snow Hill station en route for Wolverhampton (Low Level) in March 1961.

FARES

From	To	First Class (Ordinary)		Second Class (Ordinary)		Supplementary Charges (single journeys)	
		Single	Return	Single	Return	1st	2nd

Second Class Saloon

◄ The BR leaflet for the inaugural 'The Birmingham Pullman' and 'The Bristol Pullman', 12 September 1960.

nose, the streamlined power cars at each end of the train were each fitted with 1,000hp North British Locomotive/ MAN diesel engines driving electric transmission, with a top speed of 90mph. The two London Midland Region sets were six-car formation (this included the two non-accommodating power cars) providing 132 first class seats; the three Western Region sets were eight-car formations, providing 108 first class and 120 second class seats.

Following delays caused by extended trials and modifications, the first Blue Pullmans entered revenue-earning service on the LMR between St Pancras and Manchester on 4 July 1960 (see 'The Midland Pullman'). Blue Pullman services on the Western Region between Paddington and Bristol and Paddington and Wolverhampton (Low

◄ Standing in for a failed 'Blue Pullman', 'Western' class diesel hydraulic D1046 'Western Marquis' heads through Acocks Green on the outskirts of Birmingham with the substitute rake of normal Pullman coaches on a cold day in January 1963. Built at Crewe in December 1962 the loco was scrapped at Swindon in November 1976.

► A down 'Bristol Blue Pullman' speeds through Box station in the early 1960s while a single car diesel unit calls at the station with a local stopping train.

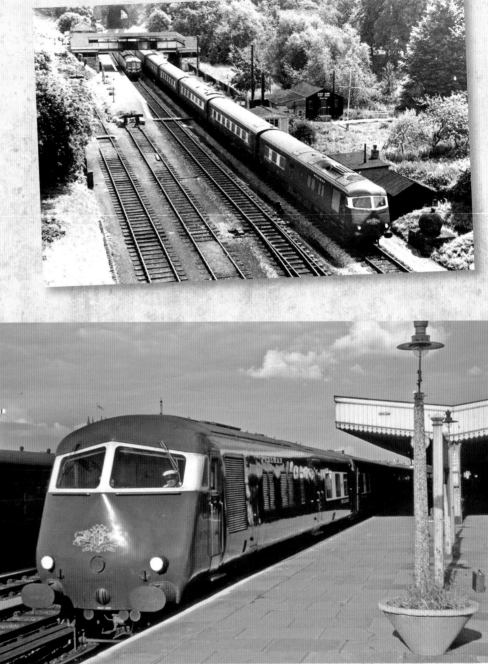

Level) commenced on 12 September 1960. An additional service was introduced between Paddington and Swansea in the summer of 1961. A steam-hauled (and later diesel-hauled) set of traditional brown and cream Pullman cars was always kept in reserve at Old Oak Common. Following the completion of electrification between Euston and Manchester Piccadilly the two LMR sets were transferred to the Western Region in March 1967, which allowed the introduction of an additional service to Bristol and a new service to Oxford. However, the introduction of High Speed Trains on the WR led to the demise of Blue Pullman services with the last train, an enthusiasts' special, running on 5 May 1973. None have been preserved.

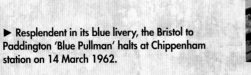

► Resplendent in its blue livery, the Bristol to Paddington 'Blue Pullman' halts at Chippenham station on 14 March 1962.

THE BON ACCORD

GLASGOW (BUCHANAN STREET) TO ABERDEEN

Introduced by the London Midland & Scottish Railway in 1937, the 'Bon Accord' was named after the motto of the city of Aberdeen which, in English, translates as 'good agreement'. ('Bon Accord' was also the name of an unfortunate Aberdeen football team that in 1885 suffered the worst defeat (36-0) in any British senior football match!) The train was one of four named express trains that once ran between Glasgow (Buchanan Street) and Aberdeen along the former Caledonian Railway's route via Forfar. Of these four the 'Bon Accord' and the 'The Saint Mungo' were timed to cover the 153 miles in three hours (Mondays to Fridays only). With a load of only seven coaches and a restaurant car the LMS 'Jubilee' 4-6-0s usually employed put up a spirited performance leaving Glasgow at 10.05am and running non-stop to Perth. The train then ran non-stop to Stonehaven before arriving in Aberdeen at 1.05pm. The return run had the same two intermediate stops, arriving back in Glasgow at 6.20pm.

The service was suspended during the Second World War but reinstated in 1949 with an early morning departure from Aberdeen and an early afternoon return from Glasgow. As with all of the Glasgow to Aberdeen three-hour expresses, the 'Bon Accord' saw Gresley 'A4' haulage from 1962 until 1966 following the displacement of those famous streamlined locomotives ended the East Coast Main Line by 'Deltic' diesels. The 'A4' swansong ended on 3 September 1966 with diesels taking over until closure of the route from Stanley Junction to Kinnaber Junction via Forfar on 4 September 1967. Glasgow's Buchanan Street closed two months later and the train was then diverted to run to and from Queen Street, eventually losing its title in May 1968.

◀ Class 'A4' 4-6-2 No. 60009 'Union of South Africa' heads the up 'Bon Accord' from Aberdeen to Glasgow (Buchanan Street) through Bridge of Allan in June 1964. The loco was built at Doncaster in 1937 and withdrawn in June 1966. It has since been preserved.

THE BOURNEMOUTH BELLE

LONDON (WATERLOO) TO BOURNEMOUTH (WEST)

Pullman cars had been used on the London & South Western Railway since the late nineteenth century. These were single cars attached to scheduled services and they had gone out of fashion by 1911. However, other railway companies in southern England, such as the London Brighton & South Coast Railway's 'Pullman Limited' and the 'Southern Belle' between Victoria and Brighton, were having more success. These all-Pullman trains became part of the Southern Railway in the 1923 Grouping and their success led the company to experiment with a similar train between Waterloo and Bournemouth. The 'Bournemouth Belle' first ran in 1931 but operated only on summer Sundays until 1936 when it became a regular daily working and, apart from its suspension during the Second World War, continued to run until its demise in 1967.

▲ Headed by 'Merchant Navy' 4-6-2 No. 35022 'Holland-America Line', the down 'The Bournemouth Belle' nears the end of its journey as it passes Pokesdown west of Christchurch on 13 September 1964. The loco was built at Eastleigh in 1948, rebuilt in 1956, withdrawn in May 1966 and is now awaiting preservation.

▲ The stylish leaflet issued by British Railways in 1951 for 'The Bournemouth Belle' Pullman train.

◄ Tickets please! Last minute ticket inspection for 'The Bournemouth Belle' passengers at Waterloo in 1965.

▼ The summer 1953 leaflet and timetable for 'The Bournemouth Belle'.

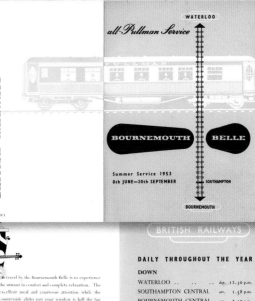

In its pre-war years the 'Belle' was usually hauled by a 'Lord Nelson' 4-6-0 and travelled non-stop between Waterloo and Southampton before calling at Bournemouth Central and terminating at Bournemouth West. Following the end of the war the train was reinstated in 1946 but this time it was hauled by one of Bulleid's new 'Merchant Navy' Class 4-6-2s. So popular was the train that it often extended to 12 carriages with a total weight of around 500 tons, a weight just within the 'Merchant Navy's' excellent capabilities.

By 1963 the 79¼ miles between Waterloo and Southampton Central were being covered in 1hr 21min, with arrival at Bournemouth Central exactly two hours after departure from London – a leisurely average speed of 54mph for the 108-mile journey. Bournemouth West station closed on 6 September 1965 after which the 'Bournemouth Belle' started or terminated its journey at Bournemouth Central. Steam clung to life on the route until the summer of 1967 providing the 'Merchant Navy' locos with their swansong. The 'Belle', for the final few months diesel-hauled, last ran on 9 July when third-rail electrification was switched on.

◄ A foreign invader – ex-LNER 'V2' Class 2-6-2 No. 60893 heads the down 'The Bournemouth Belle' at Bournemouth (Central) in May 1953. This and other 'foreign' locomotives were temporarily lent to the Southern Region following a major crank axle failure on one of Bulleid's 'Merchant Navy' Class locomotives, after which the whole class was temporarily withdrawn.

▲ Eagerly watched by some young trainspotters, 'Merchant Navy' Class 4-6-2 No. 35029 'Ellerman Lines' gets ready to leave Waterloo with the down 'The Bournemouth Belle' in the summer of 1964. The loco was built at Eastleigh in 1949, rebuilt in 1959 and withdrawn in September 1966. It is now on show as a sectioned exhibit at the National Railway Museum in York.

◄ The up 'The Bournemouth Belle' gets ready to leave Bournemouth (West) station behind 'Merchant Navy' Class 4-6-2 No. 35017 'Belgian Marine' on 15 September 1964. The loco was built at Eastleigh in 1945, rebuilt in 1957 and withdrawn in July 1966.

BRIGHTON BELLE

LONDON (VICTORIA) TO BRIGHTON

Pullman cars were introduced by the London, Brighton & South Coast Railway in 1875. Six years later the company introduced the first all-Pullman train in the UK, the 'Pullman Limited', between London Victoria and Brighton. At the beginning of the twentieth century the company changed the livery of all its coaches, including the Pullmans, to the now familiar brown umber and cream. This colour scheme was soon used on all Pullman coaches throughout Britain, including the three new 35-ton 12-wheel vehicles introduced on the LBSCR service.

The LBSCR introduced a new Pullman train between Victoria and Brighton in 1908. Named the 'Southern Belle', this train made two returns each way on weekdays, taking exactly 60 minutes for the 50½-mile journey. It continued to operate as a steam-hauled service until 1933 when the London to Brighton line was electrified using third-rail pick-up. Three five-car all-Pullman electric multiple units (EMUs) then took over and the service was renamed the 'Brighton Belle' in 1934. In common with many other Pullman coaches the non-driving cars all received female names such as 'Hazel', 'Doris', 'Audrey', 'Vera', Gwen'

▲ A pre-war postcard depicting the 'Brighton Belle' at speed in the Kentish countryside.

▶ The stylish summer 1951 leaflet and timetable for the 'Brighton Belle'.

▶ The summer 1953 leaflet and timetable for the 'Brighton Belle'.

▲ The 'Brighton Belle' speeds through Burgess Hill in October 1963.

and 'Mona'. The service was suspended during the Second World War but reinstated in 1946. By the early 1960s the train was operating three return journeys each weekday and two on Sundays, but its age was beginning to show. Although refurbished and repainted in the BR Pullman livery of blue and grey, the ageing electric units were nearing the end of their life and despite patronage by the great and the good the service was withdrawn by British Railways on 30 April 1972.

Passengers travelling on the train on its last day were presented with a souvenir brochure and menu. The bar tariff makes interesting reading just one year after the introduction of decimalisation: ¼ bottle of champagne 75p; miniature Dubonnet 22p; miniature 'Royal Scot' whisky 37p; can of Guinness 15½p; can of Bulmer's Cider 12½p; small bottle ginger beer 8p. Those were the days!

Fortunately this wasn't the end for the 'Brighton Belle's' Pullman coaches as nearly all of them were saved – some ended up in pub gardens, two survived on the Keith & Dufftown Railway, while others were lovingly restored for use on the Venice Simplon Orient Express. Moves are now afoot to restore two of the driving cars and reunite them with their coaches so that the 'Brighton Belle' can run once again.

▲ Resplendent in the burnt umber and cream Pullman livery, the 'Brighton Belle' (made up of 5 BEL set No. 3051) makes its way past Preston Park depot on the outskirts of Brighton on 23 June 1968.

▲ By the end of its life the 1930s-style decor of the 'Brighton Belle' was a reminder of a bygone age.

Farewell to the
BRIGHTON BELLE

Sunday 30 April 1972

▶ The 'Brighton Belle' made its last run between London (Victoria) and Brighton on 30 April 1972.

Today is the end of an era.
The final chapter in an unforgettable episode of railway history. The last run of the Brighton Belle.
It's goodbye to Hazel, Doris, Audrey, Vera, Gwen and Mona. And their frilly lamp shades and old-world charm.
It's a sad day. We will miss them. But one can't survive on nostalgia.
Let us remember them fondly but realistically – as ladies in retirement.

▲ 1930s-style Pullman opulence was still alive on the 'Brighton Belle' as late as 1972.

◄ This charming sentiment about the 'Brighton Belle' was printed in the souvenir brochure handed out on the last day of services.

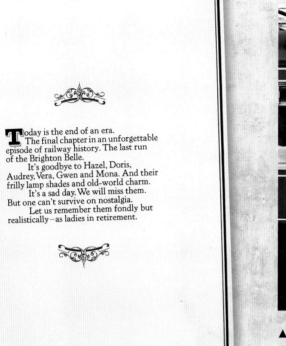

▲ Newly outshopped in the new blue and grey livery, the 'Brighton Belle' (5 BEL set No. 3052) calls at London Bridge station on 19 April 1969.

▲ The 'Brighton Belle' waits to depart for Brighton from Platform 13 at London's Victoria Station in the last year of its operation.

THE BRISTOLIAN

LONDON (PADDINGTON) TO BRISTOL (TEMPLE MEADS)

'The Bristolian' express was introduced in 1935 to mark the centenary of the Great Western Railway. Travelling non-stop between Paddington and Bristol, the lightweight train of only seven carriages was initially hauled by 'King' Class 4-6-0s and was timed to take 1hr 45min for the outward journey of 118¼ miles via Bath and for the return journey of 117½ miles via the Badminton cut-off. Before the Second World War, when the train was temporarily suspended, the up 'The Bristolian' left Paddington at 10am and the down train left Bristol at 4.30pm.

The service was reinstated in 1954 with an 8.45am departure from Paddington and a 4.30pm return from Bristol, thus giving businessmen more time for their meetings in Bristol. Still usually 'King'-hauled the timings were identical to pre-war days but the modification of some 'Castle' Class 4-6-0 locos soon brought some electrifying performances.

▲ The locomotive headboard of 'The Bristolian' carried the coats of arms of the cities of London and Bristol.

► The winter 1958/59 timetable for 'The Bristolian'.

Table 1

THE BRISTOLIAN
RESTAURANT CAR SERVICE
(LIMITED ACCOMMODATION)

LONDON
and
BRISTOL

in each direction in
1 hour 45 minutes

WEEK DAYS
(Mondays to Fridays)

					am
LONDON (Paddington)	..	..	..	..	dep 8A45
BRISTOL (Temple Meads)	..	..	..	..	arr 10 30

					pm
BRISTOL (Temple Meads)	..	..	..	..	dep 4A30
LONDON (Paddington)	..	..	..	..	arr 6 15

A—Seats can be reserved in advance on payment of a fee of 2s. 0d. per seat (see page 23).

► 'Blood-and-custard' days! Fitted with an alloy headboard, 'King' Class 4-6-0 No. 6019 'King Henry V' thunders past Thingley Junction south of Chippenham with the newly-reinstated down 'The Bristolian' in 1954. The loco was built at Swindon in 1928 and withdrawn in September 1962.

Built in 1949, 'Castle' Class No. 7018 'Dryslllwyn Castle' was the first of its class to be fitted with a double chimney and four-row superheater. Emerging from Swindon Works with its modifications in May 1956, the Bristol (Bath Road)-allocated loco was soon putting up 100mph performances on 'The Bristolian'. Soon other 'Castles' were similarly modified and the train occasionally completed the up journey via Badminton in under 94 minutes at an average speed of 75mph. The introduction of Swindon-built 'Warship' Class diesels in 1959 soon put an end to this steam spectacular – the last up steam-hauled train being hauled by No. 5085 'Evesham Abbey' on 12 June. The 'Warship' and later 'Western' Class diesel hydraulics carried on hauling the train until it lost its name in June 1965.

However, this famous train was not forgotten and in 2010 restored 'Castle' Class 4-6-0 No. 5043 'Earl of Mount Edgcumbe' hauled a commemorative 'The Bristolian' to mark the 175th anniversary of the GWR. Its return journey from Bristol to Paddington was completed in just under 1hr 50min, only five minutes slower than the 1950s schedule, arriving at its destination 45 minutes early – Messrs Churchward and Collett must have had smiles on their faces when looking down from GWR Heaven!

◄ Headed by a new 'Warship' Class diesel hydraulic, the up 'The Bristolian' accelerates past Stapleton Road Junction, north of Bristol Temple Meads, and begins the long ascent of Ashley Hill Bank to Filton Junction in 1959.

► 'Castle' Class 4-6-0 No. 7024 'Powis Castle' heads the down 'The Bristolian' near Pangbourne in the late 1950s. Built by British Railways at Swindon in 1949 this fine loco was withdrawn in February 1965.

THE BROADSMAN

LONDON (LIVERPOOL STREET) TO SHERINGHAM

'The Broadsman' was one of several short-lived named trains introduced by the newly formed Eastern Region of British Railways in the early years following nationalisation. Already served in the summer by through coaches carried on 'The Norfolkman' between Liverpool Street and Cromer, the seaside resort of Sheringham gained its own named train when 'The Broadsman' was introduced in 1950. The difference between these two trains was that 'The Norfolkman' had an early morning departure from Liverpool Street while 'The Broadsman' had a similarly timed departure from Sheringham. A restaurant car was conveyed between London and Cromer, (High station closed in 1954) whereupon trains were rerouted to Beach station where the Sheringham coaches were detached or attached.

The introduction of the new BR Standard 'Britannia' Class 4-6-2s between Liverpool Street and Norwich in 1951 brought a massive improvement to services, with journey times being slashed by 26 minutes. Over the following two years the service was speeded up again and despite stops at Diss, Stowmarket and Ipswich the down train was covering the 115 miles from Liverpool Street to Norwich in only two hours. The summer 1955 timetable shows the down train taking 73 minutes for the 68¾ miles to Ipswich (where there was a three-minute wait), then only 44 minutes for the 46¼ miles from there to Norwich. Sadly this steam spectacular did not last long as new English Electric Type 4 diesels were introduced in 1958 and the 'Britannias' soon dispersed to other parts of BR. The train was withdrawn in June 1962.

THE BROADSMAN

SHERINGHAM, CROMER, NORWICH, IPSWICH

AND

LONDON (Liverpool Street)

WEEKDAYS

	am			pm
Sheringham .. ..dep	7 33	London (Liverpool Street).. ..dep		3 30
West Runton.. .. .. .. ,,	7 38	Ipswich .. ..arr		4 51
Cromer (Beach) .. .. .. ,,	7 52	,, ...dep		4 54
North Walsham (Main).. .. ,,	8 12	Norwich (Thorpe) .. .. ..arr		5 40
Wroxham .. .. ,,	8 24	Salhouse .. .. ,,		6 0
Norwich (Thorpe).. .. .. ,,	8 45	Wroxham .. .. ,,		6 7
Ipswich .. ..arr	9 30	Worstead .. .. ,,		6 16
,, ...dep	9 32	North Walsham (Main) .. .. ,,		6 23
		Gunton.. .. .. ,,		6 34
London (Liverpool Street) arr	10 55	Cromer (Beach) .. .. .. ,,		6 48
		West Runton .. .. .. ,,		7 1
		Sheringham .. .. .. ,,		7 5

Restaurant Car available between Cromer and London (Liverpool Street).

Passengers travelling from Liverpool Street, Sheringham and Cromer (Beach) also from Norwich to Ipswich and Liverpool Street and Ipswich to Liverpool Street, by this service, can reserve seats in advance on payment of a fee of 2s. 0d. per seat.

▲ The early summer 1961 timetable for 'The Broadsman' express.

▲ The summer 1955 leaflet and timetable for the four named trains serving East Anglia.

◄ BR Standard 'Britannia' Class 4-6-2 No. 70002 'Geoffrey Chaucer' is serviced at the Liverpool Street depot before departing on 'The Broadsman' to Norwich in the mid-1950s. The loco was built at Crewe in 1951 and withdrawn in January 1967.

C THE CALEDONIAN

LONDON (EUSTON) TO GLASGOW (CENTRAL)

Introduced in 1957 by the London Midland and Scottish Regions of British Railways, 'The Caledonian' was the successor to the pre-war 'The Coronation Scot' streamlined train between London (Euston) and Glasgow (Central). With one intermediate stop at Carlisle the train left Glasgow at 8.30am and Euston at 4.15pm. Hauled by Stanier's de-streamlined 'Duchess' Pacifics, the train was ten minutes slower than the 'The Coronation Scot' even though it had one less coach. The average speed between Euston and Carlisle was just over 60mph and between Carlisle and Glasgow just under. An up test run in September 1957 saw the train arrive 37 minutes ahead of time at Euston but, despite this amazing performance, there was no change to the schedule. The train was one of very few to carry its name on a front headboard attached to the locomotive and also at the rear of the last coach.

The Caledonian

Restaurant Car Express

GLASGOW CENTRAL and LONDON EUSTON

MONDAYS TO FRIDAYS

(except Friday, 3rd and Monday, 6th August)

Glasgow Central	dep	am 8 30	London Euston	dep	pm 3 35
Carlisle		10 21	Stafford	"	5 54
Preston	arr	11 57	Carlisle	arr	9 6
Stafford		pm 1 24	Glasgow Central	"	11 0
London Euston		3 55			

Tariff for meals:—

	1st class s. d.	2nd class s. d.
Breakfast—full	8 6	8 6
—plain	5 0	5 0
Luncheon	13 6	12 6
Tea	3 6	3 6
Dinner	15 6	13 6

Seats may be reserved in advance for passengers travelling from London and Glasgow and Carlisle to London on payment of a fee of 2s. 0d. per seat.

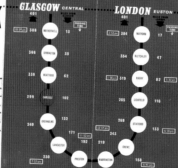

▲ The summer 1962 timetable for 'The Caledonian'.

◄ The leaflet and timetable issued by British Railways in 1957 for the new 'The Caledonian' express.

▶ Stanier's magnificence personified! 'Coronation' Class 4-6-2 No. 46240 'City of Coventry' waits to depart from Glasgow Central with the up 'The Caledonian' on 21 July 1959. The loco was built with a streamlined casing at Crewe in 1940, de-streamlined in 1947 and withdrawn in October 1964. One of the loco's nameplates is on display at Coventry station.

An additional 'The Caledonian' was introduced in 1958, this time leaving Euston at 7.45am and from Glasgow at 4pm. These were known as the 'Morning Caledonian' and the 'Afternoon Caledonian' respectively but were withdrawn less than a year later. With electrification of the West Coast Main Line gathering pace the train's schedule was slowed in 1962 and, by the following year, with English Electric Type 4 diesels now in control, three more stops had been added: in addition to Carlisle it now called at Stafford, Crewe and Wigan. The train was withdrawn at the end of the summer timetable in September 1964.

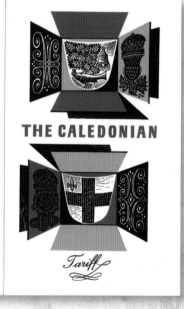

The Caledonian

You are sitting in *The Caledonian*, the latest named train on the West Coast Route between England and Scotland.

With *The Royal Scot* and *The Mid-day Scot* this train provides the limited stop daytime service between London Euston and Glasgow Central Stations, a distance of 401¼ miles.

Few journeys can in so short time give so varied a picture of Britain. Look out in particular for the wild beauty of the upper Lune Gorge south of Tebay and the upper reaches of the Clyde north of Beattock.

Do not miss the crossing of the Border by Gretna, just north of Carlisle, and your only view of the sea between London and Carlisle at Hest Bank near Lancaster. You get three more glimpses of the sea between Carlisle and Lockerbie and if the weather be clear you will see Skiddaw in the Lake District too.

Spare a glance, even, for the Manchester Ship Canal by Warrington no less than for the Lake hills west of Penrith. All these, and more, you can see in comfort from your seat in *The Caledonian*.

If you enjoy the comfort of *The Caledonian*, and are travelling again, we would remind you that all seats are reservable, and should be booked in advance, as the accommodation is limited.

THE CALEDONIAN

Tariff

▲ The stylish cover of the restaurant car tariff for 'The Caledonian' issued by British Railways in 1957.

▲ English Electric Type 4 (Class 40) diesel D319 passes through Ashton with the up 'The Caledonian' on 11 May 1961.

CAMBRIAN COAST EXPRESS

LONDON (PADDINGTON) TO ABERYSTWYTH AND PWLLHELI

A new weekday restaurant car express between Paddington and West Wales was introduced by the Great Western Railway in 1921, a year or so before it had taken control of the Cambrian Railways. With portions for Aberystwyth and Pwllheli that were attached or detached at Machynlleth, the train was officially named the 'Cambrian Coast Express' in 1927. Initially the train ran only on summer Fridays and Saturdays with a departure from Paddington at 10.10am and a fast run to Birmingham (Snow Hill) broken by a stop at Leamington. Motive power between Paddington and Wolverhampton (Low Level) was normally provided by a 'Castle' Class loco. At Wolverhampton the 'Castle' was taken off, to be replaced by a couple of 'Duke' Class 4-4-0s for the run to Welshpool and beyond, via the Abbey Foregate avoiding line at Shrewsbury. From 1938 the new 'Manor' Class 4-6-0s started to take over this leg of the journey.

The 'CCE' was withdrawn during the Second World War but was reinstated as a Saturdays-only service in 1951. Taking two hours to reach Birmingham, the train continued to Shrewsbury station where it changed locomotives and reversed direction. In 1954 it became a full weekday service

The Cambrian Coast Express

Tariff

◀ With artwork by 'CWB' this stylish restaurant car tariff was issued to passengers wishing to dine on the 'Cambrian Coast Express' in the 1950s.

Table 12

CAMBRIAN COAST EXPRESS
RESTAURANT CAR SERVICE (¶)
LONDON, ABERDOVEY, TOWYN, BARMOUTH, PWLLHELI and ABERYSTWYTH

WEEK DAYS

	am			am
London (Paddington) ..dep	10A10	Aberystwyth .. ..dep	11A45	
				pm
Banbury General ..	{arr 11 22	Borth .. .. .. „	12A 5	
	{dep 11 24	Dovey Junction .. ..arr	12 25	
	pm			
Birmingham	{arr 12 13			am
(Snow Hill)	{dep 12 17	Pwllheli .. .. ..dep	9A55	
Wolverhampton	{arr 12 39	Criccieth .. .. „	10A14	
(Low Level)	{dep 12 43	Portmadoc .. .. „	10A25	
Shrewsbury ..	{arr 1 19	Harlech .. .. .. „	10A50	
	{dep 1 23	Barmouth .. .. „	11A20	
Welshpool .. .. .. „	..arr 2 1	Barmouth Junction.. .. „	11A26	
Newtown .. .. .. „	2 30	Fairbourne .. .. „	11A29	
Machynlleth .. .. .. „	3 20	Llwyngwril .. .. „	11A40	
		Tonfanau .. .. .. „	11 48	
Machynlleth .. ..dep	3 40	Towyn .. .. .. „	11A59	
Penhelig Halt .. ..arr	4 2			pm
Aberdovey .. .. „	4 6	Aberdovey .. .. „	12A 6	
Towyn .. .. .. „	4 14	Penhelig Halt .. .. „	12 10	
Tonfanau .. .. .. „	4 21	Dovey Junction .. ..arr	12 23	
Llwyngwril .. .. „	4 32			
Fairbourne .. .. „	4 40	Dovey Junction ..dep	12A33	
Barmouth Junction .. „	4 44	Machynlleth .. .. „	12A43	
Barmouth .. .. „	4 50	Newtown .. .. „	1 35	
Harlech .. .. .. „	5 17	Welshpool .. .. „	2 7	
Portmadoc .. .. „	5 38	Shrewsbury	{arr 2 42	
Criccieth .. .. „	5 50		{dep 2 52	
Pwllheli .. .. .. „	6 10	Wolverhampton	{arr 3 31	
		(Low Level)	{dep 3 35	
Machynlleth .. ..dep	3 25	Birmingham	{arr 3 55	
Borth .. ..arr	3 45	(Snow Hill)	{dep 4 0	
Aberystwyth .. .. „	4 5	Leamington Spa	{arr 4 23	
		General	{dep 4 25	
		London (Paddington) ..arr	4 0	

A—Seats can be reserved in advance on payment of a fee of 2s. 0d. per seat (see page 23).

¶—Restaurant Car available between London (Paddington) and Aberystwyth, in each direction.

▶ The winter 1958/59 timetable for the 'Cambrian Coast Express'.

▲ Not all named trains featured powerful express locomotives at their head. Here, '4575' Class 2-6-2T No. 5517 is seen heading the Pwllheli portion of the down 'Cambrian Coast Express' at Barmouth in July 1958.

▲ 'Manor' Class 4-6-0 No. 7823 'Hook Norton Manor' and an unidentified '4300' Class 2-6-0 halt at Moat Lane Junction with the up 'Cambrian Coast Express' in August 1962. The loco was built by British Railways at Swindon in 1950 and was withdrawn in July 1964.

(Monday to Saturday) with the Aberystwyth and Pwllheli portions splitting or joining at Dovey Junction. Diesel traction took over the Paddington to Shrewsbury leg in 1963 although 'Manor' Class locos continued to haul the train over the steeply graded Cambrian Line until 1965 when BR Standard Class 4 4-6-0s took over. The last steam-hauled 'CCE' over this section ran on 11 February 1967 and the train was withdrawn less than a month later.

► Headed by BR Standard Class 4 4-6-0 No. 75033 the special steam-hauled final up 'Cambrian Coast Express' approaches Talerddig Summit on 4 March 1967. Built at Swindon in 1953 this loco was withdrawn from Carnforth shed in December 1967.

CAMBRIDGE BUFFET EXPRESSES

LONDON (KING'S CROSS) TO CAMBRIDGE

Officially known as the 'Garden Cities and Cambridge Buffet Expresses', a series of five express trains began operating between London (King's Cross) and Cambridge in 1932. With intermediate stops at Welwyn Garden City, Letchworth Garden City (hence the rather long name of the train) and Hitchin, they provided a rapid and comfortable journey between the university city and the capital. Motive power was usually 'B17' or 'B1' Class 4-6-0s until the advent of new Brush Type 2 diesels in the late 1950s. All trains included an open buffet car which proved extremely popular with travellers, as the author – a regular user in the early 1970s – can verify. It was shoulder to shoulder, standing room only, in the smoke-filled Gresley buffet car as the train rattled northwards in the early evening rush hour! The trains ceased running following electrification of the route from King's Cross to Royston in 1978.

◀ Class 'B17/1' 4-6-0 No. 61623 'Lambton Castle' speeds along the East Coast Main Line near Potters Bar with a down 'Cambridge Buffet Express' made up of Gresley 'blood-and-custard' coaches in 1951. This Gresley-designed loco was built at Darlington in 1931 and withdrawn from Cambridge shed in July 1959.

THE CAPITALS LIMITED

LONDON (KING'S CROSS) TO EDINBURGH AND ABERDEEN

By 1939, thanks to corridor tenders allowing crew members to change without stopping, the 'Flying Scotsman' express had become the longest regular non-stop run in the world, covering the 393 miles between King's Cross and Edinburgh in just seven hours. The outbreak of war stopped this golden age of high-speed travel, which was only resumed in 1949 when the new 'The Capitals Limited' was inaugurated as the new non-stop express between the two capitals – by then the 'Flying Scotsman' had already been downgraded with an intermediate stop at Newcastle. Running only during the summer months with a 9.30am departure from King's Cross and a 9.45am departure from Edinburgh, the new train also carried through coaches to and from Aberdeen. Hauled by an 'A4' Pacific, it was a very heavy train consisting of 13 coaches including a kitchen car, buffet car, two restaurant cars and a ladies' rest room, but strangely had only a limited number of first class seats. By 1952 the train had been speeded up to nearly match the pre-war schedules and in 1953 it was renamed as 'The Elizabethan' in honour of Queen Elizabeth II's coronation.

▲ The 1950 restaurant car tariff for The Capitals Limited.

◄ Not a perfect photo technically but a rare shot of 'A4' Class 4-6-2 No. 60024 'Kingfisher' at the head of the down 'The Capitals Limited' near Retford in 1948. The loco is finished in experimental ultramarine lined in red and straw. The loco was built at Doncaster in 1936 and withdrawn in September 1966 after hauling the three-hour Glasgow–Aberdeen expresses.

CAPITALS UNITED

LONDON (PADDINGTON) TO CARDIFF

The 'Capitals United Express' was inaugurated early in 1956, just six weeks after Cardiff had officially become the capital of Wales. It provided a non-stop restaurant car service to London for Welsh businessmen, departing from Cardiff at 8am, and arriving at Paddington at 10.50am. The return service left Paddington at 3.55pm and arrived back in Cardiff at 6.53pm (winter 1958/59 timetable). It also conveyed through coaches to and from Swansea, Carmarthen and Fishguard Harbour. Engines were changed at Cardiff with a Cardiff Canton 'Britannia' or 'King' normally in charge for the non-stop run to and from Paddington. The name was dropped in the summer of 1965.

▲ The stylish cover of the restaurant car tariff for the 'Capitals United' express.

Table 9

CAPITALS UNITED EXPRESS
RESTAURANT CAR SERVICE
LONDON AND CARDIFF
WEEK DAYS

	pm
LONDON (Paddington) .. .. dep	3**A**55
CARDIFF (General) .. .. arr	6 53

	am
CARDIFF (General) .. .. dep	8**A**0
LONDON (Paddington) .. .. arr	10 50

A—Seats can be reserved in advance on payment of a fee of 2s. 0d. per seat (see page 23).

◀ The winter 1958/59 timetable for the 'Capitals United' express.

◄ 'King' Class 4-6-0 No. 6028 'King George VI' speeds along with the up 'Capitals United' express near Wootton Bassett in September 1960. Built at Swindon in 1930 this loco was withdrawn from Cardiff Canton shed in November 1962.

► Cardiff Canton's BR 'Britannia' Class 4-6-2 No. 70026 'Polar Star' enters Sonning Cutting at speed with the up 'Capitals United' express in the late 1950s. The loco was built at Crewe in 1952 and withdrawn from Stockport Edgeley shed in January 1967.

CATHEDRALS EXPRESS

LONDON (PADDINGTON) TO OXFORD, WORCESTER/KIDDERMINSTER AND HEREFORD

Introduced by the Western Region of British Railways in 1957, the 'Cathedrals Express' featured an attractive locomotive headboard featuring a bishop's mitre atop the train name, which was picked out in white on a blue background in what can only be described as an 'Olde English' typeface. Running between Paddington and Hereford, this restaurant car express left Hereford at 7.45am and arrived at Paddington at 11.30am, returning at 4.45pm and reaching Hereford at 8.30pm (winter 1958/59 schedule). Despite a fast non-stop run between London and Oxford, the train also stopped at Moreton-in-Marsh and Evesham – at Worcester (Shrub Hill) the Kidderminster coaches were attached or detached before the train effectively became a stopping service to and from Hereford. The 'Cathedrals Express' became the last steam-hauled named train to operate to and from Paddington, with Worcester shed's usually immaculate 'Castle' Class locos being replaced by Brush Type 4 diesels in 1965 when the train's name was dropped.

Table 13

THE CATHEDRALS EXPRESS

RESTAURANT CAR SERVICE

LONDON, OXFORD, WORCESTER and HEREFORD

WEEK DAYS

	pm			am
London (Paddington) .. .. dep	4A45	Hereford .. .. dep	7A45	
Oxford .. .. { arr	5 58	Ledbury .. .. „	8 7	
Oxford .. .. { dep	6 4	Colwall .. .. „	8 18	
Moreton-in-Marsh .. .. .. arr	6 41	Malvern Wells.. .. .. .. „	8 23	
Evesham .. .. „	7 0	Great Malvern .. .. .. „	8A27	
Worcester (Shrub Hill).. .. „	7 20	Malvern Link .. .. „	8 31	
		Worcester (Foregate Street){ arr	8 42	
Fernhill Heath .. .. .. arr dd		Worcester (Foregate Street){ dep	8 43	
Droitwich Spa .. .. .. „	7 46	Worcester (Shrub Hill).. .. arr	8 47	
Hartlebury .. .. „	7 56			
Kidderminster .. .. .. „	8 3	Kidderminster .. .. .. dep	8A19	
		Droitwich Spa .. .. .. „	8A32	
Worcester (Shrub Hill).. .. dep	7 28			
Worcester (Foregate Street).. „	7 32	Worcester (Shrub Hill).. .. dep	9A 0	
Malvern Link .. .. .. arr	7 43	Evesham .. .. „	9 18	
Great Malvern .. .. .. „	7 47	Moreton-in-Marsh .. .. .. „	9 42	
Colwall .. .. „	7 56	Oxford .. .. { arr	10 16	
Ledbury .. .. „	8 7	Oxford .. .. { dep	10 21	
Hereford .. .. „	8 30	London (Paddington) .. .. arr	11 30	

A—Seats can be reserved in advance on payment of a fee of 2s. 0d. per seat (see page 23).

dd—Calls to set down passengers on notice to the Guard.

▶ The winter 1958/59 timetable for the 'Cathedrals Express'.

◄ Fitted with a Hawksworth tender, 'Castle' Class 4-6-0 No. 5042 'Winchester Castle' heads the 'Cathedrals Express' through Sonning Cutting in August 1959. Built at Swindon in 1935, the 'Castle' was withdrawn from Gloucester Horton Road shed in June 1965.

◄ With a headboard featuring a bishop's mitre, 'Castle' Class 4-6-0 No. 7027 'Thornbury Castle' is seen passing Scours Lane, Reading, with the up 'Cathedrals Express' in the late 1950s. Built by BR at Swindon Works in 1949, this loco was withdrawn from Reading shed in December 1963 and has since been preserved.

CHANNEL ISLANDS BOAT TRAINS

LONDON (PADDINGTON) TO WEYMOUTH

LONDON (WATERLOO) TO WEYMOUTH

Connecting with railway-owned ferries to and from the Channel Islands at Weymouth Quay, the Great Western Railway's 'Channel Islands Boat Train' (sometimes called the 'Channel Islands Boat Express') to and from Paddington continued to run until 1960. The service was then concentrated on the Waterloo to Weymouth route, usually behind Bulleid Pacifics until 1967, and continued to operate in some form or another until 1987.

During the early BR era the down Western Region restaurant car service left Paddington at 8.20am (weekdays, winter 1958/59 timetable) and called at Reading, Trowbridge, Westbury and Yeovil (Pen Mill) before arriving at Weymouth Quay at 12.17pm. The last mile of this journey was through the streets of Weymouth along the Harbour Tramway, with the train being preceded by a railwayman with a red flag! The up train left Weymouth at 3.40pm with stops at Yeovil (Pen Mill) and Frome before arriving back at Paddington at 6.46pm. In later years the train was hauled by Class 73 electro-diesels between Waterloo and Bournemouth – between here and Weymouth it was hauled by a Class 33 diesel.

◀ With the 'St Julien' steamer moored nearby, Class '1366' 0-6-0PT No. 1368 hauls an up Western Region 'Channel Islands Boat Train' through the streets of Weymouth in July 1959. One of only five members of this class, this loco was built at Swindon in 1934 and withdrawn from Wadebridge shed in October 1964.

◄ A railtour following the path of the 'Channel Island Boat Trains' slowly eases its way through the busy streets of Weymouth behind Class 33 diesel No. 33114 on 10 December 1988.

► Banked in the rear by a BR Standard Class 5 4-6-0 locomotive, an up 'Channel Islands Boat Train' approaches Bincombe Tunnels near Upwey & Broadwey station behind rebuilt 'West Country' Class 4-6-2 No. 34097 'Holsworthy' in the mid-1960s. This loco was built by BR at Brighton in 1949, rebuilt in 1961 and withdrawn in April 1967.

C CHELTENHAM FLYER

LONDON (PADDINGTON) TO GLOUCESTER AND CHELTENHAM SPA

The 1920s and 1930s were the heyday of rail companies' efforts to run the fastest scheduled passenger services in the world. The introduction of Collett's 'Castle' Class 4-6-0s in 1923 led to an increase of speed for these trains, one of which was named the 'Cheltenham Spa Express' – it soon earned the nickname the 'Cheltenham Flyer'. Timings were increasingly accelerated until 1929 when the 77¼ miles between Swindon and Paddington was scheduled to take only 70 minutes at an average speed of 66.2mph. In 1931 the timing for Swindon to Paddington was further accelerated to an average speed of 69.2mph – by now the tantalising 70mph average speed was within the Great Western Railway's reach.

On 6 June 1932 Driver Ruddock and Fireman Thorp of Old Oak Common shed handed the GWR publicity department a glittering prize when they shattered all previous timings and broke all railway speed records. Headed by No. 5006 'Tregenna Castle', the 'Cheltenham Flyer' left the town of its name promptly at 2.30pm and after a leisurely journey through the Cotswolds reached Swindon for its final stop before Paddington. At 3.48pm 'Tregenna Castle' and its six coaches left Swindon and then the fireworks started – the train accelerated continuously until Didcot (24.2 miles from Swindon) was passed after only 18min 55sec, at a speed of over 90mph. This high speed was maintained for mile after mile and despite a slight slowing past Twyford the train was still travelling at 84.4mph just two miles short of Paddington, which was reached in 56min 47sec from Swindon at an average speed of 81.6mph. What a journey! Three months later the 'Cheltenham Flyer' was accelerated again and was rescheduled to take only 65 minutes between Swindon and Paddington at an average speed of 71.3mph – it was now officially the fastest scheduled train in the world. Within a few years the GWR lost this title to high-speed diesel trains in the USA and Germany, and the world-beating service for the gentry of Cheltenham Spa was soon consigned to the history books.

▲ A luggage label issued to passengers on the 'World's Fastest Train' in the 1930s.

▼ An unidentified Great Western 'Castle' Class 4-6-0 enters Paddington with the up 'Cheltenham Flyer', circa 1934. With a start to stop speed between Swindon and Paddington booked at 71.3mph the 'Flyer' could rightfully make claim to being the 'World's Fastest Train' – a claim highlighted by the train's headboard which was proudly carried from 1931 to 1935.

C

CHELTENHAM SPA EXPRESS

LONDON (PADDINGTON) TO GLOUCESTER AND CHELTENHAM SPA

As we have already seen, the original 'Cheltenham Spa Express' was introduced in 1923 and during the pre-war years received the nickname of the 'Cheltenham Flyer'. The high-speed service was brought to an end in 1939 and was only revived in 1956 when the Western Region of British Railways gave the name to the 8am departure from Cheltenham St James and the 4.55pm return service from Paddington. As the author can testify the eight-coach restaurant car train was hauled between Cheltenham and Gloucester Central by a tank engine – these were normally '5101' Class 2-6-2Ts but on occasions even the '9400' Class 0-6-0PTs or '5700' Class 0-6-0PTs could be seen manfully struggling with the load. The train reversed direction at Gloucester with a Horton Road (85B) 'Castle' in charge for the 8.19am run up to London and

back. Locos such as No. 5017 'The Gloucestershire Regiment 28th, 61st', No. 5042 'Winchester Castle' and No. 5071 'Spitfire' were regular performers – the immaculately groomed 'Castle' and the eight brown and cream coaches made a stirring sight for the author on his way to school each morning. On both up and down trains a Swindon stop was avoided with the train running non-stop between Kemble and Paddington.

By 1964 'Western' Class diesel hydraulics were in charge, the loco headboard had disappeared and the reversal at Gloucester Central became a thing of the past when a new connection was laid in at Standish Junction. This allowed trains to run through the ex-Midland Railway station of Gloucester Eastgate. The name was dropped in 1973.

▲ This 1950s restaurant car tariff from the 'Cheltenham Spa Express' features the coat of arms of the city of London and the town of Cheltenham Spa.

Table 10			
CHELTENHAM SPA EXPRESS			
RESTAURANT CAR SERVICE			
LONDON, KEMBLE, STROUD, GLOUCESTER and CHELTENHAM			
WEEK DAYS			
	pm		am
LONDON (Paddington) ...dep	4A55	Cheltenham Spa (St. James')...dep	8A 0
Kemble ... ...arr	6 33	Cheltenham Spa (Malvern Rd.) ,,	8A 2
Stroud ... ... ,,	6 54	Gloucester Central ,,	8A19
Gloucester Central ... ... ,,	7 12	Stonehouse (Burdett Road)... ,,	8A33
Cheltenham Spa (Malvern Rd.) ,,	7 33	Stroud ... ... ,,	8A41
Cheltenham Spa (St. James')... ,,	7 35	Kemble ... ... ,,	9A 4
		LONDON (Paddington) ...arr	10 35
A—Seats can be reserved in advance on payment of a fee of 2s. 0d. per seat (see page 23).			

► The up 'Cheltenham Spa Express' speeds through West Ealing behind Gloucester Horton Road's 'Castle' Class 4-6-0 No. 7034 'Ince Castle' in March 1962. The loco was built by British Railways at Swindon in 1950 and withdrawn in June 1965.

◄ The winter 1958/59 timetable for the 'Cheltenham Spa Express'.

THE COMET

LONDON (EUSTON) TO MANCHESTER LONDON ROAD/PICCADILLY

'The Comet' was introduced by the London Midland & Scottish Railway in 1932. The up service had an early evening departure from Manchester with one intermediate stop at Stafford. From there to Euston it travelled at just over a mile-a-minute to Euston and was one of the fastest scheduled runs on the LMS. The slower down service left Euston just before noon and had intermediate stops at Crewe and Stockport. Both trains were normally hauled by a 'Royal Scot' Class 4-6-0 but strangely the down train (loading up to 14 coaches) included through coaches for Liverpool which were detached at Crewe. The train was withdrawn for the duration of the Second World War but was reintroduced by the London Midland Region of British Railways in 1949. The down train was brought forward to depart from Euston at 9.45am, running non-stop to Stoke-on-Trent and then calling at Macclesfield and Stockport. By 1954 both the up and down journeys were booked to take 3½ hours. With electrification of the West Coast Main Line gathering pace, 'The Comet' was withdrawn in 1962.

▲ The eye-catching wine tariff from 'The Comet' with artwork by 'Hundleby'.

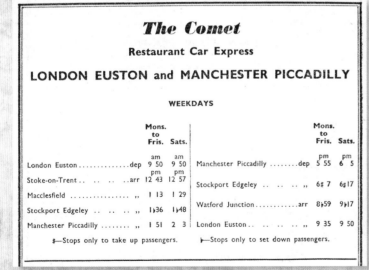

The Comet
Restaurant Car Express
LONDON EUSTON and MANCHESTER PICCADILLY
WEEKDAYS

	Mons. to Fris.	Sats.		Mons. to Fris.	Sats.
	am	am		pm	pm
London Euston ....dep	9 50	9 50	Manchester Piccadilly ....dep	5 55	6 5
	pm	pm			
Stoke-on-Trent .. ..arr	12 43	12 57	Stockport Edgeley .. .. .. ,,	6♯7	6♯17
Macclesfield .... ,,	1 13	1 29			
Stockport Edgeley .. .. .. ,,	1▶36	1▶48	Watford Junction............arr	8▶59	9▶17
Manchester Piccadilly .... ,,	1 51	2 3	London Euston.. .. .. .. ,,	9 35	9 50

♯—Stops only to take up passengers.   ▶—Stops only to set down passengers.

▲ The final timetable of 'The Comet' prior to its withdrawal in the autumn of 1962.

▲ Experimentally fitted with Westinghouse air-pumps, BR 'Britannia' Class 4-6-2 No. 70043 is seen at the head of 'The Comet' in 1954. At that time the loco was only one year old, had not been fitted with smoke deflectors and was still waiting to be named 'Lord Kitchener'. It was withdrawn from Crewe South shed in 1965 after only 12 years of service.

C

CONDOR

LONDON (HENDON) TO GLASGOW (GUSHETFAULDS)

The forerunner of today's container trains, the 'Condor' first ran on 16 March 1959 – the name was derived from the 'container door-to-door' service which provided a vastly improved overnight delivery for customers. Taking ten hours for the journey, the train consisted of vacuum-braked long-wheelbase flat wagons each carrying two containers; these could each hold up to four tons of goods of any type. Initially hauled by a pair of the new Metropolitan Vickers 1,200hp Co-Bo Type 2 diesels, the overnight train was booked to run non-stop between London and Carlisle using the Midland route via Leicester, Sheffield and the Settle & Carlisle line. The unreliable 'Metro-Vicks' did not last long and they were replaced in 1960 by more reliable steam haulage until new BR-built Sulzer Type 2 diesels took over the duty in 1961. A second overnight 'Condor' was introduced between Aston (Birmingham) and Glasgow in early 1963. Both trains were replaced by the first Freightliner service in 1965.

◄ Metro-Vick Co-Bo (Class 28) diesel D5718 heads the down 'Condor' container express through Silkstream Junction between Mill Hill and Hendon in May 1960. Twenty of these locos were built in 1958/59 by Metropolitan-Vickers but they proved so unreliable that they had all been taken out of service by 1961. Following remedial work the whole class was banished to Barrow-in-Furness and, apart from one example, had all been withdrawn by 1969. The sole survivor, D5705, awaits full restoration.

CORNISH RIVIERA EXPRESS

LONDON (PADDINGTON) TO PENZANCE

Until 1906 trains from Paddington to Devon and Cornwall had to travel the 'Great Way Round' via Bristol, but with the opening of new lines between Patney & Chirton to Westbury in 1900 and from Castle Cary to Cogload Junction (near Taunton) in 1906, the journey was shortened by just over 20 miles. New track bypassing Westbury and Frome opened in 1933 and further reduced travelling times.

With the new, shorter route in mind the Great Western Railway held a competition in 1904 to find a name for the daily premier express between Paddington and Penzance – thus the 'Cornish Riviera Limited' was born. Initially the train ran via Bristol but in 1906 it took the shorter route via Castle Cary. Slip coaches were included to serve other popular holiday destinations such as Weymouth, Ilfracombe and Newquay. The train became

▲ This luncheon menu for the 'Cornish Riviera' dates from 31 October 1922.

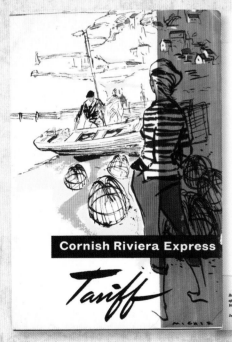

◄ With stylish artwork by 'Michie', this 'Cornish Riviera' restaurant car tariff dates from July 1958.

o popular with holidaymakers that it ran in wo portions on summer Saturdays until the First World War when it was suspended. The rain resumed service in 1919, and in 1923 the ntroduction of new carriages and the 'Castle' Class locomotives saw a further improvement in service. The introduction of the more powerful King' Class locos in 1927 allowed heavier rains to reach Plymouth in four hours and wo years later through coaches were added for Falmouth and St Ives. In 1935 new 'Centenary' carriages were introduced and the regular 0.30am departure from Paddington carried reserved seat passengers only and ran (officially) non-stop to Truro – in fact the train halted at Devonport to change engines, the 'King' being oo heavy to cross the Royal Albert Bridge. On ummer Saturdays such was the demand for he train that it ran 'non-stop' to St Erth with passengers for Falmouth and Helston being conveyed in a relief express.

▲ Circa 1923, this postcard depicts the 'Cornish Riviera' at speed behind Charles Collett's new 'Castle' Class 4-6-0 No. 4073 'Caerphilly Castle'. This milestone loco was built at Swindon in 1923, withdrawn from Cardiff Canton shed in May 1960, and has since been preserved.

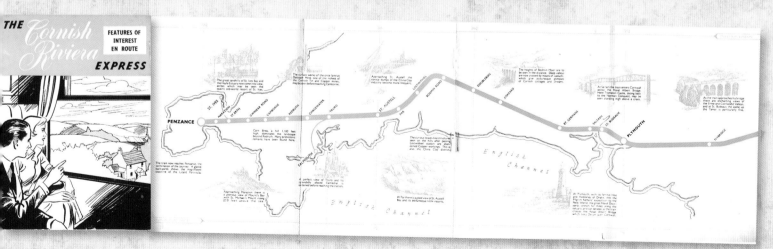

▲ A 1950s route guide to the journey of the 'Cornish Riviera Express' through Cornwall.

Table 3

CORNISH RIVIERA EXPRESS

RESTAURANT CAR SERVICE

LONDON, PLYMOUTH, TRURO and PENZANCE

WEEK DAYS and SUNDAYS

	WEEK DAYS	SUN-DAYS		WEEKDAYS	SUN-DAYS
	am	am		am	am
London (Paddington) dep	10A30	10A30	Penzance .. dep	10A 0	9A45
Exeter (St. David's). arr	..	pm 2 3	St. Erth .. ,,	10A12	9A55
Newton Abbot ..	..	3 35	Gwinear Road .. ,,	10A24	
Plymouth .. ,,	2 30	3 35	Camborne .. ,,	..	10A11
Liskeard .. ,,	..	4 16			
Par .. .. ,,	3 33	4 45	Truro .. ,,	10A53	10A38
St. Austell .. ,,	..	4 57			
Truro .. .. ,,	4 33	5 20	Par .. .. ,,	11A25	11A10
Redruth .. .. ,,	..	5 44		pm	pm
Camborne .. ,,	..	5 53	Plymouth .. .. ,,	12A30	12A20
Gwinear Road .. ,,	4 33		Exeter (St. David's) ,,	..	
Hayle .. .. ,,	..	6 3			1 50
St. Erth .. ,,	4 43	6 10	London (Paddington) arr	4 40	5 30
Penzance .. ,,	4 55	6 25			

A—Seats can be reserved in advance on payment of a fee of 2s. 0d. per seat (see page 23).

▲ The winter 1958/59 timetable for the 'Cornish Riviera Express'.

By 1939 the 'Limited' normally consisted of eight portions: the main portion with restaurant car for Penzance; one through coach each for St Ives, Falmouth, Newquay and Kingsbridge; the Taunton slip with coaches for Ilfracombe and Minehead; and the two Weymouth coaches slipped at Westbury. The train continued to run during the Second World War but via Bristol, and it wasn't until 1955 that pre-war schedules had been regained. By

that date the train had become the 'Cornish Riviera Express'. Steam haulage was ousted in the late 1950s with the introduction of 'Warship' Class diesel hydraulics, followed in the 1960s by the more powerful 'Western' Class locos. By the end of the decade the journey time to Penzance had reduced to 5hrs 35min. More progress was in the pipeline – following haulage for some years by Class 47 and Class 50 diesel electrics, the 'Cornish Riviera' (as it was then known) became an HST working in 1979 and by 1983 Plymouth was being reached in 3hrs 13min and Penzance in 4hrs 55min. The ageing HSTs still operate this service.

▼ The 'Cornish Riviera' at speed behind 'streamlined' 'King' Class 4-6-0 No. 6014 'King Henry VII'. This cosmetic attempt by the GWR to cash in on the high-speed streamlined age failed miserably and all of the casing, apart from the V-shaped cab, was removed in 1943. Built at Swindon in 1928 the loco was withdrawn in September 1962.

▲ Less than three months old, NBL 'Warship' Class diesel hydraulic D601 'Ark Royal' climbs out of Dainton Tunnel with the down 'Cornish Riviera Express' on 19 June 1958. The loco had a very short life and was withdrawn along with its four classmates in December 1967.

C

THE CORNISHMAN

WOLVERHAMPTON (LOW LEVEL) TO PENZANCE

Although not officially named as such, 'The Cornishman' was originally the premier train from Paddington to Penzance via Bristol during the broad gauge era. Running non-stop between London and Exeter via the Bristol avoiding line, it was by far the longest such service in the world. The unofficially named train disappeared in 1904 upon the inauguration of the 'Cornish Riviera Limited' (see 'Cornish Riviera Express').

Forty-eight years later in 1952 the Western Region of British Railways revived the train's name, which was given to a daily restaurant car service running between Wolverhampton (Low Level) and Penzance. An express it definitely was not as its route took it via

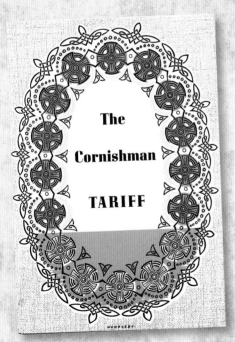

◀ Featuring artwork by 'Hundleby', this tariff graced the tables in the restaurant car of 'The Cornishman' in the late 1950s.

Table 14

THE CORNISHMAN
RESTAURANT CAR SERVICE
BETWEEN
WOLVERHAMPTON, BIRMINGHAM, GLOUCESTER, BRISTOL
AND THE
WEST OF ENGLAND
Via Stratford-upon-Avon

WEEK DAYS

WOLVERHAMPTON				PENZANCE			
			am				am
(Low Level)	... ...	..dep	9 A 0	St. Erth	... ...	..dep	10A10
Bilston Central ...	... ...	,,	9 A 6	Gwinear Road ...	... ...	,,	10A22
Wednesbury Central..	... ...	,,	9A12	Camborne ...	... ...	,,	10A35
West Bromwich ...	... ...	,,	9A20	Redruth ...	... ...	,,	10A43
Birmingham (Snow Hill)	...	,,	9A40	Truro ...	... ...	,,	10A52
Stratford-upon-Avon	... ...	,,	10 19	St. Austell ...	... ...	,,	11A12
Cheltenham Spa (Malvern Rd.)		,,	11 2	Par ...	... ...	,,	11 37
Gloucester Eastgate ...	...	,,	11 20	...	... ...	,,	11 46
			pm				pm
Bristol (Temple Meads)	...	..arr	12 15	Bodmin Road ...	... ...	,,	12 1
Taunton ...	... ...	,,	1 15	Liskeard ...	... ...	,,	12 20
Exeter (St. David's)	...	,,	1 58	Plymouth ...	... ...	,,	1 0
Dawlish.. ...	... ...	,,	2 33				
Teignmouth ...	... ...	,,	2 41	Kingswear ...	... ...	,,	12A15
Newton Abbot ...	... ...	,,	2 51	Churston (for Brixham)..	...	,,	12A30
				Goodrington Sands Halt	...	,,	12B40
Torre ...	... ...	,,	3 8	Paignton ...	... ...	,,	12A55
Torquay ...	... ...	,,	3 11	Torquay ...	... ...	,,	1 A 2
Paignton ...	... ...	,,	3 18	Torre ...	... ...	,,	1 7
Goodrington Sands Halt	...	,,	3B24	Kingskerswell ...	... ...	,,	1 15
Churston (for Brixham)..	...	,,	3 30				
Kingswear ...	... ...	,,	3 41	Newton Abbot ...	... ...	,,	1 23
				Teignmouth ...	... ...	,,	1 34
Plymouth ...	... ...	,,	3 20	Dawlish... ...	... ...	,,	1 42
Liskeard ...	... ...	,,	3 59	Exeter (St. David's)	...	,,	2 24
Bodmin Road ...	... ...	,,	4 15	Taunton ...	... ...	,,	3 5
Par ...	... ...	,,	4 28	Bristol (Temple Meads)	...	,,	4 8
St. Austell ...	... ...	,,	4 39	Gloucester Eastgate ...	...	..arr	5 3
Truro ...	... ...	,,	5 3	Cheltenham Spa (Malvern Rd.)		,,	5 21
Redruth ...	... ...	,,	5 29	Stratford-upon-Avon ..	...	,,	6 5
Carn Brea ...	... ...	,,	5 34	Birmingham (Snow Hill)	...	,,	6 49
Camborne ...	... ...	,,	5 40	West Bromwich ...	...	,,	7 4
Hayle.. ...	... ...	,,	5 50	Wednesbury Central..	...	,,	7 12
St. Erth ...	... ...	,,	5 57	Bilston Central ...	... ...	,,	7 18
Penzance ...	... ...	,,	6 10	Wolverhampton (Low Level)	...	,,	7 25

A—Seats can be reserved in advance on payment of a fee of 2s. 0d. per seat (see page 23).
B—Commences 4th May, 1959.

▲ The winter 1958/59 timetable for 'The Cornishman'.

Stratford-upon-Avon, Cheltenham (Malvern Road) and Gloucester (Eastgate) before heading along the ex-Midland Railway route to Yate and then via Filton to Bristol Temple Meads, where the Wolverhampton (Stafford Road) 'Castle' was taken off in favour of a Bristol (Bath Road) locomotive for the run down to Plymouth. Here the engine was changed once again for the run down to Penzance

with a 'County', 'Hall' or 'Grange' normally in charge. Journey time for the down train was a leisurely 9hrs 10min (winter 1958/59 times), and for the up train five minutes longer. During the winter months the train also conveyed through carriages for Torquay and Kingswear which were attached or detached at Exeter. In the summer the Kingswear portion ran as a separate train.

▲ Plymouth Laira's 'Hall' Class 4-6-0 No. 6913 'Levens Hall' heads out of Truro with the down 'The Cornishman' on 19 August 1954. The loco was built at Swindon in 1941 and withdrawn in June 1964.

◄ The time is 11.20am – Wolverhampton Stafford Road's 'Castle' Class 4-6-0 No. 5031 'Totnes Castle' heads out of Gloucester Eastgate over Barton Street Crossing with the down 'The Cornishman' on 26 September 1961. Less than a year later this train was diverted to run over the former Midland route between Birmingham and Bristol with 'Peak' diesel haulage. The 'Castle' was built at Swindon in 1934 and withdrawn from Wolverhampton (Stafford Road) shed in October 1963.

The last steam-hauled 'The Cornishman' ran along its original route on 7 September 1962. Type 4 'Peak' diesels without headboards were then introduced with the train now originating or ending its journey at Sheffield Midland and running via the ex-Midland line through Birmingham New Street to Bristol. In 1965 Bradford became the northern terminus until the train finally lost its name in 1975. It has since been revived in timetables to describe a First Great Western express.

◄ 'County' Class 4-6-0 No. 1009 'County of Carmarthen' climbs to Whiteball Summit with the down 'The Cornishman' in the late 1950s. The loco was built at Swindon in 1945 and withdrawn from Bristol (St Philip's Marsh) shed in February 1963.

THE CORONATION

LONDON (KING'S CROSS) TO EDINBURGH (WAVERLEY)

The 1930s were the golden age of high-speed rail travel. Worldwide, railway companies were introducing luxurious trains that competed with each other for the title of the world's fastest train. First on the scene was the Great Western Railway's 'Cheltenham Flyer' but this was soon eclipsed in 1935 when the London & North Eastern Railway introduced its streamlined 'Silver Jubilee' non-stop service between King's Cross and Newcastle. Introduced in July 1937 to commemorate the coronation of King George VI, the LNER's

'The Coronation' went one step further by introducing the first high-speed streamlined service between London and Scotland. Much heavier than 'The Silver Jubilee', this train called at York and Newcastle before reaching Edinburgh (Waverley) in six hours flat. Unlike the German and American streamlined trains which were diesel-hauled, the LNER's train was hauled by Nigel Gresley's 'A4' 4-6-2s of which five, all named after countries of the British Empire, were allocated for this service. Both loco and the nine coaches (four

▼ Stylishly designed in gold and red by 'FN' and featuring 'A4' 4-6-2 No. 4489 'Dominion of Canada', the LNER's publicity booklet of 1937 gives details of the seating plan and schedules for this streamlined train. The down train covered the journey from London to York at an average speed of 71.9mph.

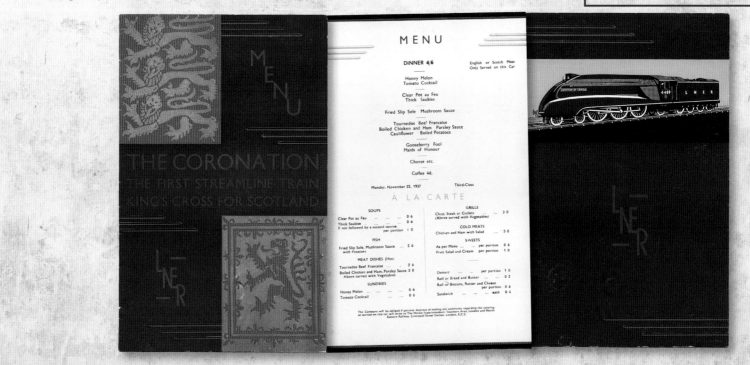

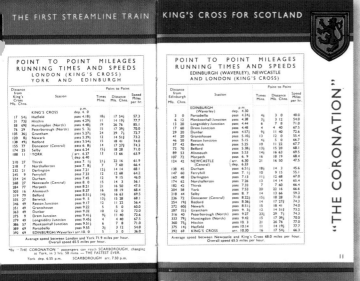

▲ Fine dining at speed – the restaurant car menu for the pre-war 'The Coronation'. The back cover features 'A4' 4-6-2 No. 4489 'Dominion of Canada'. After withdrawal in May 1965 the loco was shipped out to Canada in 1967 where it was displayed at the Exporail Museum in Montreal. It has recently arrived back in the UK for a grand reunion with the four UK-based locos of this class along with No. 60008 'Dwight D. Eisenhower' from the National Railroad Museum in the USA.

WILL'S CIGARETTES

No 4489

"CORONATION" EXPRESS. L.N.E.R.

twin articulated coaches and a streamlined 'beaver tail' observation car – the latter only carried in the summer) were colour co-ordinated, with the engine finished in a deep 'garter blue' and the stock finished in a two-tone blue. The latest in air conditioning and sound proofing was incorporated into the coaches and the two kitchen cars provided meals served at the customers' seats.

◄ This pre-war Will's Cigarettes card immortalises the stylish lines of 'The Coronation'.

CORONATION 1729 CORONATION

L.N.E.R. "THE CORONATION" – TAIL END.

The down train left King's Cross at 4pm while the up train left Edinburgh (Waverley) at 4.30pm and both proved to be very popular with travellers. Sadly the onset of the Second World War in September 1939 saw an end to this luxurious service. The two sets of coaches were then stored at remote locations in Scotland but the train was never to return in its pre–war guise.

LONDON & NORTH EASTERN RAILWAY
EDINBURGH WAVERLEY
THE CORONATION

L.N.E.R. "THE CORONATION" ENGINE END.

▲ The luggage label supplied to passengers on the pre-war 'The Coronation'.

◄ These two pre-war postcards feature 'A4' Pacific No. 4492 'Dominion of New Zealand' at the front end of 'The Coronation' and the 'beaver tail' observation car at the rear. The loco was built at Doncaster in 1937 and withdrawn as No. 60013 from King's Cross shed in April 1963.

THE CORONATION SCOT

LONDON (EUSTON) TO GLASGOW (CENTRAL)

Not to be outdone by the London & North Eastern Railway's 'The Coronation', the London Midland & Scottish Railway introduced its own Anglo–Scottish streamlined train in 1937. Confusingly named 'The Coronation Scot', the train was hauled by streamlined versions of William Stanier's new 'Coronation' Class 4-6-2s. No. 6200 'Coronation' briefly held the world speed record for steam traction when it reached 114mph during a test run south of Crewe in June of that year. Departure for both up and down trains was at 1.30pm and, with one intermediate stop

at Carlisle, Euston and Glasgow Central were both reached in 6½ hours with both trains booked to pass each other at Preston. Initially both locomotive and coaches were finished in a matching blue with horizontal white lines and a 'speed whisker' at the front. Unlike the LNER's train, 'The Coronation Scot' made use of standard coaching stock until more luxurious versions were introduced in 1939. The livery was also changed at the same time with the locos and coaches painted in LMS red and gold lining. This new train was shipped across the

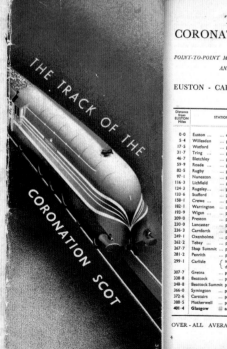

THE TRACK OF THE CORONATION SCOT

THE CORONATION SCOT

POINT-TO-POINT MILEAGES, RUNNING TIMES AND SPEEDS

EUSTON – CARLISLE – GLASGOW

Distance from EUSTON Miles	STATION		Time Mins.	Distance Miles	Speed M.P.H.
			p.m.		
0·0	Euston	dep.	1 30		
5·4	Willesden	pass	1 39	9	5·4	36·0
17·5	Watford	pass	1 50	11	12·1	66·0
31·7	Tring	pass	2 3	13	14·2	65·5
46·7	Bletchley	pass	2 15	12	15·0	75·0
59·9	Roade	pass	2 26	11	13·2	72·0
82·5	Rugby	pass	2 46	20	22·7	68·1
97·1	Nuneaton	pass	3 0	14	14·6	62·6
116·3	Lichfield	pass	3 17	17	19·2	67·8
124·3	Rugeley	pass	3 23	6	8·0	80·0
133·6	Stafford	pass	3 32	9	9·3	62·0
158·1	Crewe	pass	3 54	22	24·5	66·8
182·1	Warrington	pass	4 16	22	24·0	65·5
193·9	Wigan	pass	4 28	12	11·8	59·0
209·0	Preston	pass	4 44	16	15·1	56·6
230·0	Lancaster	pass	5 4	20	21·0	63·0
236·3	Carnforth	pass	5 9	5	6·3	75·6
249·1	Oxenholme	pass	5 21	12	12·8	64·0
262·2	Tebay	pass	5 36	15	13·1	52·4
267·7	Shap Summit	pass	5 44	8	5·5	41·3
281·2	Penrith	pass	5 56	12	13·5	67·5
299·1	Carlisle	arr. 6 13 / dep. 6 15		17	17·9	63·2
307·7	Gretna	pass	6 24	9	8·6	56·2
338·8	Beattock	pass	6 50	26	31·1	71·8
348·8	Beattock Summit	pass	7 5	15	10·0	40·0
366·0	Symington	pass	7 20	15	17·2	68·8
372·6	Carstairs	pass	7 25	5	6·6	
388·5	Motherwell	pass	7 43	17	15·9	56·1
401·4	Glasgow	arr.	8 0	17	12·9	45·5

OVER-ALL AVERAGE SPEED 61·7 M.P.H.

4

THE CORONATION SCOT

POINT-TO-POINT MILEAGES, RUNNING TIMES AND SPEEDS

GLASGOW – CARLISLE – EUSTON

Distance from GLASGOW Miles	STATION		Time Mins.	Distance Miles	Speed M.P.H.
			p.m.		
0·0	Glasgow	dep.	1 30		
12·9	Motherwell	pass	1 48	18	12·9	43·0
28·8	Carstairs	pass	2 13	15	15·9	47·7
35·4	Symington	pass	2 14	6	6·6	66·0
52·6	Beattock Summit	pass	2 31	18	17·2	57·3
62·6	Beattock	pass	2 42	10	10·0	68·0
93·7	Gretna	pass	3 7	25	31·1	74·6
102·3	Carlisle	arr. 3 15 / dep. 3 17		8	8·6	64·5
120·2	Penrith	pass	3 38	21	17·9	51·1
133·7	Shap Summit	pass	3 53	15	13·5	54·0
139·2	Tebay	pass	3 58	5	5·5	66·0
152·3	Oxenholme	pass	4 10	12	13·1	65·5
165·1	Carnforth	pass	4 21	11	12·8	69·8
171·4	Lancaster	pass	4 26	5	6·3	75·6
192·4	Preston	pass	4 45	19	21·0	66·7
207·5	Wigan	pass	5 14	13	15·1	53·3
219·3	Warrington	pass	5 14	12	11·8	59·0
243·3	Crewe	pass	5 36	22	24·0	65·0
267·8	Stafford	pass	6 0	24	24·5	61·3
277·1	Rugeley	pass	6 9	9	9·3	62·0
285·1	Lichfield	pass	6 15	6	8·0	80·0
304·3	Nuneaton	pass	6 33	18	19·2	64·0
318·9	Rugby	pass	6 47	14	14·6	67·4
341·5	Roade	pass	7 6	22	22·7	68·1
354·7	Bletchley	pass	7 17	11	13·2	72·0
369·7	Tring	pass	7 31	14	15·0	64·4
383·9	Watford	pass	7 42	11	14·2	77·5
396·0	Willesden	pass	7 52	10	12·1	72·6
401·4	Euston	arr.	8 0	8	5·4	40·5

OVER-ALL AVERAGE SPEED 61·7 M.P.H.

5

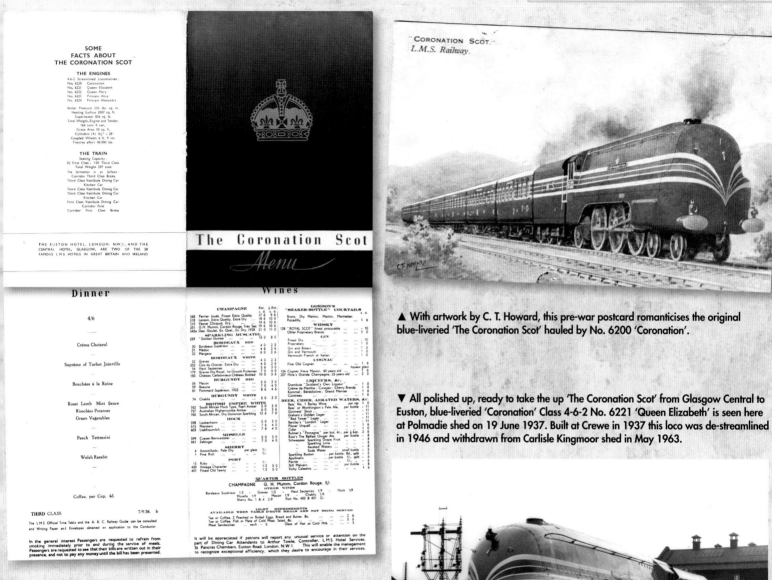

SOME FACTS ABOUT THE CORONATION SCOT

THE ENGINES

4-6-2 Streamlined Locomotives:
No. 6220 Coronation
No. 6221 Queen Elizabeth
No. 6222 Queen Mary
No. 6223 Princess Alice
No. 6224 Princess Alexandra

Boiler Pressure 250 lbs. sq. in.
Heating Surface 2807 sq. ft.
Superheater 856 sq. ft.
Total Weight, Engine and Tender,
164 tons 9 cwt.
Grate Area 50 sq. ft.
Cylinders (4) 16½" × 28"
Coupled Wheels 6 ft. 9 ins.
Tractive effort 40,000 lbs.

THE TRAIN

Seating Capacity:
82 First Class; 150 Third Class
Total Weight 297 tons

The formation is as follows:
Corridor Third Class Brake
Third Class Vestibule Dining Car
Kitchen Car
Third Class Vestibule Dining Car
Third Class Vestibule Dining Car
Kitchen Car
First Class Vestibule Dining Car
Corridor First
Corridor First Class Brake

THE EUSTON HOTEL, LONDON, N.W.1, AND THE
CENTRAL HOTEL, GLASGOW, ARE TWO OF THE 28
FAMOUS L.M.S. HOTELS IN GREAT BRITAIN AND IRELAND

The Coronation Scot
Menu

"CORONATION SCOT."
L.M.S. Railway.

▲ With artwork by C. T. Howard, this pre-war postcard romanticises the original blue-liveried 'The Coronation Scot' hauled by No. 6200 'Coronation'.

▼ All polished up, ready to take the up 'The Coronation Scot' from Glasgow Central to Euston, blue-liveried 'Coronation' Class 4-6-2 No. 6221 'Queen Elizabeth' is seen here at Polmadie shed on 19 June 1937. Built at Crewe in 1937 this loco was de-streamlined in 1946 and withdrawn from Carlisle Kingmoor shed in May 1963.

Dinner

4/6

6224

Crème Choiseul

Suprême of Turbot Joinville

Bouchées à la Reine

Roast Lamb Mint Sauce
Rissolées Potatoes
Green Vegetables

Peach Tettrazini

Welsh Rarebit

Coffee, per Cup, 4d.

THIRD CLASS   7/9/38. b

The L.M.S. Official Time Table and the A.B.C. Railway Guide can be consulted and Writing Paper and Envelopes obtained on application to the Conductor.

In the general interest Passengers are requested to refrain from smoking immediately prior to and during the service of meals. Passengers are requested to see that their bills are written out in their presence, and not to pay any money until the bill has been presented.

Wines

It will be appreciated if patrons will report any unusual service or attention on the part of Dining Car Attendants to Arthur Towle, Controller, L.M.S. Hotel Services, St. Pancras Chambers, Euston Road, London, N.W.1. This will enable the management to recognize exceptional efficiency, which they desire to encourage in their services.

▲ The third class menu of 'The Coronation Scot' for the journey taken on 7 September 1938.

◄ Point-to-point running times, speeds and a route description for 'The Coronation Scot' were published in this booklet produced by the LMS in 1937.

Atlantic to appear at the New York World's Fair but got trapped in the USA when the Second World War broke out. The loco, No. 6220 'Coronation', was eventually returned to Britain during the war but the set of coaches, used as accommodation for army officers, remained in the USA until after the war. Following the war the train was not reinstated and Stanier's 'Coronation' Pacifics soon had their streamlined casing removed.

▼ In its new red and gold livery, 'Coronation' Class 4-6-2 No. 6222 'Queen Mary' thunders towards Berkhamsted with the down 'The Coronation Scot' on 12 July 1939. Built at Crewe in 1937 this loco was de-streamlined in 1946 and withdrawn from Polmadie shed in October 1963.

No 22 L.M.S. ENGINE AND TENDER 6220 "CORONATION" WITH NEW TYPE CAB, LAMP AND BELL.
L.M.S. 4-6-2 Engine No. 6220 "Coronation." Attained 114 m.p.h. on test in June 1937, then a British record.
Weight 165 tons. Length 74 ft. Tractive effort 40,000 lbs. Driving Wheels 6 ft. 9 ins in diameter.

◄ ▼ Red and gold-liveried No. 6220 'Coronation' and a new train of 'The Coronation Scot' stock visited the New York World's Fair in 1939. The loco was fitted with a bell and headlight for its visit to the USA. The first of its class, this loco was built at Crewe in 1937, de-streamlined in 1946 and withdrawn from Carlisle Kingmoor in April 1963.

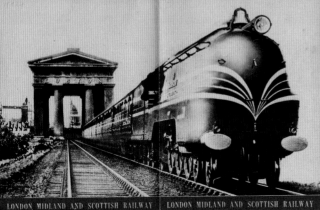

◄ This leaflet issued to visitors at the New York World's Fair in 1939 extolled the virtues of rail travel on the London, Midland & Scottish Railway in Britain.

THE DAY CONTINENTAL

LONDON (LIVERPOOL STREET) TO HARWICH PARKESTON QUAY

The successor to the pre-war 'Flemish Continental', the 'Day Continental' was introduced by the London & North Eastern Railway in 1947. It was one a trio of post-war luxury restaurant car expresses (the others were the 'Scandinavian' and the 'Hook Continental') that connected with cross-Channel ferries to and from the Hook of Holland and Esbjerg (on Denmark's Jutland coast) at Parkeston Quay in Harwich. In their early years these expresses were hauled by 'B1' Class 4-6-0s but with the introduction of new BR Standard 'Britannias' at Stratford Depot in 1951 their schedules were speeded up considerably. In the autumn of 1960 'The Day Continental' left Liverpool Street at 9.15am and arrived at Parkeston Quay at 10.55am while the up train left Parkeston Quay at 7pm and arrived back in London at 8.36pm. This may not seem fast but much of the journey was over some of the busiest commuter lines in the world. By this date steam had been replaced by English Electric Type 4 (Class 40) diesels followed by Type 3 (Class 37) and finally Brush Type 4 (Class 47) locos. The train lost its name in 1987.

▲ Immaculate BR Standard 'Britannia' Class 4-6-2 No. 70037 'Hereward the Wake' is seen here at Stratford shed prior to hauling the down 'The Day Continental' from Liverpool Street to Parkeston Quay in May 1956. The loco was built at Crewe in 1952 and was withdrawn from Carlisle Kingmoor shed in November 1966.

◄ 'B1' Class 4-6-0 No. 61372 of Parkeston shed prepares to leave Liverpool Street with the down 'The Day Continental' in April 1960. Built for BR by the North British Locomotive Company in 1950 this loco was withdrawn from Colwick shed in June 1965.

THE DEVON BELLE

The "Devon Belle"

LONDON (WATERLOO) TO ILFRACOMBE/PLYMOUTH

Unlike the 'Bournemouth Belle' and the all-electric 'Brighton Belle', 'The Devon Belle' had an extremely short existence. Hauled by the latest Bulleid 4-6-2s as far as Exeter Central, this all-Pullman train was introduced by the Southern Railway in June 1947. Departing from Waterloo at 12 noon, the 12 or 14 coach train was officially non-stop to Sidmouth Junction (in fact, engines were changed out of sight at Wilton to the west of Salisbury), making this the only train booked to run non-stop through Salisbury since an accident there in 1906. At Exeter the train was split, with one portion going on to Ilfracombe and the other to Plymouth. Bulleid's new light Pacifics were ideal locomotives for this second leg of the journey, although banking assistance was always needed up the steep Braunton Bank and on the return past the Slade Reservoirs out of Ilfracombe.

Unusually the Ilfracombe portion of the train carried an observation car at the rear. This was not the first time such cars had been used in Britain – the short-lived 'Coronation' run by the London & North Eastern Railway before the war carried an observation car and after the war these were used on Highland tourist routes in Scotland. Paying a supplement, observation car passengers on 'The Devon Belle' must have had a wonderful close-up view of the banking engine as the train struggled up the 1-in-36 Braunton Bank between Barnstaple and Ilfracombe. Naturally the observation car had to be turned on a turntable at the end of each journey.

Sadly, patronage of the Plymouth portion was poor and this was discontinued in 1950, leaving the summer-only 'Belle' as a Waterloo-Ilfracombe service (Fridays, Saturdays and Sundays for the down train and Saturdays, Sundays and Mondays for the up train) until September 1954 when it, too, was finally withdrawn. The two observation cars later saw service on the Inverness to Kyle of Lochalsh and the Glasgow to Oban lines into the 1960s. Fortunately both of them have survived and can be seen in action on the Paignton & Dartmouth Railway and the Swanage Railway respectively.

◀ The summer 1951 sales leaflet and timetable for 'The Devon Belle' Pullman train.

▶ Exmouth Junction's 'West Country' Class 4-6-2 No. 34017, appropriately named 'Ilfracombe', passes through Exeter St David's station with the down 'The Devon Belle' in the early 1950s. Built at Brighton in 1945 this loco was rebuilt in 1957 and withdrawn in October 1966.

THE DEVONIAN

BRADFORD TO PAIGNTON/KINGSWEAR

One of just a small number of named cross-country trains, 'The Devonian' was first introduced by the London Midland & Scottish Railway in 1927. During the winter months it was an express between Bradford and Bristol where three coaches were then detached and taken forward by a slow GWR stopping train to Paignton. During the summer months the entire train of LMS coaches and restaurant car ran between Bradford and Kingswear, and on summer Saturdays ran in several portions. Although discontinued during the Second World War the train was reinstated in October 1946. Until the advent of 'Peak' Class 45 diesels in 1961 the train was normally hauled between Leeds City and Bristol Temple Meads by a Holbeck (55A) 'Jubilee'

Class 4-6-0. Probably the last year that saw steam haulage was the summer of 1962 when the Saturdays-only main train left Bradford Forster Square at 9.05am, reversed direction at Leeds City and arrived at Paignton at 6pm – the normal weekday stops at Sheffield Midland, Derby, Birmingham New Street and Gloucester were all omitted. In the reverse direction the train left Paignton at 9.30am and arrived at Bradford at 6.57pm but this time omitted stops at Bristol, Cheltenham and Birmingham. Quite a journey! Despite the advent of the 'Peak' diesels in the early 1960s journey times saw little improvement and the train's name was dropped in 1975 to herald in that bland era of modernity then so favoured by our state-run railway.

The Devonian
Restaurant Car Express
between
BRADFORD, LEEDS, TORQUAY AND PAIGNTON
WEEKDAYS ONLY

NORTH TO WEST			WEST TO NORTH		
	am	am		am	am
	9* 5	10*15			
Bradford Forster Square...dep	9* 5	10*15	Kingswear................dep	9b 0	....
Shipley . . . . "	9 13	10 22	Churston (for Brixham) .. .. "	9b10	....
Leeds City . . . . "	9*36	10*45	Paignton . . . . "	9b30	9*30
		pm	Torquay .. .. "	9b40	9*40
Sheffield Midland . . . . "	..	12 3	Torre .... "	....	9 47
Chesterfield .... "	11 18	..	Newton Abbot .. .. .. "	9b58	10 3
Derby Midland .... "	..	12 55	Teignmouth .... "	....	10 12
Birmingham New Street .. .. "	..	1 53	Dawlish.. .. .. "	....	10 20
Cheltenham Spa Lansdown...arr	..	2 49	Exeter St. David's .. .. .. "	....	10 40
Gloucester Eastgate ...... "	pm	3 4	Taunton .... "	....	11 18
Bristol Temple Meads .. .. "	3 8	3 56	Bridgwater .... "	....	11 38
Weston-super-Mare General .. "	..	4 31	Weston-super-Mare General .. "	pm	pm
Bridgwater .. .. "	..	4 54	Bristol Temple Meads .. .. "	....	12 1
Taunton .. .. "	..	5 12	Gloucester Eastgate ...... "	....	12 40
Exeter St. David's .. .. "	4 48	5 55	Cheltenham Spa Lansdown.. "	1 24	1 35
Dawlish.. .. .. "	..	6 21	Birmingham New Street.. .arr	....	1 52
Teignmouth .. .. "	5 16	6 29	Burton-on-Trent .. .. .. "	....	2 51
Newton Abbot .... "	5 25	6 38	Derby Midland .... "	3 28	3 33
Torre .. .. "	..	6 55	Chesterfield Midland ...... "	3 49	3 52
Torquay .. .. "	5 47	7 0	Sheffield Midland .... "	4 31	4 29
Paignton .. .. "	6 0	7 10	Rotherham Masborough .... "	4 54	4 52
			Normanton .. .. "	5 10	5 7
			Leeds City .... "	6 3	5 59
			Shipley .. .. "	6 48	6 40
			Bradford Forster Square.... "	6 57	6 49

A Buffet service is also available on this train.

*—Seats can be reserved in advance on payment of a fee of 2s. 0d. per seat.

b—Passengers travelling by this train are required to hold Regulation Tickets.

◀ The summer 1962 timetable for 'The Devonian'.

▲ Fitted with a Fowler tender, Leeds Holbeck's 'Jubilee' Class 4-6-0 No. 45597 'Barbados' gets ready to leave Derby with 'The Devonian' express in July 1957. The loco was built by the North British Locomotive Company in 1935 and withdrawn from Holbeck shed in January 1965.

◄ Fitted with an early style alloy headboard, 'Hall' Class 4-6-0 No. 6932 'Burwarton Hall' prepares to leave Bristol Temple Meads with the down 'The Devonian' in the summer of 1961. The loco was built at Swindon in 1941 and withdrawn from Oxford shed in December 1965.

► Fitted with 'The Devonian' headboard, Bristol Bath Road's BR Sulzer Type 4 diesel D93 climbs the Lickey Incline near Bromsgrove with the up train in July 1961. The heavily loaded train is being banked in the rear by one of the steam Lickey bankers based at Bromsgrove shed. Built at Crewe Works in 1961 the diesel was withdrawn as No. 45057 in January 1985.

THE EAST ANGLIAN

LONDON (LIVERPOOL STREET) TO NORWICH

To coincide with the new high-speed streamlined 'Coronation' on the East Coast Main Line, the London & North Eastern Railway introduced a similar train on the Liverpool Street to Norwich route in 1937. Luxuriously equipped, the two six-coach sets for this new train – 'The East Anglian' – were hauled by two specially streamlined 'B17' Class 4-6-0s, No. 2859 'East Anglian' and No. 2870 'City of London'. However, there the similarity ended as the trains were scheduled to take a leisurely 2¼ hours for the 115-mile journey – the streamlining was purely a cosmetic publicity stunt by the LNER. The train was withdrawn on the outbreak of the Second World War but was reinstated in 1946. The streamlined 'B17s' were soon to disappear and the train was normally worked by 'B17' or 'B1' Class 4-6-0s until the arrival of

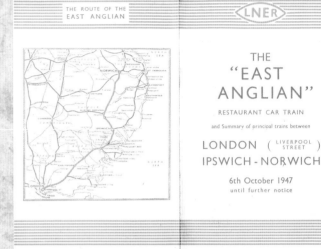

▲ The October 1947 LNER leaflet and timetable for 'The East Anglian' express.

THE EAST ANGLIAN

NORWICH, IPSWICH

and

LONDON (Liverpool Street)

WEEKDAYS

		am		**pm**
Norwich (Thorpe) ... ...dep	11 45	London (Liverpool Street) ...dep	6 30
	pm	Ipswich ... ...arr	7 51
Ipswich ... ...arr	12 30	„ ... ...dep	7 54
„ ... ...dep	12 32	Norwich (Thorpe) ... ...arr	8 40
London (Liverpool Street) ...arr	2A5		

A On Saturdays arrives 1 55 pm

Restaurant Car available

Passengers travelling from Liverpool Street and Norwich, also from Ipswich to Liverpool Street, by this service, can reserve seats in advance on payment of a fee of 2s. 0d. per seat.

▲ The winter 1960/61 timetable for the accelerated 'The East Anglian'.

► This postcard shows the LNER's pre-war streamlined Class B17 4-6-0 No. 2859 'East Anglian' and its train of luxury coaches. The loco was built at Darlington in 1936 and withdrawn as No. 61659 from Lowestoft shed in March 1960.

the BR Standard 'Britannia' 4-6-2s in 1951. These magnificent engines soon transformed express services out of Liverpool Street and cut journey times considerably. By 1960 the English Electric Type 4 diesels had taken over but the up train still left Norwich at 11.45am and, with one stop at Ipswich, reached London at 2.05pm (on Saturdays it arrived ten minutes earlier). The down train left Liverpool Street at 6.30pm and arrived back at Norwich (again with a stop at Ipswich) at 8.40pm. Although the train lost its title in 1962, the name was subsequently bestowed on a Liverpool Street to Yarmouth via Norwich service in 1980. Hauled by Class 47 diesels the train's journey time was cut to 1hr 50min for the London to Norwich leg. Today the train lives on, hauled by Class 90 electric locos with a journey time of 104 minutes and intermediate stops at Diss and Ipswich.

► BR Standard 'Britannia' Class 4-6-2 No. 70009 'Alfred the Great' heading through Marks Tey at speed with 'The East Anglian' express in July 1953. The loco was built at Crewe in 1951 and withdrawn from Carlisle Kingmoor shed in January 1967.

THE EASTERLING

LONDON (LIVERPOOL STREET) TO LOWESTOFT CENTRAL/YARMOUTH SOUTH TOWN

This short-lived named train between Liverpool Street and Lowestoft Central/Yarmouth South Town was introduced by the Eastern Region of British Railways in 1950. Running only during the summer timetable, the train travelled non-stop from London via the East Suffolk Line to Beccles where the two portions – one to or from Lowestoft Central and the other to or from Yarmouth South Town – were either divided or joined. The train was withdrawn in 1958 and the line between Beccles and Yarmouth South Town was closed the following year.

▶ The summer 1955 leaflet for four named trains serving East Anglia. The route of 'The Easterling' between Liverpool Street and Lowestoft/Yarmouth is shown on the map.

▶ A rare photograph of the up 'The Easterling' being hauled by Class B176 No. 61669 'Barnsley' in the Waveney Forest in July 1957. Named after Barnsley Football Club, the loco was built in 1937 and withdrawn from Ipswich shed in September 1958.

THE ELIZABETHAN

LONDON (KING'S CROSS) TO EDINBURGH (WAVERLEY)

The outbreak of war brought a ten-year halt to the golden age of high-speed travel on the East Coast Main Line. It was resumed in 1949 when the new 'The Capitals Limited' was inaugurated as the new non-stop express between King's Cross and Edinburgh – by then the 'Flying Scotsman' had already been downgraded with an intermediate stop at Newcastle. Running only during the summer months with a 9.30am departure from King's Cross and a 9.45am departure from Edinburgh, the new train also carried through coaches to and from Aberdeen. Hauled by an 'A4' Pacific it was a very heavy train consisting of 13 coaches including a kitchen car, buffet car, two restaurant cars and a ladies' rest room, but strangely had only a limited number of first class seats. By 1952 the train had been speeded up almost to pre-war schedules and in 1953 it was renamed 'The Elizabethan' in honour of Queen Elizabeth II's coronation. The introduction of this train saw journey times cut to 6¾ hours in both directions and a year later it was cut to 6½ hours or just about a mile-a-minute. Running only during the summer months the heavily loaded train, weighing in at around 420 tons, was probably the most demanding ever seen in Britain but Gresley's 'A4' Pacifics were certainly up to the job. Locos used on this run were fitted with corridor tenders allowing crews to change over without a stop, making this the longest scheduled non-stop railway journey in the world.

▶ The leaflet, route map and timetable for the inaugural 'The Elizabethan' in the summer of 1953.

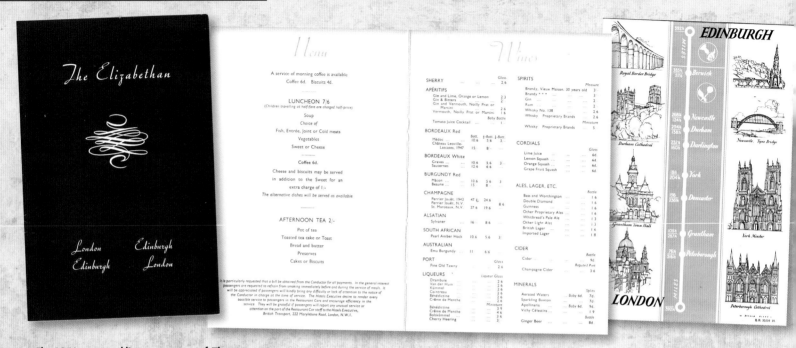

▲ The 1956 menu and linear route map of 'The Elizabethan' features line drawings by Donald Blake.

► Headed by King's Cross shed's 'A4' Class 4-6-2 No. 60033 'Seagull', the up 'The Elizabethan' of 'blood-and-custard' coaches passes Portobello soon after leaving Edinburgh Waverley for the non-stop run to King's Cross on 29 August 1956. This train was diverted via the Waverley Route due to flooding on the East Coast Main Line. The loco was built at Doncaster in 1938 and withdrawn in December 1963.

◄ King's Cross shed's 'A4' Class 4-6-2 No. 60028 'Walter K. Whigham' prepares to leave King's Cross with the down non-stop 'The Elizabethan' in the summer of 1959. Originally named 'Sea Eagle', the loco was built at Doncaster in 1937 and withdrawn from King's Cross shed in December 1962.

▼ King's Cross shed's record-breaking 'A4' 4-6-2 No. 60022 'Mallard' looks in fine fettle as it leaves Edinburgh Waverley with the down 'The Elizabethan' in September 1961. Steam haulage of this famous train ended a few days later. The loco was built at Doncaster in 1938 and achieved the world record for steam haulage of 126mph on 3 July that year. 'Mallard' was withdrawn from King's Cross shed in April 1963 but has since been restored as part of the National Collection.

To celebrate this achievement British Transport Films made a highly regarded 20 minute documentary film of the train in 1954 – the film starred 'A4' Class Pacific No. 60017 'Silver Fox' and featured a journey between the two capitals accompanied by music written by Clifton Parker.

The last steam–hauled 'The Elizabethan' ran at the end of the 1961 summer timetable by which time the new 'Deltic' diesels were soon to appear on the ECML. The train ran for one more season behind these new machines but as they did not have a corridor connection a stop was made at Newcastle for a crew change – so much for progress! The train ceased to run in September 1962.

E

THE EMERALD ISLE EXPRESS

LONDON (EUSTON) TO HOLYHEAD

Passengers wishing to travel overnight to Ireland via Holyhead had for years used the trusted 8.45pm departure from London (Euston). Known as 'The Irish Mail', its arrival at Holyhead in the wee small hours left a lot to be desired for those wishing to put their head down on the ferry. To cater for travellers wanting a good night's sleep on the ferry an earlier train left Euston at 5.35pm; introduced after the Second World War this restaurant car train was given the name of 'The Emerald Isle Express' in 1954. With intermediate stops at Stafford, Crewe, Chester and Llandudno Junction the train arrived at Holyhead at 10.55pm. The up service left Holyhead at 7.30am and arrived back at Euston at 1.18pm. Motive power was usually provided by BR Standard 'Britannia' Pacifics until these were replaced by new English Electric Type 4 diesels in the early 1960s. By then, with West Coast Main Line electrification gathering pace, the arrival time at Holyhead had slid to 11.13pm with the arrival of the up train at Euston put back to 1.30pm (Sunday to Thursday) and 1.40pm (Friday and Saturday). From April 1966 the train was diverted with electric haulage between Euston and Coventry and then diesel haulage to and from Holyhead via Birmingham New Street – the result was

▲ The wine list from 'The Emerald Isle Express' from May 1959.

that the train became even slower. Things improved once electrification was completed between Euston and Crewe in 1967 with no fewer than 90 minutes shaved off the schedule of the up train – strangely the down train was still diverted via Birmingham New Street yet still managed to cut nearly half an hour off the journey time. The train lost its title in May 1975.

◄ Hauled by English Electric Type 4 (Class 40) diesel D343, 'The Emerald Isle Express' heads through Camden in August 1961. The long-wheelbase utility van behind the loco must have virtually rattled along at express speed! The loco was built at the Vulcan Foundry in 1961 and withdrawn as No. 40143 in January 1985.

◄ Holyhead shed's BR Standard 'Britannia' Class 4-6-2 No. 70048 approaches Headstone Lane with the up 'The Emerald Isle Express' on 15 April 1957. Seen here unnamed, the loco was named 'The Territorial Army 1908-1958' by the Duke of Norfolk on 23 July 1958. No. 70048 was built at Crewe in 1954 and withdrawn from Carlisle Kingmoor shed in September 1967.

E ENTERPRISE

BELFAST TO DUBLIN

Introduced by the Great Northern Railway (Ireland) in August 1947, the 'Enterprise' was the first non-stop service between Belfast (Great Victoria Street) and Dublin (Amiens Street). Covering the 112¼ miles in 2¼ hours the train was hauled in its early years by the GNR(I)'s blue-liveried 'V' Class 4-4-0s. Although introduced in 1915, an additional five locos were built by Beyer Peacock in 1947 specifically for this service. Passengers needed to arrive 30 minutes before departure for passport checks but once on the train they could relax in a cocktail bar and buffet car. The service was extended beyond Dublin to Cork in 1950 but this proved unpopular as the total journey time to or from Belfast was now 6½ hours! The Cork extension was dropped in 1953, the year that the GNR(I) was nationalised. The year 1958 saw the nationalised Great Northern Railway Board divided between Córas Iompair Éireann (CIE) and the Ulster Transport Authority (UTA); the introduction of diesel multiple units was soon to follow on the cross-border service before they in turn were replaced

GNR DUBLIN BELFAST BY ENTERPRISE EXPRESSES

Quiet comfort... THE NEW ENTERPRISE EXPRESSES

provide fast **non-stop** services between the capital cities at convenient times with a high standard of travel comfort.

...in bright surroundings...

accommodation for first and third class passengers is roomy and well-appointed

...perhaps a cocktail...

the 112½ miles is covered in 2¼ hours, giving ample time for a visit to the cocktail bar and a meal in the buffet car...

by diesel locomotive hauled stock. Although interrupted on numerous occasions during the period of 'The Troubles' in the 1970s and 1980s, the 'Enterprise' lives on today and gives its name to all express services between Belfast and Dublin. Since 1976 the northern terminus for this service has been Belfast Central while in Dublin Amiens Street station has been renamed Connolly.

▶ Diesel multiple unit No. 134 speeds along near Tandragee with an 'Enterprise' express in July 1965.

...with a meal to follow!

it is advisable to be at the station about half an hour before departure time for Customs examination. Please book in advance.

▲ GNR (I) 4-4-0 No. 86 is featured on this cigarette card hauling a Dublin to Belfast express.

▲ Featuring a blue-liveried GNR (I) 4-4-0, this late 1940s pocket-sized fold-out leaflet colourfully displays the delights of travelling on the 'Enterprise' express between Belfast and Dublin.

THE FAIR MAID

LONDON (KING'S CROSS) TO PERTH

Following in the footsteps of the pre-war 'Coronation', the introduction of 'The Talisman' between King's Cross and Edinburgh in 1956 was hailed such a success that an additional morning working was inaugurated in 1957. The start of the winter timetable in that year saw this 'Morning Talisman' renamed as 'The Fair Maid' with the northern terminus extended to Perth. With intermediate stops at Darlington, Newcastle, Berwick and Edinburgh the down train took 8hrs 28min to complete its journey while the up train took 8hrs 50min. The new extended working was not successful and a year later the train lost its name and reverted to the 'Morning Talisman' service between King's Cross and Edinburgh.

▼ The 1957 menu for the short-lived 'The Fair Maid'. The linear route map features line drawings by Donald Blake.

▲ King's Cross shed's 'A1' Class 4-6-2 No. 60158 'Aberdonian' is seen here at the head of 'The Fair Maid' at Darlington in August 1958. A month later this short-lived named train was withdrawn. The loco was built at Darlington in 1949 and withdrawn from Doncaster shed in December 1964.

THE FENMAN

LONDON (LIVERPOOL STREET) TO HUNSTANTON/BURY ST EDMUNDS

Working express trains out of Liverpool Street along some of the busiest commuter lines in the world was no mean feat. Needless to say journey times between the capital and Cambridge via Broxbourne were fairly lethargic and it was into this scene that the Eastern Region's new named buffet car train, 'The Fenman', was introduced between Liverpool Street and the Norfolk seaside resort of Hunstanton in the summer of 1949. Running Mondays to Fridays, departure for the up train from Hunstanton was at 6.45am, then all stations to King's Lynn where the train reversed direction before heading south to London. There were then intermediate stops at Downham, Ely and Cambridge where a portion from Bury St Edmunds was attached before reaching Liverpool Street at 10.04am. The down train left the capital at 4.30pm and with the same stops arrived at Hunstanton at 8.05pm. The train was speeded up in 1953, losing the Bury St Edmunds portion but adding one for March and Wisbech which was attached or detached at Ely. Until the advent of the Brush Type 2 and English Electric Type 3 diesels the train was normally hauled by 'B17' Class or 'B1' Class 4-6-0s. However, the rot had set in by 1960 with the Wisbech portion dropped, and the train starting

or terminating its journey at King's Lynn – passengers to or from Hunstanton then had to travel in a separate diesel multiple unit. The train lost its name in 1968 and the Hunstanton branch was closed a year later.

▲ The summer 1950 leaflet, route map and timetable for 'The Fenman'.

◄ Ex-GER Class 'D16/3' 4-4-0 No. 62606 leaves King's Lynn with 'The Fenman', circa 1956. The loco bears a 31C shedplate and was a King's Lynn engine from 1954 to 1959. Designed by Nigel Gresley, it was built at Stratford Works in 1911 and withdrawn in September 1959.

FIFE COAST EXPRESS

GLASGOW (QUEEN STREET/BUCHANAN STREET) TO ST ANDREWS

A summer-only train with this name had been operated from Glasgow to the East of Fife coastal line since before the First World War. The Second World War put an end to this service for holidaymakers but it was reintroduced by the Scottish Region in 1949. Running between Glasgow Queen Street and the golfing capital of St Andrews, the train was normally hauled by 'B1' 4-6-0s and for some years passengers were treated to a ride in a set of articulated luxury coaches that had once seen service on the pre-war 'Silver Jubilee'. The train was diverted to Glasgow (Buchanan Street) in 1957 and lost its title at the end of the 1959 summer timetable. Despite this, steam-hauled trains continued to run along this route during the summer months until 6 September 1965 when the coastal line closed between St Andrews and Leven.

◄ After arriving at Glasgow Queen Street with the 'Fife Coast Express' on 12 July 1956, 'B1' Class 4-6-0 No. 61197 pushes the empty stock up the 1-in-41 of Cowlairs Bank to the carriage sidings. A Class 'J83' 0-6-0T was assisting at the other end. The 'B1' was built by the North British Locomotive Company in 1947 and was withdrawn from Ayr shed in June 1964.

THE FLYING SCOTSMAN

LONDON (KING'S CROSS) TO EDINBURGH

By 1860 services on the East Coast Main Line between London King's Cross and Edinburgh Waverley were under the control of the Great Northern Railway, the North Eastern Railway and the North British Railway. Through services between the two capitals were hindered by the lack of standard passenger carriages and in that year the three companies formed the East Coast Joint Stock to remedy this situation.

By 1862 new rolling stock for the first 'Special Scotch Express' was ready and the train became a regular feature departing each day at 10am from King's Cross and Waverley stations. At that time the train took a leisurely 10½ hours to complete the 393 miles including a stop at York where the passengers disembarked for lunch. This leisurely pace did not last long and when Patrick Stirling, the GNR's Chief Mechanical Engineer, designed his famous Stirling Single locomotives in 1870, the East Coast route saw a rapid acceleration of schedules with a whole two hours soon being lopped off the King's Cross to Edinburgh journey.

By 1888 there had also developed a serious rivalry between the operators of the West Coast Main Line (L&NWR and CR) and the East Coast Main Line (GNR, NER, NBR) to achieve the fastest possible time between London and Aberdeen. This resulted in what became known as the 'Race to the North' and on 20 August that year, with the surefooted help from the Stirling Singles as far as York, the ECML between King's Cross and Edinburgh was covered in 6hrs 19min at an average speed of 62.2mph. The rivalry continued until 1896 when an Anglo-Scottish express, operated by the L&NWR, was derailed at Preston – safety limits had been flouted and a speed limit was imposed on the two rivals which stayed in place until 1932.

▲ This late 1950s restaurant car menu from 'The Flying Scotsman' features line drawings by Donald Blake on the linear route map.

The beginning of the twentieth century brought major improvements to the 'Special Scotch Express', with modern corridor carriages and dining cars. The heavier and longer trains were now headed by Ivatt's new 'Atlantics' as far as York but timings remained the same due to the 1896 speed restriction. The arrival of Nigel Gresley as Locomotive Engineer of the Great Northern Railway in 1911 led to the building of a series of groundbreaking 'Pacific' locomotive types. Two of his Class 'A1' 4-6-2s were built at Doncaster in 1922 and ten more had been ordered

The
FLYING SCOTSMAN
1862–1962

Luncheon

12/6

Tomato Juice
or
Ox-tail Soup

Whiting Bercy

Roast Chicken, Bread Sauce
Garden Peas   Carrots Vichy
Roast and Boiled Potatoes

Fruit Flan
or
Cheese, Salad, Biscuits and Butter

Coffee, 1/-

Cheese & Biscuits etc. may be served in addition
to the Sweet for an extra charge of 1/6

BRITISH TRANSPORT CATERING SERVICE

Sc.R / K31

◄ This Scottish Region restaurant car luncheon menu celebrates the hundredth anniversary of 'The Flying Scotsman' in 1962.

▼ The stylish pre-war luggage label for use by 'The Flying Scotsman' passengers.

THE FLYING SCOTSMAN
RESTAURANT CAR EXPRESS

LONDON (King's Cross)
NEWCASTLE AND EDINBURGH (Waverley)

WEEKDAYS

	SX am	SO am			A am	B am
LONDON (King's Cross) .. dep	10 0	10 0	EDINBURGH (Waverley) .. dep	10 0	10 0	10 0
	pm	pm			pm	pm
Newcastle .. { arr	2 45	3 12	Newcastle .. { arr	12 14	12 20
{ dep	2 51	3 18	{ dep	12 20	12 26
EDINBURGH (Waverley) .. arr	5 2	5 35	LONDON (King's Cross) arr	5 5	5 30

A—Saturdays excepted. Conveys Through Carriage from Aberdeen (depart 6.10 am) to London (King's Cross).
B—Saturdays only. Conveys Through Carriage from Aberdeen (depart 6.10 am) to London (King's Cross).
SO—Saturdays only.
SX—Saturdays excepted.

Restaurant Car for Table d'Hôte meals.
Miniature Buffet Car for light refreshments.
Seats are reservable in advance for passengers travelling from King's Cross and Edinburgh on payment of a fee of 2s. 0d. per seat.

◄ The summer 1961 timetable for 'The Flying Scotsman' – the following year new 'Deltic' diesels were in charge.

LONDON & NORTH EASTERN RAILWAY
EDINBURGH
WAVERLEY
THE FLYING SCOTSMAN

▶ This postcard, circa 1930, features Gresley's unique 'W1' Class ('Hush-Hush') 4-6-4 No. 10000 at the head of 'The Flying Scotsman'.

just before the 'Big Four' Grouping of 1923. As Chief Mechanical Engineer of the newly-formed LNER, Gresley went on to develop this design into the 'A3' and later 'A4' streamlined Pacifics.

The 'Special Scotch Express' became officially know as 'The Flying Scotsman' in 1924 and one of Gresley's 'A1' locos, No. 4472, was also named in honour of the train. To reduce the journey time between King's Cross and Edinburgh some of the 'A1' locos were fitted with larger tenders containing not only more coal but also with a corridor linking the engine to the first coach of the train. The latter allowed a crew changeover halfway through the journey and so 'The Flying Scotsman' became a non-stop service in May 1928, complete with a host of on-board facilities. The speed limitation agreement was abolished in 1932 and the gloves were off – by 1938 the journey time for the down 'The Flying Scotsman' had been reduced to 7hrs 20min. The austerity measures of the Second World War soon brought an end to high-speed rail travel and it took some years before pre-war schedules were being reattained. With the introduction of the record-breaking non-stop 'The Elizabethan' express in

▲ The down 'The Flying Scotsman' passes non-stop through York behind 'A1' Class 4-6-2 No. 60156 'Great Central' (fitted with Timken roller bearings) on 10 April 1954. This loco was built at Doncaster in 1949 and withdrawn from York North shed in May 1965.

► Fitted with Timken roller bearings, 'A1' Class 4-6-2 No. 60157 'Great Eastern' storms through Finsbury Park with the down 'The Flying Scotsman' in the late 1950s. The loco was built at Doncaster in 1949 and withdrawn from Doncaster shed in January 1965.

1954 (taking only 6½ hours to cover the 393 miles) the 'Flying Scotsman' had reverted to an intermediate stop at Newcastle – even though the journey time by 1961 had come down to 7hrs 2min with the introduction of the new 'Deltic' (Class 55) diesels.

The introduction of 100mph running along many stretches of the ECML gave the 'Deltics' their racing ground and timings for 'The Flying Scotsman' continued to tumble. In turn, the 'Deltics' were replaced by HST sets between 1976 and 1981, and the opening of the Selby diversion improved matters further. Electrification was completed in 1990 and since then InterCity 225 sets with a maximum permissible speed of 125mph have provided an even faster service. Since privatisation the train has continued to run, with a speeded up service complete with special 'Flying Scotsman' livery being introduced in 2011 – the up train now takes only four hours between the two capitals. Strangely, the slower 10am down working from King's Cross now does not carry the name.

◄ 'Deltic' (Class 55) diesel D9018 'Ballymoss' climbs to Stoke Summit at Little Ponton with the up 'The Flying Scotsman' in July 1962. Introduced new from Vulcan Foundry in November 1961, the loco was named after a famous racehorse and was withdrawn in October 1981.

GOLDEN ARROW

LONDON (VICTORIA) TO PARIS (GARE DU NORD)

During the late nineteenth century, years before the advent of air transport, the only way to travel between London and Paris was by boat and train. Compared to the current Eurostar service through the Channel Tunnel, the journey was leisurely and involved a ferry journey between Dover or Folkestone and Calais. In 1906 the London Brighton & South Coast Railway introduced luxury Pullman cars and within a few years these were included in their boat trains from Victoria station. Soon after the formation of the Southern Railway in the 1923 Grouping, an all-Pullman boat train was introduced and in 1929 it was officially named the 'Golden Arrow' – on the French side of the Channel the corresponding train between Calais and Paris was called 'Flèche d'Or'. In 1936 the SR built a luxury ferry, the 'Canterbury', for the sole use of its first class

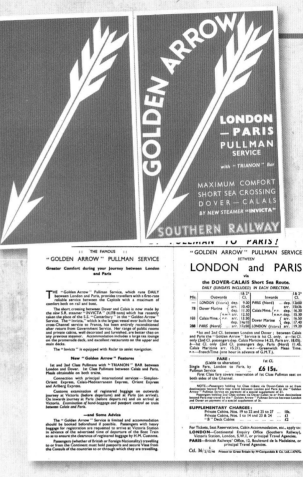

▲ Dated 2 December 1946, this Southern Railway leaflet announces cross-Channel sailings for 'Golden Arrow' passengers aboard the new company-owned steamer SS *Invicta*.

▲ The stylish luggage label for the pre-war 'Golden Arrow'.

passengers on the London to Paris route. The ship was also fitted with rails on the cargo deck which carried through coaches of the luxury 'The Night Ferry' sleeper train between the two capitals.

The outbreak of the Second World War brought an end to the service, which returned in April 1946. Bulleid's new air-smoothed 'Merchant Navy' and light Pacific locomotives based at Stewarts Lane shed were now in charge of the train which, by 1951, had been augmented by the introduction of new Pullman cars and was temporarily renamed the 'Festival of Britain Golden Arrow'. Locomotives hauling the train were

▲ The colourful BR leaflet for the 'Golden Arrow' service for November 1959 to May 1960.

▶ BR Standard 'Britannia' Class 4-6-2 No. 70004 'William Shakespeare' is cleaned at Stewarts Lane depot prior to hauling the 'Golden Arrow' to Dover in the mid-1950s. The loco was built at Crewe in 1951 and withdrawn from Carlisle Kingmoor in December 1967.

▼ The summer 1963 timetable for the 'Golden Arrow'.

LONDON and PARIS
BY
"GOLDEN ARROW"
PULLMAN SERVICE
EVERY DAY IN EACH DIRECTION

Miles				1st Class Luxe
—	LONDON (Victoria)	…	dep	11 0 am
78	Dover Marine	{ arr		12 22 pm
		dep		12 50 pm
103	Calais Maritime	{ arr		2 10 pm
		dep		2 37 pm
288	PARIS (Nord)	…	arr	5 50 pm
				1st Class Luxe
	PARIS (Nord)	…	dep	12 39 pm
	Calais Maritime	{ arr		3 45 pm
		dep		4 10 pm
	Dover Marine	{ arr		5 30 pm
		dep		6 10 pm

grandly adorned with a long golden arrow on each side and on the smokebox door. The Union Jack and French Tricolore fluttered from the bufferbeam. Two of the first batch of brand new BR Standard 'Britannia' Class locos, No. 70004 'William Shakespeare' and No. 70014 'Iron Duke', were specifically allocated to Stewarts Lane in 1951 to haul the upgraded 'Golden Arrow', a job they continued to do until they were transferred to Longsight, Manchester, in 1958.

▲ Unrebuilt 'West Country' Class 4-6-2 No. 34092 'City of Wells' under the coaling tower at Stewarts Lane depot prior to hauling the down 'Golden Arrow' in the late 1950s. The loco was built at Brighton in 1949, withdrawn in November 1964 and has since been preserved.

► The up 'Golden Arrow' storms through Folkestone Junction behind BR 'Britannia' Class 4-6-2 No. 70004 'William Shakespeare' in the mid-1950s. On the right is 'H' Class 0-4-4T No. 31322 on more humble shunting duties.

During the 1950s the popularity and speed of air travel between London and Paris spelt the end for this luxury train which was now made up of first class Pullman cars and standard second class stock. Electric haulage by BR–built (Class 71) Bo–Bo locos (E5000–E5023) was introduced in June 1961 and continued until September 1972 when this famous train ceased to run.

► This colourful postcard shows a new Class 71 Bo-Bo electric locomotive hauling the 'Golden Arrow' in the early 1960s.

◄ Rebuilt 'West Country' 4-6-2 No. 34101 'Appledore' heads the down 'Golden Arrow' through Folkestone Warren in July 1962 – this was one of the last steam-worked 'GA' trains. The loco was built at Eastleigh in 1950, rebuilt in 1960, withdrawn in July 1966 and has since been preserved.

G

GOLDEN HIND

LONDON (PADDINGTON) TO PLYMOUTH

Introduced on 15 June 1964, the all-new 'Golden Hind' provided a much-needed early morning express for businessmen from Plymouth up to London with a late afternoon return from Paddington. Hauled by 'Western' Class diesel hydraulics, the lightweight restaurant car train of seven coaches (later increased to eight) set the fastest-ever scheduled time between Plymouth and London of 3hrs 50min – the return service was five minutes longer. With intermediate stops at Newton Abbot, Exeter and Taunton, the last leg of the up journey took only 2hrs 7min. New Mk 2 coaches introduced in 1970 accompanied an even faster schedule and in 1972 the service was extended to Penzance. Unusually for a named train, the last coach had a nameboard attached to its rear end. HSTs had taken over from the locomotive hauled stock by the early 1980s and the train continues in this form today – the up service taking only 3hrs 7min for the journey from Plymouth to Paddington.

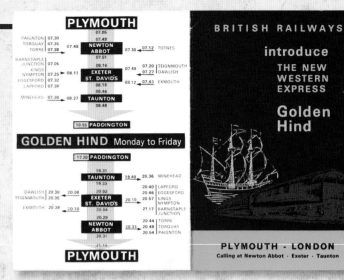

▲▼ The leaflet and menu issued by BR for the new 'Golden Hind' express in the summer of 1964.

▲ English Electric Type 4 (Class 50) diesel No. 50048 'Dauntless' speeds through West Ealing with the down 'Golden Hind' on 22 April 1975. Built in 1968 at the Vulcan Foundry, the loco was withdrawn in March 1978.

G

THE GRAMPIAN

GLASGOW (BUCHANAN STREET) TO ABERDEEN

In the early twentieth century the Caledonian Railway operated a series of luxurious trains between Glasgow (Buchanan Street) and Aberdeen via Perth and Forfar. Known as 'The Grampian Corridor' (after the new 12-wheeled corridor stock used for the trains) and 'The Granite City', the trains were discontinued on the outbreak of the First World War. They resumed after the war but were no longer named. In 1922 the 7.15am departure from Glasgow (which included a Pullman breakfast car) was scheduled to arrive at Aberdeen at 11.50am. The service continued to run with newer LMS coaching stock and refurbished Pullman cars until the outbreak of the Second World War.

The name was reintroduced by the Scottish Region of BR in 1962 and applied to the 8.25am departure from Glasgow which took exactly three hours to reach Aberdeen. With more intermediate stops, the return service left Aberdeen at 1.30pm and arrived back at Glasgow at 5.30pm – both trains included a miniature buffet car. As with the other Glasgow to Aberdeen three-hour expresses, 'The Grampian' saw Gresley's 'A4' Pacifics perform their swansong between 1962 and 3 September 1966 when diesel haulage took over. Trains such as 'The Grampian' ceased to operate along this route on 4 September 1967 when the former Caledonian main line between Stanley Junction and Kinnaber Junction via Forfar was closed. They were then diverted via Dundee but with slower timings.

◄ Banished from its duties on the East Coast Main Line, 'A4' Class 4-6-2 No. 60031 'Golden Plover' enters Gleneagles station with the up 'The Grampian' express in September 1963. The loco was built at Doncaster in 1937 and withdrawn from St Rollox shed in October 1965.

THE GRANITE CITY

GLASGOW (BUCHANAN STREET) TO ABERDEEN

'The Granite City' was first applied in 1906 to a luxurious restaurant car train operated by the Caledonian Railway between Glasgow and Aberdeen. The name was dropped on the outbreak of the First World War but reinstated by the London Midland & Scottish Railway in 1933 and given to the 10.05am departure from Buchanan Street, returning from Aberdeen at 5.35pm. During the Second World War the train continued to run although the name was quietly dropped. It was reintroduced in 1949, this time with a 10am departure from Buchanan Street and a 5.15pm departure for the return working from Aberdeen. Both trains carried a restaurant car but the down service took 3hrs 41min while the up journey was achieved in three hours. As with other Glasgow to Aberdeen three-hour expresses 'The Granite City' was hauled by Gresley's 'A4' Pacifics between 1962 and 1966. Diesel haulage then took over but the train was rerouted via Dundee following the closure of the Forfar line in 1967. It lost its name in 1968.

◄ Sporting a loco nameboard with a train of 'blood-and-custard' Gresley coaches, 'The Granite City' prepares to leave Aberdeen for Glasgow behind BR Standard Class 5 4-6-0 No. 73007 in April 1954. The loco was built at Derby in 1951 and withdrawn from Stirling shed in March 1966.

THE HOOK CONTINENTAL

LONDON (LIVERPOOL STREET) TO HARWICH (PARKESTON QUAY)

By the early twentieth century the ferry port of Parkeston Quay in Harwich was being served by luxurious Great Eastern Railway trains from Liverpool Street which connected with the company's steamers to and from the Hook of Holland. The port assumed even greater importance after the First World War when a new service to and from Zeebrugge in Belgium was introduced, followed by a steamer service to and from Flushing in 1927. With the addition of Pullman cars after the war the Hook of Holland train was one of the heaviest to

be operated by the Great Eastern Railway and was entrusted to the powerful Holden '1500' Class 4-6-0s from Parkeston Quay shed. Under the London & North Eastern Railway a new luxury train – officially named 'The Hook Continental' – was introduced in 1927 with the down train leaving Liverpool Street in the evening and the up train returning the next morning. Timings were tight especially for the up train which had to battle its way through heavy morning commuter traffic into the capital.

The Second World War naturally brought

an end to all of these Continental services but the luxurious 'The Hook Continental' was reintroduced in November 1945. The train was speeded up when new BR Standard 'Britannia' Pacifics were introduced in 1951 – the down journey time was slashed to only 1hr 20min. Steam was replaced by English Electric Type 4 diesels in 1958, followed by Class 37 and Class 47 haulage until electrification in 1986. With the introduction of electric multiple units the train lost its name in 1987.

▲ Stratford shed's brand new BR 'Britannia' Class 4-6-2 No. 70001 'Lord Hurcomb' prepares to haul 'The Hook Continental' at Liverpool Street in the summer of 1951. Built at Crewe, the loco was withdrawn in August 1966.

THE HEART OF MIDLOTHIAN

LONDON (KING'S CROSS) TO EDINBURGH

For many years the two early afternoon departures from Edinburgh and King's Cross remained nameless but in 1951 British Railways bestowed the name of 'The Heart of Midlothian' on these trains to commemorate the Festival of Britain. Consisting of 12 brand-new all-steel BR standard (Mk 1) coaches, each train included the largest kitchen car ever put into service in Britain – cooking was carried out using a flexible source from either anthracite or electricity. Both up and down trains departed at 2pm and, with stops at Peterborough, York, Darlington

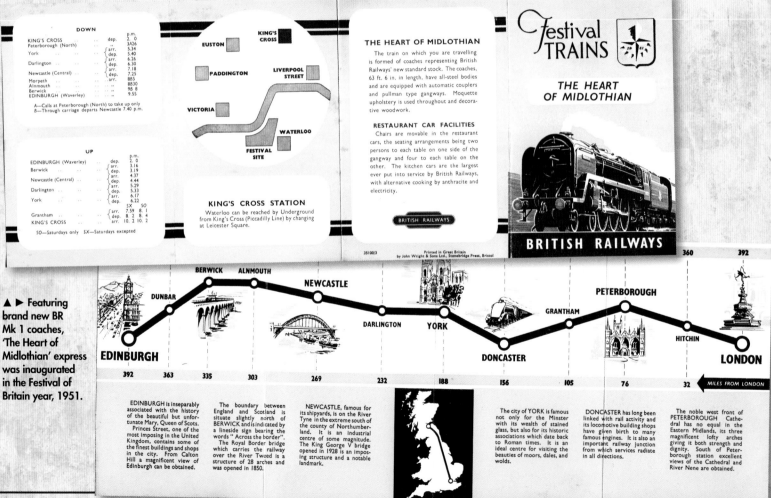

DOWN			
			p.m.
KING'S CROSS	..	dep.	2. 0
Peterborough (North)	..	"	3A26
York	..	{ arr.	5.34
		dep.	5.40
Darlington	..	{ arr.	6.26
		dep.	6.30
Newcastle (Central)	..	{ arr.	7.18
		dep.	7.25
Morpeth	..	arr.	8 8 5
Alnmouth			8 8 30
Berwick			98. 8
EDINBURGH (Waverley)			9.55

A—Calls at Peterborough (North) to take up only
B—Through carriage departs Newcastle 7.40 p.m.

UP			
			p.m.
EDINBURGH (Waverley)	..	dep.	2. 0
Berwick	..	{ arr.	3.16
		dep.	3.19
Newcastle (Central)	..	{ arr.	4.37
		dep.	4.44
Darlington	..	{ arr.	5.29
		dep.	5.33
York	..	{ arr.	6.17
		dep.	6.22
			SX SO
Grantham	..	{ arr.	7.59 8. 1
		dep.	8. 2 8. 4
KING'S CROSS	..	arr.	10. 2 10. 2

SO—Saturdays only   SX—Saturdays excepted

KING'S CROSS STATION

Waterloo can be reached by Underground from King's Cross (Piccadilly Line) by changing at Leicester Square.

THE HEART OF MIDLOTHIAN

The train on which you are travelling is formed of coaches representing British Railways' new standard stock. The coaches, 63 ft. 6 in. in length, have all-steel bodies and are equipped with automatic couplers and pullman type gangways. Moquette upholstery is used throughout and decorative woodwork.

RESTAURANT CAR FACILITIES

Chairs are movable in the restaurant cars, the seating arrangements being two persons to each table on one side of the gangway and four to each table on the other. The kitchen cars are the largest ever put into service by British Railways, with alternative cooking by anthracite and electricity.

BRITISH RAILWAYS

35100/3

Printed in Great Britain by John Wright & Sons Ltd., Stonebridge Press, Bristol

Festival TRAINS

THE HEART OF MIDLOTHIAN

BRITISH RAILWAYS

▲ ► Featuring brand new BR Mk 1 coaches, 'The Heart of Midlothian' express was inaugurated in the Festival of Britain year, 1951.

EDINBURGH 392 — DUNBAR 363 — BERWICK 335 — ALNMOUTH 303 — NEWCASTLE 269 — DARLINGTON 232 — YORK 188 — DONCASTER 156 — GRANTHAM 105 — PETERBOROUGH 76 — HITCHIN 32 — LONDON

360   392

MILES FROM LONDON

EDINBURGH is inseparably associated with the history of the beautiful but unfortunate Mary, Queen of Scots. Princes Street, one of the most imposing in the United Kingdom, contains some of the finest buildings and shops in the city. From Calton Hill a magnificent view of Edinburgh can be obtained.

The boundary between England and Scotland is situate slightly north of BERWICK and is indicated by a lineside sign bearing the words "Across the border". The Royal Border bridge which carries the railway over the River Tweed is a structure of 28 arches and was opened in 1850.

NEWCASTLE, famous for its shipyards, is on the River Tyne in the extreme south of the county of Northumberland. It is an industrial centre of some magnitude. The King George V bridge opened in 1928 is an imposing structure and a notable landmark.

The city of YORK is famous not only for the Minster with its wealth of stained glass, but also for its historic associations which date back to Roman times. It is an ideal centre for visiting the beauties of moors, dales, and wolds.

DONCASTER has long been linked with rail activity and its locomotive building shops have given birth to many famous engines. It is also an important railway junction from which services radiate in all directions.

The noble west front of PETERBOROUGH Cathedral has no equal in the Eastern Midlands, its three magnificent lofty arches giving it both strength and dignity. South of Peterborough station excellent views of the Cathedral and River Nene are obtained.

and Newcastle, the down train arrived at Edinburgh at 9.55pm. Carriages for Morpeth, Alnmouth and Berwick were removed at Newcastle and followed on as a slower train. The up train called at Berwick, Newcastle, Darlington, York and Grantham and arrived at King's Cross at 10.02pm.

An experiment in 1957 to extend the service northwards to serve Stirling and Perth failed to attract customers and was soon withdrawn. 'Deltic' diesels took over in 1962 and timings were slashed to give a 6½-hour journey for the up train and 6¾ hours for the down service. The train lost its name in 1968.

▲ 'A1' Class 4-6-2 No. 60152 'Holyrood' heads 'The Heart of Midlothian' through Grantshouse in June 1958. The loco was built at Darlington in 1949 and withdrawn in June 1965.

THE HEART OF MIDLOTHIAN

LONDON (King's Cross),
YORK, DARLINGTON, NEWCASTLE
and
EDINBURGH (Waverley)

WEEKDAYS

	pm			A pm
London (King's Cross) dep	1 0	Edinburgh (Waverley) dep		1 30
Peterborough (North) ,,	2 32	Berwick-upon-Tweed ,,		2 40
York ... ... arr	4 39	Newcastle ... ... ,,		3 57
Darlington ... ... ,,	5 32	Darlington ... ... ,,		4 48
Newcastle ... ... ,,	6 20	York ... ... ,,		5 35
Alnmouth ... ... ,,	7 7	Grantham ... ...arr		7 7
Berwick-upon-Tweed ,,	7 47	London (King's Cross) ,,		9 20
Dunbar ... ... ,,	8 21			
Edinburgh (Waverley) ,,	8 54			

A Conveys Through Carriage from Aberdeen (dep 9 45 am) to London (King's Cross)

Restaurant Cars for Table d'Hote Meals.

Ladies' retiring room with attendant.

Seats are reservable in advance for passengers travelling from London (King's Cross) and Edinburgh (Waverley) on payment of a fee of 2s. 0d. per seat.

▲ Minus its headboard, the up 'The Heart of Midlothian' passes Beningborough north of York behind Gateshead's filthy 'A4' Class 4-6-2 No. 60020 'Guillemot' on 6 August 1961. Soon to lose these top link duties to 'Deltic' diesels, this loco was built at Doncaster in 1938 and withdrawn from Gateshead shed in March 1964.

◄ The summer 1961 timetable for 'The Heart of Midlothian'.

THE HULL PULLMAN AND THE HULL EXECUTIVE

LONDON (KING'S CROSS) TO HULL

Replacing previous Pullman services to Leeds, Bradford and Harrogate, 'The Yorkshire Pullman' received its name in 1935 and conveyed Pullman carriages to or from Hull that were detached from or attached to the main train at Doncaster. Although withdrawn for the duration of the Second World War the train returned in 1946 and continued to run with the Hull portion until March 1967 when a new train, 'The Hull Pullman', was introduced. Initially hauled by Class 47 diesels, the seven-coach up train put in a spirited performance with a

10.35am departure from Hull reaching King's Cross in 189 minutes. Departing from King's Cross in the early evening the down train took 195 minutes – both trains called at Doncaster, Goole and Brough. 'Deltic' haulage was introduced in the early 1970s, when the train was lengthened and continued to run in this guise until 1978, when it was replaced by the new non-Pullman 'The Hull Executive'. The latter train continued to run until replaced by HSTs in 1981. The name is still used to describe a daily express service between Hull and King's Cross.

▲ 'Deltic' (Class 55) diesel No. 55017 'The Durham Light Infantry' leaves Doncaster with the up 'The Hull Pullman' on 22 June 1977. Introduced in 1962, this loco was withdrawn at the end of 1981.

THE HULL PULLMAN

HULL
Retford
Doncaster
Goole
Brough

D

BR21717/33

◄ A window sticker from the 'Deltic'-hauled 'The Hull Pullman' era.

▼ Belching diesel fumes, 'Deltic' (Class 55) diesel No. 55003 'Meld' prepares to haul 'The Hull Executive', circa 1979. Introduced in 1961, this loco was withdrawn at the end of 1980.

THE INTER-CITY

LONDON (PADDINGTON) TO BIRMINGHAM (SNOW HILL) AND WOLVERHAMPTON (LOW LEVEL)

Introduced by the Western Region of British Railways in 1950, 'The Inter-City' provided a fast service for businessmen between London and the West Midlands. Hauled by 'Castle' or 'King' Class 4-6-0s, the down train left Paddington at 9am and called at High Wycombe before reaching Birmingham (Snow Hill) at 11.10am – Wolverhampton was reached a leisurely 25 minutes later. The up train took an extra five minutes calling at Leamington and High Wycombe before reaching

▼ A 1950s BR leaflet giving details of the route of 'The Inter-City' through the scenery of the West Midlands.

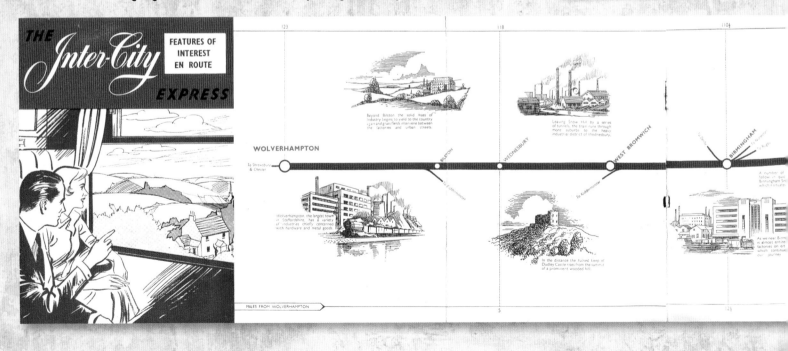

Paddington at 7.05pm. The schedule was speeded up in 1954 with the down train taking exactly two hours to reach Snow Hill. 'Western' Class diesel hydraulics took over in 1962 and the train lost its name three years later. Losing its definite article, 'Inter-City' was then used very successfully by British Railways as a brand name and was even licensed for use by the German and Irish state railways.

Table II

THE INTER-CITY
RESTAURANT CAR SERVICE
LONDON, BIRMINGHAM and WOLVERHAMPTON
WEEK DAYS
(Mondays to Fridays)

		am			pm
London (Paddington) .. .. dep	9A 0		Wolverhampton (Low Level).. dep	4A35
High Wycombe .. .. .. ,,	9 32		Birmingham (Snow Hill) .. ,,	5A 0
Birmingham (Snow Hill) .. arr	11 0		Leamington Spa General .. ,,	5 26
Wolverhampton (Low Level) ,,	11 25		High Wycombe .. .. arr	6 34
			London (Paddington) .. .. ,,	7 10

◄ The winter 1958/59 timetable for the Western Region's 'The Inter-City'.

◄ The stylish cover of the restaurant car tariff for 'The Inter-City' express, circa 1957.

▼ An unidentified Old Oak Common 'King' Class 4-6-0 hauls the down 'The Inter-City' near Saunderton in the late 1950s.

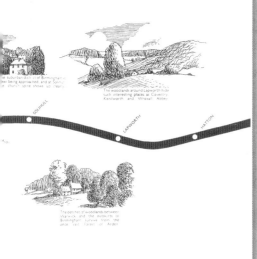

THE IRISH MAIL

LONDON (EUSTON) TO HOLYHEAD

'The successful debut of railways operated by locomotives in 1830, the introduction of the Penny Post in 1840, and a demand for faster mail services between London and Dublin were sequences in a cycle of events which led directly to the construction of the Chester & Holyhead Railway (1844-1850) and the establishment of the first all-railway owned route to Ireland. The Chester & Holyhead railway built four ships for the new service; two of their names are perpetuated today by the 5,000-ton motor ships *Cambria* and *Hibernia*.' (BR publicity blurb, 1955)

There were in fact two Irish Mail services between Euston and Holyhead – the daytime service carried restaurant cars while the night service conveyed sleeping cars. Both services also conveyed two Post Office sorting carriages – from as early as the 1870s these were also able to pick up mailbags at speed from lineside postal apparatus. The introduction of the world's first water troughs at Mochdre on the London & North Western Railway's main line between Chester and Holyhead in 1860 also greatly assisted in speeding up services.

Officially receiving the name 'The Irish Mail' in 1927 both the daytime and night-time services were amongst the heaviest to be operated on Britain's railways – the advent of Fowler's 'Royal Scot' Class in the same year saw these engines hauling up to 17 bogie coaches unassisted along the North Wales coast line, the

▼ Featuring a superbly designed cover and a map of LMS hotels, this menu for the first class restaurant car of 'The Irish Mail' is dated 30 January 1934.

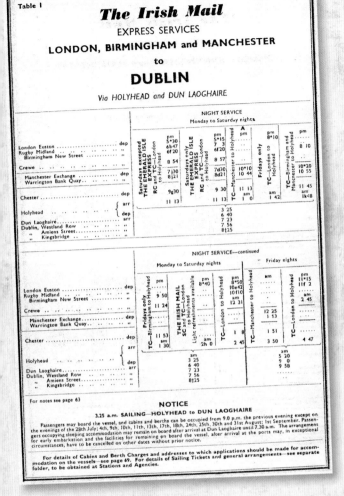

▲ The summer 1962 timetable for the down 'The Irish Mail' and the preceding 'Emerald Isle Express'.

▶ BR Standard 'Britannia' Class 4-6-2 No. 70047 stands at Holyhead shed prior to hauling the up 'The Irish Mail' in August 1959. Built at Crewe in 1954, this loco was the only one of its class not to be named and was withdrawn from Carlisle Kingmoor shed in July 1967.

same engine and crew working the train for the entire 263 miles between Euston and Holyhead. Only the daytime service survived for the duration of the Second World War with the night service being reinstated in 1946. At this stage the daytime service became a summer-only working. By the early 1950s the trains were being hauled by new BR Standard 'Britannia' 4-6-2s and even 'Coronation' Class 4-6-2s for a short while after their demotion from West Coast Main Line duties in the late 1950s and early 1960s. By this time the down night train (8.40pm out of Euston) was booked to run non-stop between Euston and Holyhead (scheduled to arrive at 2am). The up train was slower with stops at Chester, Crewe and Rugby. Such was the demand for seats on the night service that relief trains to both up and down trains were also run. Steam had been replaced by English Electric Type 4 diesels by the early 1960s and in 1966 the switch-on of the electrified West Coast Main Line between Euston and Crewe introduced the first ever change of locos for the train at the latter junction station. With the demise of mail being carried by rail, the onset of cheap air travel and faster ferry crossings, the 'Irish Mail' sadly bit the dust in 1985.

The Great Western Railway also operated its own 'Irish Mail' train services between Paddington and Fishguard from 1906 to 1939.

THE JACOBITE

FORT WILLIAM TO MALLAIG

The Jacobite

Fort William - Glenfinnan - Arisaig - Mallaig

WEST COAST RAILWAYS
The UK's Leading Special Trains Operator

WWW.WESTCOASTRAILWAYS.CO.UK   **TEL. 01524 732100**

◀ The coach window sticker for 'The Jacobite' steam train between Fort William and Mallaig.

'The Jacobite' is a steam-hauled tourist train that operates along the scenic 41-mile Mallaig Extension (opened in 1901) between Fort William and Mallaig. It was originally introduced as 'The West Highlander' by British Railways in 1984 to increase patronage on this remote route which last saw regular steam haulage in 1961. Later renamed 'The Lochaber' the train subsequently passed into the ownership of the West Coast Railway Company (based at Carnforth) in 1995 following privatisation of British Railways. Since then it has been named 'The Jacobite' with steam locomotives based for the season at Fort William and taken from a pool of preserved privately owned locomotives. In recent years it has become so popular with tourists and enthusiasts that a second daily service was added in 2011. The train (known as the 'Hogwarts Express') and route also featured in the highly successful Harry Potter films.

▲ Preserved Stanier 'Black 5' 4-6-0 No. 44871 heads the westbound 'The Jacobite' train near Polnish on 30 October 2011. The loco was built at Crewe in 1945 and withdrawn from Carnforth shed in August 1968. It was one of the locos used to haul the very last steam-hauled train on British Railways – the famous 'Fifteen Guinea Special' – on 11 August 1968.

THE KENTISH BELLE

LONDON (VICTORIA) TO RAMSGATE/CANTERBURY

Luxury Pullman trains between London (Victoria) and Kent were first introduced by the South Eastern & Chatham Railway in 1921. Known as the 'Thanet Belle' the train ran non-stop between London and Margate, ending or starting its journey at Ramsgate Harbour. The train was continued by the Southern Railway from 1923 but by 1931 the Pullman content of the train had dwindled to just one coach. Suspended during the Second World War the train was reintroduced for the summer seasons of 1948-1950 as the 'Thanet Belle' but this time consisting of all-Pullman stock with a non-stop run between London and Whitstable. The Festival of Britain year of 1951 saw the train renamed as 'The Kentish Belle' with through coaches for Canterbury East being detached or attached at Faversham during the week. At weekends this portion was not included and the Faversham stop omitted. The Canterbury portion was not successful and had been dropped altogether by 1953 when two return services were provided on Saturdays and Sundays. The train was withdrawn at the end of the 1958 summer season, and replaced by characterless electric multiple units when Phase 1 of the Kent Coast electrification scheme was completed in June 1959.

▲ The summer 1951 BR leaflet and timetable for 'The Kentish Belle'.

◄ Unrebuilt 'Battle of Britain' Class 4-6-2 No. 34077 '603 Squadron' heads the all-Pullman 'The Kentish Belle' out of Broadstairs, circa 1955. The loco was built by BR at Brighton in 1948, rebuilt in 1960 and withdrawn in March 1967.

THE LAKES EXPRESS

LONDON (EUSTON) TO WINDERMERE/WORKINGTON

Hardly justifying the title of express, 'The Lakes Express' was introduced as a summer-only train by the London Midland & Scottish Railway in 1927. Within a few years a weekend service with the same name had also been introduced in the winter.

In its pre-war years the restaurant car train carried portions for Preston and Blackpool (detached or attached at Wigan), Barrow-in-Furness, Whitehaven and Workington (detached or attached at Lancaster) and Windermere (detached or attached at Oxenholme) before the remainder of the train continued to Keswick and

The Lakes Express
Restaurant Car Express between LONDON and THE LAKE DISTRICT
WEEKDAYS ONLY

	am	am
London Euston ... dep	11 35	11 35
	pm	
Crewe ...	3 11	
Wigan North Western ...	3 55	3 53
Preston ...	4 27	
Lancaster Castle ...	4 53	4 53
Oxenholme ...	5 16	5 17
Kendal ... arr	5 34	5 39
Burneside ...	5 41	5 46
Staveley ...	5 48	5 53
Windermere† ...	5 58	6 3
Penrith* ... arr		6 10
Keswick ...	6 55	6 55
Braithwaite ...	7 7	7 7
Bassenthwaite Lake ...	7 16	7 16
Cockermouth‡ ...	7 27	7 27
Brigham ...	7≠35	7≠35
Workington Main ...	7 53	7 53

(left column: Saturdays excepted 2nd July to 31st August; right column: Saturdays only Until 1st September)

	am	am
Workington Main ... dep	9 5	8 40
Brigham ...	9 21	
Cockermouth† ...	9 29	9 3
Bassenthwaite Lake ...	9 39	9 13
Braithwaite ...	9 48	
Keswick ...	10 5	9 38
Penrith* ...	10 50	10 26
Tebay ...	11 25	
Windermere† ... dep	11 5	10 50
Staveley ...	11 14	10 59
Burneside ...	11 19	11 4
Kendal ...	11 28	11 13
Oxenholme ... dep	11 49	11 30
	pm	
Carnforth ... arr	12 4	11 46
Lancaster ...	12 14	12 0
		pm
Preston ...	12 48	12≠43
Wigan North Western ...	1 18	
Warrington Bank Quay ...	1 37	
Crewe ...	2 12	1 46
London Euston ... arr	5 30	5 10

(left column: Saturdays excepted 2nd July to 31st August; right column: Saturdays only)

NOTES

≠—Stops only to take up passengers.
—Stops to set down passengers on notice being given to the guard at Cockermouth.
‡—Station for Buttermere.
†—Station for Bowness (1½ miles) and Ambleside (4½ miles).
*—Station for Ullswater (Pooley Bridge) (5¾ miles).

Restaurant Buffet Car and Through Carriages between London and Windermere. Through Carriages between London and Keswick also London and Workington, via Penrith.

Seats on these trains may be reserved in advance for passengers travelling from London, Windermere, Workington and Keswick on payment of a fee of 2s. 0d. per seat.

▲ The summer 1962 timetable for 'The Lakes Express'.

◄ Unrebuilt 'Patriot' Class 4-6-0 No. 45513 makes easy going of the three-coach Keswick portion of 'The Lakes Express' at Peat Lane, Oxenholme in May 1962. The loco was built at Crewe in 1932, named 'Sir W. A. Stanier' in 1943 and withdrawn from Edge Hill shed in September 1962. The loco lost its name in 1947 when new 'Coronation' Class 4-6-2 No. 46256 was named 'Sir William A. Stanier, F.R.S.'

▲ The down 'The Lakes Express' passes Scout Green halfway up Shap Bank at speed, headed by 'Coronation' Class 4-6-2 No. 46252 'City of Leicester'. At this stage the train consisted of only four or five coaches, as the Windermere portion had already been detached at Oxenholme. The loco was built without streamlining at Crewe in 1944 and withdrawn from Camden shed in June 1963.

Workington via Penrith – the latter portion arrived in Workington over half an hour before the portion that had been detached at Lancaster! Until the introduction of Ivatt Class 2 2-6-0s after the war the Keswick and Workington portion was hauled westwards from Penrith by ancient nineteenth century ex-LNWR locos. The train lost its name during the Second World War but it was reinstated in the summer of 1950. By the early 1960s it had lost the Blackpool and Barrow/Whitehaven portions; in 1962 the down train left Euston at 11.35am and arrived at Workington at 7.53pm, while the up train left Workington at 8.40am and arrived at Euston at 5.10pm. The train survived until 1965, after which the Penrith to Workington line went into its death throes – Keswick to Workington went in 1966 and Penrith to Keswick in 1972. Windermere continued to be served by a nameless train from Euston for a few more years but electrification of the West Coast Main Line saw an end to this service.

THE LANCASTRIAN

LONDON (EUSTON) TO MANCHESTER (LONDON ROAD/PICCADILLY)

Given its name officially in 1928, 'The Lancastrian' provided a fast service primarily between Manchester and London and, until the Second World War, also conveyed through coaches from Colne and Rochdale which were attached to the up train at Wilmslow – between here and Euston the train ran non-stop usually behind a 'Royal Scot' Class 4-6-0. The train lost its name on the outbreak of the Second World War and was only reinstated in 1957. One peculiarity of 'The Lancastrian' was that the up and down services took different routes – between Mondays and Fridays (departure from Euston at 7.45am) the down train travelled via Crewe and Stockport, arriving in Manchester Piccadilly at 11.38am. However the up service (departure from Manchester at 4.05pm) travelled via the more difficult Macclesfield and Stoke-on-Trent route, reaching Euston at 8.05pm (Monday to Friday). On Saturdays both up and down trains travelled via Stoke (all times courtesy of the LMR summer 1962 timetable.) The train's sister, 'The Mancunian', also took both routes but in the opposite directions. The train was discontinued at the end of the summer timetable in 1962 when most expresses between London and Manchester were re-timetabled to run via the Midland route to and from St Pancras to make way for the electrification of the West Coast Main Line.

The Lancastrian

Restaurant Car Express

LONDON EUSTON and MANCHESTER PICCADILLY

WEEKDAYS

	Mons. to Fris.	Sats.		Mons. to Fris.	Sats.
	am	am		pm	pm
London Euston ....dep	7 45	8 30	Manchester Piccadilly ....dep	4 5	4 10
Watford Junction ... ... „	8‡10	8‡58			
Rugby Midland ....„		10 28	Stockport Edgeley ... ... „	4 17	4 24
Nuneaton Trent Valley .. „ ..		10 44	Macclesfield ....„	4 36	4 43
Stoke-on-Trent ....„		11 57			
		pm	Stoke-on-Trent .. .. „	5 9	5 13
Macclesfield ... ...„		12 28			
Crewe..........................„	10 59	....	Watford Junction ....arr	7↓29	7↓43
Stockport Edgeley .. ..arr	11 27	12 48			
Manchester Piccadilly .... „	11 38	1 3	London Euston .. ..arr	8 5	8 15

‡—Stops only to take up passengers.　　→—Stops only to set down passengers.

Seats may be reserved in advance for passengers travelling from London and Manchester on payment of a fee of 2s. 0d. per seat.

▲ The summer 1962 timetable for 'The Lancastrian'.

THE MAN OF KENT

LONDON (CHARING CROSS) TO FOLKESTONE (CENTRAL)

Introduced in 1953, 'The Man of Kent' was the only named train to operate out of Charing Cross during the British Railways era. It was named after the Association of Men of Kent and Kentish Men which was founded by ten benevolent Kentish businessmen in 1897. Normally hauled by 'Schools' Class 4-4-0s or Bulleid Light Pacifics, the down train left Charing Cross at 4.15pm, briefly calling at Waterloo East, and arrived at Folkestone at 5.35pm before ending its journey via Dover and Deal at Ramsgate. Starting its journey at Sandwich, the up working left Folkestone at 11.10am and arrived at Charing Cross at 12.30pm. The Kent Coast electrification soon put paid to this train, which was withdrawn in 1961.

▲ 'Schools' Class 4-4-0 No. 30925 'Cheltenham' calls at Waterloo East with 'The Man of Kent' on 30 May 1959. The loco was built at Eastleigh in 1934 and withdrawn in 1962. It is now preserved as part of the National Collection.

▶ Unrebuilt 'Battle of Britain' Class 4-6-2 No. 34084 '253 Squadron' speeds through Chelsfield with 'The Man of Kent' on 5 September 1957. The loco was built by BR at Brighton in 1948 and withdrawn in October 1965.

MANCHESTER AND LIVERPOOL PULLMANS

LONDON (EUSTON) TO MANCHESTER (PICCADILLY)/LIVERPOOL (LIME STREET)

Following completion of West Coast Main Line electrification between Euston and Manchester in 1966, the blue diesel 'The Midland Pullman' between St Pancras and Manchester was withdrawn. It was replaced by electric locomotive haulage along the WCML with a new eight-coach all-Pullman train running two return journeys each weekday. By 1967 the schedule had been cut to 2½ hours between the two cities. A similar service was provided between Liverpool and Euston but in this case the train consisted of only four Pullman cars plus four normal second class coaches. The latter service ended in 1975 but the 'Manchester Pullman' (from 1985 onwards the Pullman coaches were replaced by new Mk 3 coaches) continued in operation until 1997, making it the last surviving Pullman service in Britain.

▲ The up 'Manchester Pullman' leaves Manchester Piccadilly behind Class 86/2 electric loco No. 86228 on 8 June 1984. The loco was built at Vulcan Foundry in 1965 and withdrawn in September 2008.

THE MANCUNIAN

LONDON (EUSTON) TO MANCHESTER (LONDON ROAD/PICCADILLY)

Introduced by the London Midland & Scottish Railway in 1927, 'The Mancunian' offered a restaurant car service with a morning departure from Manchester and an early evening departure from Euston. As with 'The Lancastrian', the up and down trains took different routes but in the case of 'The Mancunian' it travelled down via Stoke-on-Trent and up via Crewe and Wilmslow. Strangely, the through coaches from Colne and Rochdale, attached to the up 'The Lancastrian' at Wilmslow, were conveyed back by the down 'The Mancunian' and detached at Wilmslow. The train was discontinued during the Second World War but revived by British Railways in 1949. By the summer of 1962, with electrification of the West Coast Main Line already underway, the weekday train was making slow progress with the 9.40am departure from Manchester running non-stop to Euston in 3hrs 40min – the down train took 3hrs 55min with a stop at Wilmslow. The Saturday services were even slower. In the autumn of that year almost all services to and from Manchester were diverted to run via the Midland route to and from St Pancras – 'The Mancunian' was the only exception, continuing to run to and from Euston until April 1966 when it was withdrawn.

▲ Longsight's 'Royal Scot' Class 4-6-0 No. 46140 'The King's Royal Rifle Corps' speeds over Whitmore Troughs with the up 'The Mancunian' on 15 June 1957. The loco was built in 1927, rebuilt in 1952 and withdrawn from Carlisle Kingmoor shed in November 1965.

THE MANCUNIAN

The first train to bear the name *The Mancunian* ran from Manchester to London in 1927, although an unnamed train had provided a similar service for many years previously, and the departure time has not varied much over the years.

The Mancunian is one of British Railways' principal 'there and back in a day' services for businessmen who have the afternoon for conferences before returning home by the evening train from London.

The route of *The Mancunian* takes it through the great railway junction of Crewe, through Stafford and Lichfield, the triple spires of whose lovely cathedral can be seen. Then Nuneaton and Rugby, another important railway junction, over the Chilterns at Tring, and by Harrow with its famous school on the hill.

The Manchester Ship Canal 1894

THE MANCUNIAN

WINE LIST

▲ The wine list from 'The Mancunian', circa 1960.

▼ Unrebuilt 'Patriot' Class 4-6-0 No. 45518 'Bradshaw' speeds over Castlethorpe Troughs with 'The Mancunian' in August 1958. The loco was built at Crewe in 1933, received its name in 1939 and was withdrawn from Lancaster Green Ayre shed in October 1962.

The Mancunian

Restaurant Car Express

MANCHESTER PICCADILLY and LONDON EUSTON

WEEKDAYS

	Mons. to Fris.	Sats.		Mons. to Fris.	Sats.
	am	am		pm	pm
Manchester Piccadilly ....dep	9 40	9 40	London Euston ....dep	6 0	5 45
			Wilmslow	...	9⊾20
			Cheadle Hulme..............arr	9c37	9⊾20
London Euston .. ..arr	pm	pm	Stockport Edgeley .... ,,	....	9⊾26
	1 20	1 25	Manchester Piccadilly .... ,,	....	9⊾35
				9d55	9 50

►—Stops only to set down passengers.

c—Note ► applies.   On Fridays arrives 9 43 pm.
d—On Fridays arrives 10 4 pm.

Seats on these trains may be reserved in advance for passengers travelling from London and Manchester, on payment of a fee of 2s. 0d. per seat.

▲ The summer 1962 timetable for 'The Mancunian'.

THE MANXMAN

LONDON (EUSTON) TO LIVERPOOL (LIME STREET)

The Isle of Man had long been a popular destination for holidaymakers and to cater for this traffic 'The Manxman' (not to be confused with a silent film made by Alfred Hitchcock in 1929) was introduced by the London Midland & Scottish Railway in 1927. Running only during the summer months, the restaurant car train provided connections with steamers to and from the island at Liverpool. The train was discontinued on the outbreak of the Second World War but reintroduced by British Railways in 1951 and continued to operate until 1965.

Running Mondays to Saturdays, the 1962 down summer service left Euston at 10.20am (10.25am on Saturdays) and, with an intermediate stop at Crewe, arrived at Lime Street at 2.20pm (2.35pm on Saturdays). The up train left Lime Street at 2.05pm (2.10pm on Saturdays) and after a stop at Rugby arrived at Euston at 5.50pm (6.20pm on Saturdays). Until English Electric Type 4 diesels took over in the early 1960s, the heavily loaded train was often hauled by ex-LMS 'Princess Royal' Pacifics from Edge Hill shed. Electrification of the West Coast Main Line saw the train discontinued at the end of the 1965 summer timetable.

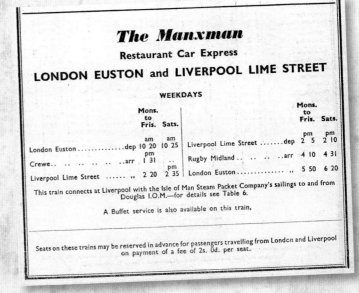

The Manxman
Restaurant Car Express
LONDON EUSTON and LIVERPOOL LIME STREET

WEEKDAYS

	Mons. to Fris.	Sats.		Mons. to Fris.	Sats.
	am	am		pm	pm
London Euston ....dep	10 20	10 25	Liverpool Lime Street ....dep	2 5	2 10
	pm				
Crewe.. .. ..arr	1 31	..	Rugby Midland .. ..arr	4 10	4 31
	pm	pm			
Liverpool Lime Street ...... "	2 20	2 35	London Euston .... "	5 50	6 20

This train connects at Liverpool with the Isle of Man Steam Packet Company's sailings to and from Douglas I.O.M.—for details see Table 6.

A Buffet service is also available on this train.

Seats on these trains may be reserved in advance for passengers travelling from London and Liverpool on payment of a fee of 2s. 0d. per seat.

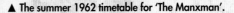

▲ The summer 1962 timetable for 'The Manxman'.

◀ Stanier 'Black 5' 4-6-0 No. 45234 and rebuilt 'Patriot' Class 4-6-0 No. 45531 'Sir Frederick Harrison' head the 'blood-and-custard' coaches of 'The Manxman' near Lichfield Trent Valley in August 1954. The former loco was built by Armstrong Whitworth in 1936 and withdrawn from Newton Heath shed in September 1967. The latter loco was built at Crewe in 1933, rebuilt in 1947 and withdrawn from Carlisle Kingmoor shed in November 1965.

THE MASTER CUTLER

LONDON (MARYLEBONE/KING'S CROSS/ ST PANCRAS) TO SHEFFIELD

For many years between the wars, the Great Central route between Sheffield and Marylebone was served by a popular morning up restaurant car express service to London and an early evening down service. Discontinued during the Second World War, it was revived by the London & North Eastern Railway in the autumn of 1947 with the title of 'The Master Cutler'. Until the introduction of Gresley 'A3' Pacifics in the mid-1950s the train was normally hauled by 'B1' 4-6-0s; the up train travelled via the direct line through Amersham while the down train was sent via the GW/GC Joint Line through High Wycombe and Princes Risborough to avoid the heavy early evening commuter traffic.

The 1948 timetable saw the train leave Sheffield Victoria at 7.40 am and, after stops at Nottingham Victoria, Leicester Central and Rugby Central, arrive at Marylebone at 11.15am. The down train left Marylebone at 6.15pm and, with the same stops, arrived back at Sheffield at 10.02pm. The downgrading of the former Great Central route saw 'The Master Cutler' transferred to King's Cross in 1958. With new English Electric Type 4 diesels the new all-Pullman train provided a much faster service for Sheffield businessmen, getting them into the capital at 10.15am with a 7.20pm departure for the return service. The only intermediate stop was at Retford. The Pullman cars were also used for the 'Sheffield Pullman' express between King's Cross and Sheffield, but with more stops, which ran during the day. The train was discontinued in 1968 but in 1971 the name was bestowed on a Sheffield Midland to St Pancras express until HSTs took over in 1985.

▶ The summer 1948 BR leaflet and route map for the Eastern Region's 'The Master Cutler'.

▼ The inaugural all-Pullman 'The Master Cutler' to run via the East Coast Main Line arrives at King's Cross from Sheffield behind English Electric Type 4 (Class 40) diesel D207 on 15 September 1958. The loco was built at Vulcan Foundry in 1958 and withdrawn as No. 40007 in February 1983.

▶ The winter 1960/61 timetable for 'The Master Cutler'.

PULLMAN CAR SERVICES
BETWEEN
SHEFFIELD (Victoria) and LONDON (King's Cross)

THE MASTER CUTLER
(Limited Train)
MONDAYS TO FRIDAYS INCLUSIVE
(Except Monday 26th December, 1960; Thursday 30th, Friday 31st March, Monday 3rd April, Friday 19th and Monday 22nd May, 1961)

	am			pm
Sheffield (Victoria) .. .. dep 7 20		London (King's Cross) .. .. dep 7 20		
Retford .. .. { arr 7 53		Retford .. .. { arr 9 39		
.. .. { dep 7 54		.. .. { dep 9 40		
London (King's Cross) .. .. .. arr 10 15		Sheffield (Victoria) .. .. .. arr 10 14		

THE MAYFLOWER

LONDON (PADDINGTON) TO KINGSWEAR/PLYMOUTH

Introduced by the Western Region in 1957, 'The Mayflower' (so named after the ship that carried the Pilgrim Fathers from Plymouth to New England) left Plymouth at 8.30am and, after stops at Newton Abbot (to attach through coaches from Kingswear), Exeter, Taunton, Westbury and Reading, arrived at Paddington at 1.25pm. In steam days the restaurant car train was normally worked by a 'King' Class 4-6-0, with the down train leaving Paddington at 5.30pm and, after calling at Taunton and Exeter (to detach the Kingswear coaches), arriving back at Plymouth at 10pm. By 1960 steam had given way to diesel haulage, with 'Warship' and later 'Western' Class diesel hydraulics taking over until 1965 when the train lost its name. The name has since been revived in timetables to describe a First Great Western express service.

Table 6

THE MAYFLOWER
RESTAURANT CAR SERVICE

LONDON, TAUNTON, EXETER, NEWTON ABBOT and PLYMOUTH

WEEK DAYS

	pm		am
London (Paddington) ... ... dep	5A30	Plymouth ... ... dep	8A30
Taunton ... ...arr	7 57		
Exeter (St. David's) ... ... ,,	8 37	Kingswear ... ... ,,	8A30
		Churston (for Brixham) ,,	8A40
Dawlish ... ... ,,	9 7	Paignton... ... ... ,,	8A50
Teignmouth ... ... ,,	9 15	Torquay ... ... ,,	8A58
Newton Abbot ... ... ,,	9 25	Torre ... ... ,,	9 3
Torre ... ... ,,	9 39	Newton Abbot... ... ... ,,	9 26
Torquay ... ... ,,	9 42	Exeter (St. David's)... ... ,,	10 0
Paignton ... ... ,,	9 55	Taunton ... ... ,,	10 40
Churston (for Brixham) ... ,,	10 5	Westbury ... ... ,,	11 37
Kingswear ... ... ,,	10 15		pm
		Reading General ... ...arr	12 42
Plymouth ... ... ,,	10 0	London (Paddington) ... ,,	1 25

A—Seats can be reserved in advance on payment of a fee of 2s. 0d. per seat (see page 23).

▲ The winter 1958/59 timetable for 'The Mayflower'.

◀ Designed by Eric Fraser, this restaurant car tariff from 'The Mayflower' circa 1958 features the ship of the same name that carried the Pilgrim Fathers to New England in 1620.

◀ Carrying one of the early alloy headboards, Old Oak Common's 'King' Class 4-6-0 No. 6002 'King William IV' passes along the sea wall at Teignmouth with the up 'The Mayflower' on 30 July 1957. The loco was built at Swindon in 1927 and withdrawn from Wolverhampton Stafford Road shed in September 1962.

▶ Fitted with a new style headboard, the down 'The Mayflower' passes White Waltham near Maidenhead behind nearly new 'Warship' Class diesel hydraulic D804 'Avenger' on 8 August 1959. The first two carriages of the train are Gresley corridor stock. The loco was outshopped new from Swindon Works on 23 April of that year and withdrawn from Laira shed in October 1971.

THE MERCHANT VENTURER

LONDON (PADDINGTON) TO WESTON-SUPER-MARE

Receiving its name in 1951, 'The Merchant Venturer' provided a restaurant car service between Paddington, Bath, Bristol and Weston-super-Mare – it was named after a charitable organisation of Bristol merchants that was founded in the thirteenth century. Strangely, the down service was much faster than the up service with fewer stops, leaving Paddington at 11.15am (winter 1958/59 timetable), stopping only at Bath before arriving at Bristol Temple Meads at 1.22pm. Here engines were changed – in steam days normally a 'King' or 'Castle' Class 4-6-0 were used as far as Bristol, with a 'Hall' 4-6-0 for

Table 2

THE MERCHANT VENTURER
RESTAURANT CAR SERVICE

LONDON, BATH SPA, BRISTOL
and WESTON-SUPER-MARE

WEEK DAYS

	am		pm
London (Paddington) .. dep	11A15	Weston-super-Mare General.. dep	4A35
		Yatton .. .. "	4 47
	pm	Nailsea and Backwell .. .. "	4 56
		Bristol (Temple Meads).. .. "	5A27
Bath Spa .. .. .. arr	1 1	Bath Spa .. .. "	5 48
		Chippenham .. .. "	6 10
Bristol (Temple Meads) .. "	1 22	Swindon .. .. "	6 40
		Reading General .. .. arr	7 21
Weston-super-Mare General "	1C56	London (Paddington) .. .. "	8 5

A—Seats can be reserved in advance on payment of a fee of 2s. 0d. per seat (see page 23).
C—On Saturdays arr 2 4 pm

The Merchant Venturer

TARIFF

The Merchant Venturer

LUNCHEON
11/-

Tomato Juice or Grape Fruit
or
Crème Pastourille

Turbot Meunière

Sauté of Beef Paysanne
or
Roast Pork, Stuffing and Apple Sauce
Vegetables   Potatoes
Assorted Cold Meats - Dressed Salad
or

Compôte of Gooseberries and Ice Cream
or
Assorted Cheeses, Salad, Biscuits & Butter

Cheese & Biscuits etc. may be served in addition
to the Sweet for an extra charge of 1/6
Savoury may be served additionally for an extra charge of 1/-

Coffee 10d.

May we draw your attention to the
interesting wines now provided at prices as
reasonable as any you will find in this country

BRITISH TRANSPORT CATERING SERVICES

W R

▲ The winter 1958/59 timetable for 'The Merchant Venturer'.

◄ The attractive restaurant car tariff and luncheon menu card from 'The Merchant Venturer', circa 1955.

the remainder of the journey to Weston – before the train ran non-stop to Weston-super-Mare arriving at 1.56pm (2.04pm on Saturdays). The up train was much slower, with stops at Yatton, Nailsea & Blackwell, Bristol (engine change), Bath, Chippenham, Swindon and Reading, with the entire journey taking a leisurely 3½ hours. The train lost its name in 1965 but has since been revived in timetables to describe a First Great Western express.

▲ 'King' Class 4-6-0 No. 6025 'King Henry III' exits St Anne's Park Tunnel on the last mile into Bristol with the down 'The Merchant Venturer', circa 1960. This loco was built at Swindon in 1930 and withdrawn from Old Oak Common shed at the end of 1962.

◄ 'Castle' Class 4-6-0 No. 7033 'Hartlebury Castle' rolls into Bath Spa with the down 'The Merchant Venturer' in 1960. This loco was built by BR at Swindon in 1950 and withdrawn from Old Oak Common shed in January 1963, even though it had potentially at least another 25 years life ahead of it. What a waste!

THE MERSEYSIDE EXPRESS

LONDON (EUSTON) TO LIVERPOOL (LIME STREET)

Introduced by the London Midland & Scottish Railway in 1927 as the 'London-Merseyside Express', this train was renamed 'The Merseyside Express' a year later. The name was discontinued during the Second World War but was revived in 1946. Loading up to 15 coaches, the heavy restaurant car train was normally hauled by an Edge Hill 'Princess Royal' Pacific and carried through coaches to and from Southport Chapel Street. By the

▼ The attractive cover of the wine list for 'The Merseyside Express', circa 1955.

The Merseyside Express

The name *The Merseyside Express* is an abbreviated version of the original title *London-Merseyside Express* which was conferred on this train in 1927.

The Merseyside Express is one of British Railways 'there and back in a day' services for men of commerce. It leaves Liverpool in the morning and returns from London in the early evening, allowing sufficient time for business conferences in London. It is possible, however, to have even more time for London meetings by travelling on *The Shamrock*, an earlier morning service from Liverpool and another of the three trains which form the principal direct overland link between the great seaport and industrial centre of Liverpool and the Capital. The third train is *The Red Rose*.

The route of *The Merseyside Express* takes it over the famous Runcorn bridge and viaducts across the Mersey, through the important junction and railway centre of Crewe, then Stafford, Lichfield, whose lovely cathedral can be seen from the train, Rugby, another important railway junction, and Harrow, with its school on the hill.

The Merseyside Express
Restaurant Car Express
LIVERPOOL LIME STREET and LONDON EUSTON

WEEKDAYS

	Mons. to Fris.	Sats.		Mons. to Fris.	Sats.
	am	am		pm	pm
Liverpool Lime Street ....dep	10‡10	10‡10	London Euston ....dep	6§10	6§ 5
			Mossley Hill .. .. ..arr	9c54	9§54
	pm	pm	Liverpool Lime Street .... ,,	10d10	10 10
London Euston .. .. ..arr	1 55	2 10			

▸—Stops to set down passengers only.
‡—Conveys through carriage from Southport Chapel Street (departs 8.50 am).
§—Conveys through carriage to Southport Chapel Street (on Fridays arrives 11.26 pm—on other days arrives 10.56 pm).
c—Note ▸ applies. Arrives 10 4 pm on Fridays.
d—Fridays arrives 10 20 pm.

Seats on these trains may be reserved in advance for passengers travelling from London, Liverpool and Southport on payment of a fee of 2s. 0d. per seat.

▲ The summer 1962 timetable for 'The Merseyside Express'.

summer of 1962 steam had given way to English Electric Type 4 haulage with the up service leaving Liverpool at 10.10am and travelling non-stop to Euston where it arrived at 1.55pm (15 minutes later on a Saturday). The down service left Euston at 6.10pm (6.05pm on Saturdays) and made an intermediate stop on the outskirts of Liverpool at Mossley Hill before reaching Lime Street at 10.10pm. The train lost its name following the completion of electrification out of Euston in 1966.

▲ 'Princess Royal' Class 4-6-2 No. 46207 'Princess Arthur of Connaught' heads the 6.05pm down 'The Merseyside Express' through Willesden Junction on 29 May 1954. This loco was built at Crewe in 1935 and withdrawn from Willesden shed in November 1961.

M

THE MID-DAY SCOT

LONDON (EUSTON) TO GLASGOW (CENTRAL)

Although not receiving its name until 1927, the early afternoon departures from Glasgow and Euston had long been known unofficially as 'The Corridor' – the train was so nicknamed as it was one of the first Anglo-Scottish expresses on the West Coast Main Line to use luxurious 12-wheeled corridor coaches. Up until the Second World War the train also carried through coaches for Aberdeen and Edinburgh, which were attached or detached at Law Junction and Symington respectively. Although shorn of these through portions during the war, 'The Mid-Day Scot' regularly loaded up to 15 coaches, necessitating Pacific haulage throughout. The train continued to run after the war – the unique BR Standard 4-6-2 No. 71000 'Duke of Gloucester' was a regular performer

▶ The summer 1962 timetable for 'The Mid-Day Scot'.

The Mid-Day Scot

Restaurant Car Express

LONDON EUSTON and GLASGOW CENTRAL

WEEKDAYS

	Mons. to Fris.	Sats.		Mons. to Fris.	Sats.
	pm	pm		pm	pm
London Euston ....dep	1 0	1 0	Glasgow Central ....dep	1 30	1 30
Crewe .. .. ,,	4 0	.	Carlisle .. .. ,,	3 21	3 27
Carlisle ....arr	6 35	7 4	Wigan North Western .....arr	5 16	.
Carstairs .. .. ,,	.	8 37	Crewe....................... ,,	5 59	6 26
Glasgow Central .... ,,	8 30	9 20	London Euston .. .. ,,	8 55	9 35

SUNDAYS

	pm			pm
London Euston ....dep	12 15	Glasgow Central ....dep	1 0
Crewe .. .. ,,	3 57		
Carlisle ....arr	6 51	Carlisle .. .. ,,	3 20
Motherwell .. .. ,,	8 53	Crewe....................arr	6 33
Glasgow Central .... ,,	9 20	London Euston .. .. ,,	10 30

A Buffet service is also available on this train on weekdays

Seats may be reserved in advance for passengers travelling from London and Glasgow and on weekdays only, Carlisle to London on payment of a fee of 2s. 0d. per seat.

▲ Crewe North's unique BR Standard Class '8P' 4-6-2 No. 71000 'Duke of Gloucester' heads the down 'The Mid-Day Scot' past Kenton on 11 March 1957. An unpopular locomotive with crews, No. 71000 was built at Crewe in 1954 and withdrawn from Crewe North shed in December 1962. After languishing for years on the scrapheap at Barry it was restored to full operational condition in 1987.

▲ Another view of No. 71000 heading the down 'The Mid-Day Scot', this time seen leaving Rugby in September 1958.

in the 1950s – and by the summer of 1962 with diesel haulage the up weekday train was departing from Glasgow at 1.30pm and, with stops at Carlisle, Wigan and Crewe, arriving at Euston at 8.55pm. The down weekday train left Euston at 1pm and with stops at Crewe, Carlisle and Carstairs arrived at Glasgow at 8.30pm. The Saturday service was slower and the Sunday service painfully so. The train lost its name in 1966.

▲ The down 'The Mid-Day Scot' passes Greenholme near to the bottom of Shap Bank, headed by 'Coronation' Class 4-6-2 No. 46238 'City of Carlisle' on 6 August 1960. Built with a streamlined casing at Crewe in 1939, this loco was 'de-streamlined' in 1946 and withdrawn from Carlisle Kingmoor shed in October 1964.

THE MIDLANDER

LONDON (EUSTON) TO WOLVERHAMPTON (HIGH LEVEL)

Receiving its name in 1950, 'The Midlander' was the successor to the pre-war two-hour expresses that ran between Euston and Birmingham New Street. Competing with the Great Western Railway's similar service between Paddington, Birmingham Snow Hill and Wolverhampton (Low Level), the London Midland & Scottish Railway trains started or ended their journeys at Wolverhampton (High Level). Running only from Mondays to Fridays, the restaurant car express was normally hauled by 'Jubilee' Class 4-6-0s until diesel haulage took over in the late 1950s. However it failed to match the pre-war two-hour schedule and by 1962 the

▲ 'Jubilee' Class 4-6-0 No. 45742 'Connaught' after arrival at Euston with the up 'The Midlander' on 21 October 1959. The loco was the last of its class to be built, emerging from Crewe Works in December 1936. It was fitted with a double chimney between 1940 and 1955, and withdrawn from Carlisle Kingmoor shed in May 1965.

11.30am from New Street with a stop at Coventry was arriving at Euston at 1.40pm. The down service left Euston at 5.40pm and, after stopping at Coventry, arrived back at New Street at 7.47pm. The train was withdrawn in 1963 when all express services between Euston and Birmingham were concentrated on the former GWR line via Leamington to make way for electrification of the West Coast Main Line. With the latter completed a new Euston to Birmingham (New Street) service was introduced in 1967. One of the peak hour return services was named 'The Executive', giving a fast journey time between Euston and Birmingham of just over 90 minutes each way. The name was dropped in 1970.

Table 11a

THE MIDLANDER
RESTAURANT CAR SERVICE
WOLVERHAMPTON, BIRMINGHAM and LONDON
WEEK DAYS
(Mondays to Fridays)

	am			pm
Wolverhampton (High Level) dep	10B55	London (Euston) .. .. .. dep	5A40
Birmingham (New Street) .. ,,	11B30	Coventry .. .. arr	7 18
Coventry .. .. ,,	11B55	Birmingham (New Street) .. ,,	7 47
	pm	Bescot .. .. ,,	8 14
London (Euston) .. .. arr	1 40	Wolverhampton (High Level) ,,	8 27

A—Seats can be reserved in advance on payment of a fee of 2s. 0d. per seat (see page 23.)

B—Except for 22nd, 23rd, 24th and 26th December, 1958, 26th, 27th, 30th and 31st March, and 14th, 15th, 18th and 19th May, 1959, seats can be reserved in advance on payment of a fee of 2s. 0d. per seat (see page 23).

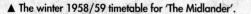

▲ The winter 1958/59 timetable for 'The Midlander'.

THE MIDLAND PULLMAN

LONDON (ST PANCRAS) TO MANCHESTER (CENTRAL)

The British Transport Commission took over the British Pullman Car Company in 1954 and a year later the British Railways Modernisation Programme was published; one of its main objectives was the replacement of steam by diesel power. A committee was soon set up to look into the introduction of diesel-hauled express passenger trains and in 1957 it was announced that the Metropolitan-Cammell Carriage & Wagon Company of Birmingham would build five high-speed diesel multiple-unit (DMU) sets. These were to be introduced in 1958 on the London Midland Region between London St Pancras and Manchester Central, and on the

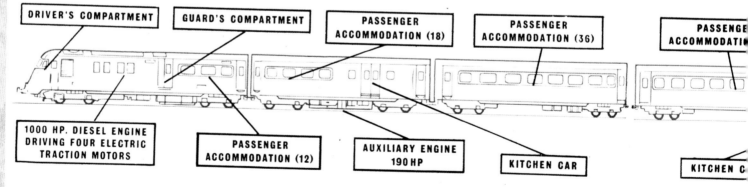

DRIVER'S COMPARTMENT

GUARD'S COMPARTMENT

PASSENGER ACCOMMODATION (18)

PASSENGER ACCOMMODATION (36)

PASSENGER ACCOMMODATION

1000 HP. DIESEL ENGINE DRIVING FOUR ELECTRIC TRACTION MOTORS

PASSENGER ACCOMMODATION (12)

AUXILIARY ENGINE 190 HP

KITCHEN CAR

KITCHEN CAR

Western Region between London Paddington and Bristol and Birmingham.

Finished in two-tone Nanking blue and white with a grey roof, the passenger coaches were fitted with double glazing, air conditioning and sumptuous seating; passengers were served at their tables by staff dressed in matching blue uniforms. The streamlined power cars at each end of the train were each fitted with 1,000hp NBL/MAN diesel engines driving electric transmission, with a top speed of 90mph. The two LMR sets were six-car formation (this included the two non-accommodating power cars) providing 132 first class seats, while the three WR sets were eight-car formation (see 'Blue Pullmans').

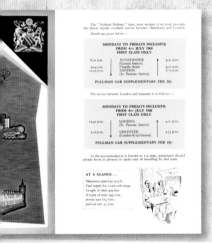

◀ Produced for the inaugural 'The Midland Pullman' service on 4 July 1960, this stylish brochure includes a seating plan, route map and timetable.

The Midland Pullman

First class only

Diesel "De Luxe" Express Services

between

MANCHESTER CENTRAL—LONDON ST. PANCRAS

LONDON ST. PANCRAS—NOTTINGHAM MIDLAND

Meals and Refreshments served at every seat

MONDAYS TO FRIDAYS

(except 3rd and 6th August)

		am				pm
Manchester Central	.. .. .. dep	7 45	London St. Pancras	.. .. ..	dep	6 10
Cheadle Heath	.. .. .. "	7‡58	Cheadle Heath	.. .. ..	arr	9⊦3
London St. Pancras	.. .. .. arr	11 0	Manchester Central	.. .. ..	"	9 20

		am				pm
London St. Pancras	.. .. .. dep	11 20	Nottingham Midland	.. .. ..	dep	3 30
		pm				
Leicester London Road	.. .. .. arr	12 45	Loughborough Midland	.. .. ..		3 47
Loughborough Midland	.. .. .. "	12 59	Leicester London Road	.. .. ..		4 2
Nottingham Midland	.. .. .. "	1 20	London St. Pancras	.. .. ..	arr	5 30

‡—Stops only to take up passengers ⊦—Stops only to set down passengers

Supplementary charges for each single journey—including children occupying seats:—

		s. d.
Between Manchester, or Cheadle Heath and London		20s. 0d.
"	London and Leicester	8s. 0d.
"	London and Loughborough	9s. 0d.
"	London and Nottingham	10s. 0d.
"	Leicester and Loughborough	1s. 0d.
"	Leicester and Nottingham	2s. 0d.
"	Loughborough and Nottingham	1s. 0d.

Tariff for meals:— s. d.
Breakfast full *table d'hote* 8 6
Afternoon Tea *light service* 3 6
Luncheon and Dinner are served *a-la-carte*

All seats are reservable on payment of supplementary charge

To ensure accommodation on these services seats should be reserved in advance

▲ The summer 1962 timetable for 'The Midland Pullman'.

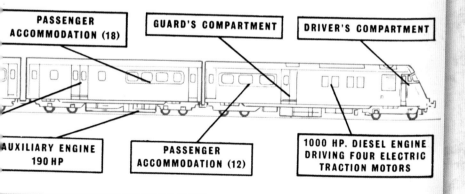

PASSENGER ACCOMMODATION (18)

GUARD'S COMPARTMENT

DRIVER'S COMPARTMENT

AUXILIARY ENGINE 190 HP

PASSENGER ACCOMMODATION (12)

1000 HP. DIESEL ENGINE DRIVING FOUR ELECTRIC TRACTION MOTORS

Following delays the first Blue Pullmans finally entered service on the LMR between St Pancras and Manchester on 4 July 1960. With West Coast Main Line electrification now underway they were to provide the fastest journey time ever between Manchester and London until this major project was completed. Running only from Mondays to Fridays, the up train left Manchester Central at 8.50am and with one stop at Cheadle Heath arrived at St Pancras at 12.03pm (by 1962 the departure had been brought forward to 7.45am with an 11am arrival in the capital). The down train left St Pancras at 6.10pm and with one stop at Cheadle Heath arrived back in Manchester at 9.21pm (9.20pm in 1962). In between these two services the 'Blue Pullman' set managed a trip from St Pancras to Leicester and back (in 1962 extended to Nottingham). The train was withdrawn in 1966 on completion of electrification between Euston and Manchester (Piccadilly).

▲ 'The Midland Pullman' passes Hathern in Leicestershire on 13 May 1965.

► The northbound 'The Midland Pullman' at speed through Mill Hill on its journey to Manchester Central – 28 June 1961.

THE NORFOLKMAN

LONDON (LIVERPOOL STREET) TO NORWICH/CROMER

Post-war successor (during the summer months) to the famous 'The Norfolk Coast Express' introduced by the Great Eastern Railway in 1907, 'The Norfolkman' was introduced by the Eastern Region of British Railways in 1948. Running between Liverpool Street and Norwich during the winter months, the train was extended to run to and from Cromer and Sheringham during the summer. Prior to the introduction of the new BR Standard 'Britannia' Pacifics in 1951 the down train left Liverpool Street at 10am and, after a three-minute stop at Ipswich en-route, arrived in Norwich at 12.20pm. In the summer it continued on, stopping at Wroxham, North Walsham, Cromer (High), West Runton and Sheringham (1.38pm). The train was slower on Saturdays. In the reverse direction the restaurant car train left Sheringham at 3.35pm and arrived back at Liverpool Street at 7.20pm. The 'Britannia' Pacifics managed to lop a full ten minutes off the Liverpool Street to Norwich run and these timings continued with English Electric Type 4 diesel haulage introduced in 1959. Sadly, the train lost its name in June 1962.

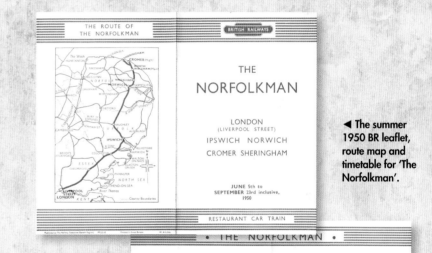

▲ The winter 1960/61 timetable for 'The Norfolkman'.

◄ The summer 1950 BR leaflet, route map and timetable for 'The Norfolkman'.

◄ Soon to be replaced by English Electric Type 4 diesels, Stratford shed's BR Standard 'Britannia' Class 4-6-2 No. 70034, 'Thomas Hardy' prepares to depart from Liverpool Street station with the down 'The Norfolkman' in May 1959. The loco was built at Crewe in 1952 and withdrawn from Carlisle Kingmoor shed in May 1967.

THE NIGHT FERRY

LONDON (VICTORIA) TO PARIS (GARE DU NORD)

'The Night Ferry' ('Ferry de Nuit') was inaugurated by the International Sleeping Car Company (Compagnie Internationale des Wagon-Lits et des Grand Express Européens) in 1936 after the completion of new train ferry terminals at Dover and Dunkerque. Providing a first class overnight sleeping car service between London and Paris and London and Brussels, the train was one of the heaviest to be operated on Britain's railways,

PARIS & BRUSSELS

BY

"THE NIGHT FERRY"

THROUGH SLEEPING CAR SERVICES

1st Class — via DOVER—DUNKERQUE

Every night in each direction

PARIS

Outwards	LONDON (Victoria)	dep	10 0 pm	
	PARIS (Nord)	arr	8 40 am	(R)
Inwards	PARIS (Nord)	dep	10 0 pm	(S)
	LONDON (Victoria)	arr	9 10 am	

BRUSSELS

Outwards	LONDON (Victoria)	dep	10 0 pm	(T)
	BRUSSELS (Midi)	arr	9 5 am	
Inwards	BRUSSELS (Midi)	dep	9 22 pm	(S)
	LONDON (Victoria)	arr	9 10 am	

R—Restaurant Car from London (Victoria) to Dover Marine; Restaurant Car from Dunkerque to Paris (Nord).
S—Restaurant Car from Dover Marine to London (Victoria).   T—Restaurant Car from London (Victoria) to Dover Marine; Continental Breakfast obtainable between Dunkerque and Brussels (Midi).

▲ The summer 1963 timetable for 'The Night Ferry'.

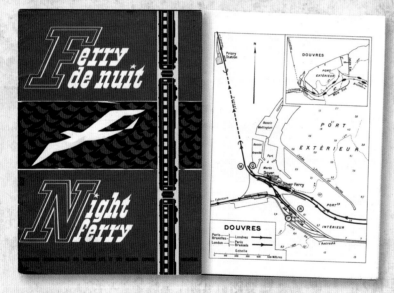

▲ With a cover designed by Peter Mann, this bilingual booklet and timetable was issued by the International Sleeping Car Company (Compagnie Internationale des Wagon-Lits et des Grand Express Européens) on 1 January 1958.

▶ Pilot engine 'L1' Class 4-4-0 No. 31789 waits to depart from London Victoria with 'The Night Ferry' to Dover and Paris in the 1950s. The loco was built by the North British Locomotive Company in Glasgow in 1926 and withdrawn in November 1961.

with up to 19 coaches being hauled between Victoria and Dover. Double heading was the order of the day until the train was withdrawn on the outbreak of the Second World War. Reinstated in 1947, the train was then hauled by Bulleid's new 'Merchant Navy' Pacifics but even these needed a pilot in the form of an 'L1' 4-4-0 on occasions until electrification of the London to Dover route in June 1959. From then until 1976 the train was in the capable hands of Class 71 Bo-Bo electric locomotives and with their demise Class 73 electro-diesels took over.

In the 1960s, departure from Victoria was at 10pm and at Dover the ten Wagon-Lits sleeping cars and a couple of French luggage vans were shunted carefully on to a train ferry before the Channel crossing to Dunkerque. Arrival in Paris was at 8.40am. In the opposite direction the train left Gare du Nord at 10pm and arrived, having attached British restaurant cars and coaches at Dover, at Victoria at 9.10am. Both trains also included through coaches either to or from Brussels. Fighting a losing battle with airline travel, in latter years the train ran in a much reduced form until its withdrawal on 1 November 1980.

▲ 'Merchant Navy' Class 4-6-2 No. 35030 'Elder Dempster Lines' leaves Dover Marine with 'The Night Ferry' to London Victoria on 11 October 1952. The last of its class, this loco was built by BR at Eastleigh in 1949, rebuilt in 1958 and withdrawn in July 1967.

► Class 71/74 Bo-Bo electric locomotive E5024 heads the up 'The Night Ferry' through Catford on 4 May 1963. Built at Doncaster Works as E5000 in 1958, this loco was renumbered to E5024 in December 1962, renumbered to E6104 in February 1968, renumbered to 74004 in December 1973 and withdrawn in December 1977.

THE NORSEMAN

LONDON (KING'S CROSS) TO TYNE COMMISSION QUAY

For some years before the Second World War the London & North Eastern Railway ran a boat train to and from King's Cross that connected with a steamer service to and from Norway at Tyne Commission Quay. Reintroduced by British Railways in 1950, by 1961 the down 'The Norseman' had various departure times on Mondays, Wednesdays, Thursdays and Saturdays (9.20am, 9.30am and 9.40am) from King's Cross and called at York before arriving at Newcastle Central at 2.24pm or 2.45pm. The Pacific loco was taken off here and the heavy train was hauled for the rest of its journey to Tyne Commission Quay, usually by a 'V3' 2-6-2 tank engine. Another boat train left King's Cross at 10.40am on summer Saturdays to connect with a steamer sailing to Stavanger (for Oslo Vest). In the opposite direction 'The Norseman' had an 11am departure from Tyne Commission Quay on Sundays and Fridays, and a 7am departure on Mondays and Thursdays. An oddity of the North Eastern Region timetable of summer 1961 was that only the up train was named 'The Norseman'. By 1962, diesels in the shape of English Electric Type 4s and 'Deltics' had usurped Pacific haulage of the train, which was withdrawn in 1966.

◄ Record-breaking 'A4' 4-6-2 No. 60022 'Mallard' accelerates through Selby with the down 'The Norseman', circa 1957. This famous loco was built at Doncaster in 1938 and withdrawn from King's Cross shed in April 1963. It has since been preserved.

◄ For its journey between Tyne Commission Quay and Newcastle Central 'The Norseman' was usually hauled by a tank engine. Here, 'V3' Class 2-6-2T No. 67691 prepares to leave Tyne Commission Quay with the up train in the late 1950s. The loco was the last of its class to be built, emerging from Doncaster Works in 1940, and was withdrawn from Gateshead shed in November 1964.

THE NORTH BRITON

LEEDS (CITY) TO EDINBURGH (WAVERLEY) AND GLASGOW (QUEEN STREET)

Although officially named 'The North Briton' by British Railways in 1949, an express restaurant car service had operated between Leeds and Edinburgh since the early twentieth century. The service had been extended to Glasgow (Queen Street) by 1914. By the outbreak of the Second World War and despite heavier loadings the schedule had seen vast improvements, with nearly an hour lopped off the timings. Named and reintroduced in 1949, 'The North Briton' became the first post-war service to include a mile-a-minute schedule (between Darlington and York). The 1950s saw new 'A1' class 4-6-2s from Leeds Neville Hill shed in charge until they were replaced by Class 47 diesels in the early 1960s. The summer 1961 timetable saw the train leaving Leeds (City) at 9.15am on weekdays and, after calling at York, Darlington, Newcastle and Dunbar, it arrived at Edinburgh (Waverley) at 1.53pm (1.44pm on Saturdays). Glasgow (Queen Street) was reached at 3.14pm. In the opposite direction the train departed Glasgow at 4pm and with the same stops reached Leeds at 10.08pm. The name was discontinued in 1968 but was reinstated between 1972 and 1975 to describe a Leeds to Dundee service.

► The summer 1961 timetable for 'The North Briton'.

THE NORTH BRITON
RESTAURANT CAR EXPRESS

LEEDS (City), YORK, DARLINGTON, NEWCASTLE, EDINBURGH (Waverley) and GLASGOW (Queen Street)

WEEKDAYS

		SX am	SO am				pm
LEEDS (City)	.. dep.	9 15	9 15	GLASGOW (Queen Street)	.. dep.		4 0
YORK	.. arr.	9 47	9 47	EDINBURGH (Wav.)	"		5 15
	.. dep.	9 51	9 51	DUNBAR	"		5 51
DARLINGTON	.. arr.	10 39	—	BERWICK-UPON-TWEED	.. arr.		6 25
	.. dep.	10 42	—		" dep.		6 28
NEWCASTLE	.. arr.	11 27	11 20	NEWCASTLE	.. arr.		7 42
	.. dep.	11 33	11 26		" dep.		7 53
		pm	pm	DARLINGTON	.. arr.		8 39
DUNBAR	.. arr.	1 19	—		" dep.		8 43
EDINBURGH (Wav.)	"	1 53	1 44	YORK	" arr.		9 25
GLASGOW (Queen Street)	"	3 14	3 14		" dep.		9 33
				LEEDS (City)	.. arr.		10 8

SX—Except Saturdays. **SO**—Saturdays only.

Seats may be reserved in advance for passengers travelling from Leeds and Glasgow on payment of a fee of 2s. 0d. per seat.

◄ The eye-catching luggage label for the steam-hauled 'The North Briton', circa 1950.

► Neville Hill's immaculate 'A3' Class 4-6-2 No. 60086 'Gainsborough' prepares to depart from Leeds City with the northbound 'The North Briton' on 25 March 1961. Built at Doncaster in 1930, this fine loco was withdrawn from Neville Hill shed in November 1963.

THE NORTHERN IRISHMAN

LONDON (EUSTON) TO STRANRAER HARBOUR

In the early years of the twentieth century the Midland Railway was operating an overnight sleeper service between St Pancras and Stranraer Harbour. Here the train, affectionately known as 'The Paddy', connected with sailings to and from Larne (for Belfast) in Northern Ireland. The route was via Leeds, Carlisle, Dumfries and the 'Port Road' to Stranraer through the wilds of Galloway. Euston station replaced St Pancras as the London terminus of this train in 1923 and the train continued to run through the Second World War. The name 'The Northern Irishman' was given to this train in 1952 and soon saw new BR Standard 'Clan' 4-6-2s in charge over the gruelling section between Dumfries and Stranraer. The summer 1962 timetable saw the train leave Euston at 7.20pm (Monday to Friday) and 7.15pm (Sunday) and, after calling at Bletchley, Rugby, Nuneaton and Crewe, where a restaurant car was detached, it called at Wigan before an engine change at Carlisle. Stranraer Harbour was reached at 5.28am the next day. In the reverse direction the train left Stranraer Harbour at 10pm and arrived back at Euston at 8.15am (8.45am on Saturdays) the next day.

The closure of the 'Port Line' between Dumfries and Challoch Junction on 14 June 1965 (steam-hauled until the end) saw 'The Northern Irishman' diverted via Girvan, Ayr and Mauchline, which added another 60 miles to the journey. The train remained steam-hauled between Stranraer Harbour and Carlisle with trains being double-headed to cope with the severe gradients of this route south of Girvan. The train lost its name in 1966 although there remained a Euston to Stranraer service until the 1980s.

Table 3

The Northern Irishman
EXPRESS SERVICES between
LONDON and BELFAST
Via STRANRAER AND LARNE
WEEK DAYS

TO BELFAST

	Monday to Friday nights THE NORTHERN IRISHMAN RC and TC—London to Stranraer Harbour	Sunday nights THE NORTHERN IRISHMAN RC and TC—London to Crewe	Saturdays excepted	Saturdays only
London Euston .... dep	7*20 pm	7*15 pm	am	am
Bletchley .... ,,	8 24	8 23		
Rugby Midland .... ,,	9 19	9 25		
Nuneaton Trent Valley .. ,,	9 40	9 49		
Crewe .... ,,	11 11 am	11 11 am		
Wigan North Western ... ,,	12 2	12 9	6d37	6c37
Carlisle .... ,,	2 19	2 25	11e0	11 17
Stranraer Harbour ..... arr	5b28	5b28		
Larne Harbour .... dep	7 0	7 0	2 30	2 30
Belfast York Road ..... arr	9 15	9 15	4 45	4 45
	10 5	10 5	5 35	5 35

FROM BELFAST

	Monday to Friday nights THE NORTHERN IRISHMAN SC and TC—Stranraer Harbour to London	Sunday nights THE NORTHERN IRISHMAN SC and TC—Crewe to London	Saturdays excepted	Saturdays only
Belfast York Road ..... dep	5 55 pm	5 55 pm	am	am
Larne Harbour .... ,,	6 50	6 50	10 5	10 5
			11 0	11 0
Stranraer Harbour ..... arr	9 5	9 5	1 15	1 15
	dep	10*0 am	10 am	1 40	1 40
Carlisle .... arr	1 19	1 19	5e 8	5h 8
Crewe .... ,,	4 28	4 28	10f8	11g52
Nuneaton Trent Valley .. ,,	5 56	5 56		
Rugby Midland .... ,,	6 7	6 23		
Bletchley .... ,,	6+50	7+20		
London Euston .... arr	8 15	8 45		

*—Seats may be reserved in advance on payment of a fee of 2s. 0d. per seat.
a—Stops only to take up passengers.
b—Stops only to set down passengers.
RC—Restaurant Car
SC—1st and 2nd class sleeping accommodation.
TC—Through Carriages.

b—Sleeping car passengers may remain in berths until 6.25 am.
c—Change at Carlisle.
d—Change at Carlisle and Dumfries.
e—Change at Dumfries.
f—Change at Dumfries, Carlisle and Preston.
g—Change at Carlisle and Preston.
h—from 7th July to 1st September arrives 4 51 pm

For details of Cabins and Berth Charges and addresses to which application should be made for accommodation on the vessels—see page 69. For details of Sailing Tickets and general arrangements—see separate folder, to be obtained at Stations and Agencies.

▲ The summer 1962 timetable for 'The Northern Irishman'.

◄ 'The Northern Irishman' was a difficult train to photograph due to its nocturnal habits. However the long daylight hours of June enabled M. Covey-Crump to snap this photo of Stanier 'Black 5' 4-6-0 No. 45126 waiting to depart from Stranraer Harbour in 1965. This train was diverted to run via Girvan and Mauchline following the closure of the 'Port Road' on 14 June. On the right is the ferry to Larne in Northern Ireland. Built by Armstrong Whitworth in 1935 this loco was withdrawn from Carlisle Kingmoor shed in May 1967.

THE NORTHUMBRIAN

LONDON (KING'S CROSS) TO NEWCASTLE-UPON-TYNE

Receiving its name in 1949, 'The Northumbrian' was effectively a relief train to the overcrowded 1pm departure from King's Cross to Edinburgh which during the Second World War had grown to over 20 coaches in length. During the last year of steam haulage in the summer of 1961 the down restaurant car train left King's Cross at 12.30pm and, after calling at Grantham, York, Darlington

BRITISH RAILWAYS

NEWCASTLE CENTRAL

THE NORTHUMBRIAN

▲ The stylish luggage label for the steam-hauled 'The Northumbrian', circa 1950.

▲ Attracting interest from a gaggle of trainspotters, 'A4' Class 4-6-2 No. 60006 'Sir Ralph Wedgwood' calls at Darlington Bank Top station with the up 'The Northumbrian' on 10 October 1953. The loco was built at Doncaster in 1938 and was originally named 'Herring Gull'. It received its new name in 1944 following the destruction of classmate No. 4469 (then named 'Sir Ralph Wedgwood') following a Luftwaffe bombing of York North shed in June 1942. No. 60006 was withdrawn from Aberdeen Ferryhill shed in September 1965.

► The summer 1961 timetable for 'The Northumbrian'.

THE NORTHUMBRIAN

LONDON (King's Cross), YORK, DARLINGTON, DURHAM and NEWCASTLE

WEEKDAYS

		pm				pm
LONDON (King's Cross) ..	dep	12 20	Newcastle	..	dep	12 30
Grantham	,,	2 27	Durham	..	,,	12 52
York	arr	3 59	Darlington	..	,,	1 25
Darlington	,,	4 51	York	..	,,	2 12
Durham	,,	5 20	Peterborough (North) ..	..	arr	4 17
Newcastle	,,	5 43	LONDON (King's Cross) ..	..	,,	5 56

Restaurant Cars for Table d'Hote meals.

Seats are reservable in advance for passengers travelling from London (King's Cross), and from Newcastle, Durham and Darlington to London (King's Cross) on payment of a fee of 2s. 0d. per seat.

and Durham, it arrived at Newcastle at 5.48pm (5.49pm on Saturdays). This train also conveyed through carriages for Scarborough which were detached at York. The up train left Newcastle at 12.50pm (11.55am on Saturdays) and, with the same stops plus Peterborough, arrived at King's Cross at 6.07pm. The Saturday service omitted the Peterborough stop and arrived in the capital at 5.48pm. Following a few years of diesel haulage the train lost its name in 1964.

▲ Peppercorn 'A1' Class 4-6-2 No. 60126 'Sir Vincent Raven' storms out of Durham to Relly Mill with the up 'The Northumbrian' on 6 January 1960. Built at Doncaster in 1949, this loco was withdrawn from York North shed in January 1965.

◀ 'A3' Class 4-6-2 No. 60106 'Flying Fox' speeds along the East Coast Main Line near Retford with the up 'The Northumbrian' on 23 August 1952. Built at Doncaster as a Gresley 'A1' in 1923, this loco was rebuilt as an 'A3' in 1947 and withdrawn from New England shed in November 1964.

OCEAN LINER EXPRESSES

LONDON (WATERLOO) TO SOUTHAMPTON DOCKS

Boat trains were run for many years by the London & South Western Railway, the Southern Railway and the Southern Region of BR between London Waterloo and Southampton Docks. Here the trains connected with ocean liners from around the world. Collectively known as the 'Ocean Liner Expresses', they ran under different names depending on the shipping line that was being met at Southampton. During the BR era the following trains ran when required between Waterloo and Southampton: 'The Cunarder' connected with RMS *Queen Mary* and *Queen Elizabeth* for the New York service; 'The

Statesman' connected with the SS *United States* for the New York service; the 'Union Castle Express' connected with Union-Castle Line sailings to and from South Africa; 'The Holland-American' connected with Holland-America Line sailings to and from New York; 'The South American' connected with Royal Mail line sailings to and from South America; 'The Greek Line' for Greek Line sailings to and from New York; 'The Sitmar Line' for Sitmar Line sailings to and from Australia; 'The Oriana' and 'The Canberra' for P&O sailings to and from Australia.

OCEAN LINER EXPRESS

Wine list

▲ Rebuilt 'West Country' Class 4-6-2 No. 34008 'Padstow' thunders down the track at Worting Junction west of Basingstoke with the 'Union Castle Express', circa 1965. The loco was built at Brighton in 1945, rebuilt in 1960 and withdrawn in June 1967.

THE PALATINE

LONDON (ST PANCRAS) TO MANCHESTER (CENTRAL)

Introduced by the London Midland & Scottish Railway in 1938 'The Palatine' was one of a pair of named trains – the other was named 'The Peak Express' – that operated over the former Midland Railway route between St Pancras and Manchester Central. The former departed from Manchester at 10am and returned from St Pancras at 4.30pm while the latter train left St Pancras at 10.30am and returned from Manchester at 4.25pm. 'The Palatine' also carried a through coach to and from Liverpool which was attached or detached at Chinley. Both named trains were discontinued during the Second World War and only 'The Palatine' was reintroduced in 1957. Until the advent of new 'Peak' Class diesels it was normally hauled by 'Jubilee' or 'Royal Scot' 4-6-0s. By the summer of 1962 the diesels had taken over and the restaurant train was departing from St Pancras at 7.55am and, after stopping at Luton, Wellingborough, Leicester, Derby, Matlock and Miller's Dale, it arrived at Manchester Central at 11.54am. The return service left Manchester at 2.25pm and with stops at Chinley, Miller's Dale, Matlock, Derby and Leicester it arrived back in the capital at 6.20pm. The train was rerouted via Nottingham from the autumn of 1962 and it was not uncommon for the train to load up to 14 coaches. It lost its name in 1964.

The Palatine
Restaurant Car Express
MANCHESTER CENTRAL and LONDON ST. PANCRAS
MONDAYS TO FRIDAYS

		am				pm
London St. Pancras	.. .. dep	7*55	Manchester Central	.. .. dep		2*25
Luton Midland Road	.. .. "	8‡29	Chinley	.. .. ..	"	2 54
Wellingborough Midland Road	.. "	9 9	Miller's Dale	.. .. ..	"	3 16
Leicester London Road	.. arr	9 45	Matlock	.. .. ..	"	3 35
Derby Midland	.. .. "	10 21	Derby Midland	.. .. ..	"	4 5
Matlock	.. .. .. "	10 48	Leicester London Road	.. .. arr		4 35
Miller's Dale	.. .. .. "	11 10	London St. Pancras	.. .. ..	"	6 20
Manchester Central	.. .. .. "	11 54				

A Buffet service is also available on this train.

‡—Stops only to take up passengers

*—Seats may be reserved in advance on payment of a fee of 2s. 0d. per seat.

▲ The summer 1962 timetable for 'The Palatine'.

► The up 'The Palatine' at speed near Darley Dale in June 1959 hauled by Stanier 'Black 5' 4-6-0 No. 44822 of Kentish Town shed. The loco was built at Derby in 1944 and was withdrawn from Newton Heath shed in October 1967.

◀ 'Jubilee' Class 4-6-0 No. 45575 'Madras' heads the up 'The Palatine' under the recently electrified Styal Loop near Didsbury in 1959. The loco was built by the North British Locomotive Company in Glasgow in 1934 and withdrawn from Burton shed in June 1963.

▶ Fitted with a Fowler tender, 'Jubilee' Class 4-6-0 No. 45616 'Malta GC' passes Knighton North Junction with the up 'The Palatine' in June 1959. The loco was built at Crewe in 1934 and withdrawn from Leicester Midland shed in January 1961.

PEMBROKE COAST EXPRESS

LONDON (PADDINGTON) TO PEMBROKE DOCK

Introduced by the Western Region in 1953, this train was a new restaurant car express linking London with South Wales and the seaside resorts of Pembrokeshire. Normally hauled for the first leg of its journey between Paddington and Carmarthen by 'Castle' Class locos, the down train left Paddington at 10.55am and ran the 133 miles to Newport non-stop in a blistering 131 minutes – the first ever mile-a-minute run on this route. Thereafter the train called at Cardiff, Swansea, Llanelli and Carmarthen, arriving there at 3.40pm. Here the train reversed direction, usually behind a 'Manor' Class 4-6-0, for the all-stations journey to Pembroke Dock, arriving at 5.26pm (all times courtesy of the Western Region 1958 summer timetable). In the reverse direction Pembroke Dock was left at 1.05pm and, with the same stops and engine changes, reached Newport at 5.20pm. From there to Paddington the train took 145 minutes, arriving in the capital at 7.45pm. The train lost its name in 1963.

Table 7

THE PEMBROKE COAST EXPRESS
RESTAURANT CAR SERVICE (¶)

LONDON, NEWPORT, CARDIFF, SWANSEA, TENBY and PEMBROKE DOCK

WEEK DAYS

				am					pm
LONDON (Paddington)	..	..	dep	10A55	Pembroke Dock ..	..	..	dep	1A 5
				pm	Pembroke ..	..	..	"	1A10
Newport ..	..	..	arr	1 6	Lamphey ..	..	..	"	1 15
Cardiff (General)	..	..	"	1 25	Manorbier ..	..	..	"	1A23
Swansea (High St.)	..	..	"	2 40	Penally ..	..	..	"	1A32
Llanelly ..	..	..	"	3 12	Tenby ..	..	..	"	1A40
Carmarthen ..	..	..	"	3 40	Saundersfoot ..	..	..	"	1A50
St. Clears ..	..	..	"	4 0	Kilgetty ..	..	..	"	1A55
Whitland ..	..	..	"	4 10	Templeton ..	..	..	"	2 0
Narberth ..	..	..	"	4 25	Narberth ..	..	..	"	2A10
Templeton ..	..	..	"	4 35	Whitland ..	..	..	"	2A25
Kilgetty ..	..	..	"	4 40	Carmarthen ..	..	..	"	2 48
Saundersfoot ..	..	..	"	4 45	Llanelly ..	..	..	"	3 15
Tenby ..	..	..	"	4 57	Swansea (High Street)	..	..	"	3A45
Penally ..	..	..	"	5 3	Cardiff (General) ..	..	..	"	5 0
Manorbier ..	..	..	"	5 10	Newport ..	..	..	"	5 20
Lamphey ..	..	..	"	5 16	LONDON (Paddington) ..	..	arr	7 45
Pembroke ..	..	..	"	5 20					
Pembroke Dock ..	..	..	"	5 26					

A—Seats can be reserved in advance on payment of a fee of 2s. 0d. per seat (see page 23).

¶—Restaurant Car available between London (Paddington) and Swansea (High St.), in each direction.

▲ The 'Pembroke Coast Express' timetable for winter 1958/59.

▲ The attractive restaurant car tariff for the 'Pembroke Coast Express', circa 1955.

▼ Looking resplendent with its attractive headboard, 'Manor' Class 4-6-0 No. 7804 'Baydon Manor' calls at Whitland station with the 'Pembroke Coast Express' in August 1963. This loco was built at Swindon in 1938 and withdrawn from Severn Tunnel Junction shed in September 1965.

P

PINES EXPRESS

MANCHESTER (LONDON ROAD/MAYFIELD) TO BOURNEMOUTH (WEST)

The opening of the Somerset & Dorset Railway's northern extension to Bath in 1874 allowed through trains to travel over the London & North Western Railway and Midland Railway between the Midlands, the North of England and Bournemouth. The forerunner of what became known as the 'Pines Express', a Manchester to Bournemouth restaurant car train, started running on weekdays throughout the year from 1 October 1910. It ceased running during the First World War but was reinstated after the war and by 1922 the train included through carriages from Bournemouth West and Swanage to Liverpool (Lime Street) and Manchester (London Road). The 248½-mile journey from Bournemouth to Manchester took 6hrs 25min.

Table 16

THE PINES EXPRESS
RESTAURANT CAR SERVICE
BETWEEN
MANCHESTER, LIVERPOOL
AND
CHELTENHAM SPA, GLOUCESTER, BATH and BOURNEMOUTH

WEEK DAYS ONLY

NORTH to SOUTH		SOUTH to NORTH	
	am		am
Manchester (London Road) .. ..dep	10A15	Bournemouth West.. .. ..dep	9A45
Stockport (Edgeley).. .. .. "	10 27	Poole .. .. "	9 54
Liverpool (Lime Street) .. .. "	10A 5	Blandford Forum .. .. "	10 20
		Stalbridge .. .. "	10 41
Crewe .. .. "	11 13	Evercreech Junction .. .. "	11 6
	pm	Shepton Mallet (Charlton Road) .. .. "	11 18
Birmingham (New Street) .. .. "	12 40		pm
		Bath Green Park .. .. "	12 1
Cheltenham Spa (Lansdown).. .. ..arr	1 39	Gloucester Eastgate .. .. "	12 57
Gloucester Eastgate .. .. "	1 59	Cheltenham Spa (Lansdown) .. .. "	1 15
Bath Green Park .. .. "	3 9		
Evercreech Junction .. .. "	4 54	Birmingham (New Street) .. ..arr	2 25
Blandford Forum .. .. "	5 12	Crewe .. .. "	3 47
Broadstone .. .. "	5 20	Hartford .. .. "	4 16
Poole .. .. "	5 32	Runcorn .. .. "	4 37
Bournemouth West.. .. .. "		Liverpool (Lime Street) .. .. "	4 55
		Wilmslow .. .. "	4 25
		Stockport (Edgeley) .. .. "	4 39
		Manchester (Mayfield) .. .. "	4B52

A—Seats can be reserved in advance on payment of a fee of 2s. 0d. per seat (see page 23)
B—Arrives London Road Station on Saturdays

▲ The winter 1958/59 timetable for the 'Pines Express'.

◄ The down 'Pines Express' comes off Midford Viaduct behind BR Standard Class '4' 4-6-0 No. 75023 and unrebuilt 'West Country' Class 4-6-2 No. 34043 'Combe Martin' in August 1962. This was the last season of through trains over the Somerset & Dorset, which came to the end of a slow and painful death on 7 March 1966. The former loco was built at Swindon at the end of 1953 and was withdrawn from Stoke shed in January 1966. 'Combe Martin' was built at Brighton in 1946 and was withdrawn in June 1963

Running via Birmingham (New Street), Gloucester (Eastgate), Mangotsfield and Bath (Green Park) this train was given the name 'Pines Express' in 1927 and it continued to run until the outbreak of the Second World War in September 1939. The 'Pines' was restored in 1949 and included a Sheffield portion except on summer Saturdays when this became a separate train. However, the journey time of 7hrs 7min by 1958 hardly meant that the train was an 'express' – it was significantly slower than the same journey 36 years before. The virtual takeover of the S&D by the Western Region in 1958 spelt the end for through workings over the line and the last 'Pines' over the route ran on 8 September 1962, appropriately hauled single-handedly by BR Standard Class '9F' 2-10-0 No. 92220 'Evening Star'. After that date the train was rerouted to run via Oxford and Basingstoke – the weekday train now taking 7hrs 11min between Bournemouth West and Manchester Piccadilly. The last ever 'Pines Express' over this new route ran on 4 March 1967.

After the Second World War the 'Pines' was normally hauled by 'Jubilee' or 'Black Five' 4-6-0s between Manchester and Bath Green Park. These were replaced by BR Sulzer Type 4s in the early 1960s but the route south from Bath was a different kettle of fish. The steeply-graded line over the Mendips necessitated double-heading of the train until the introduction of BR Standard Class '9F' 2-10-0s in 1960. Loco combinations on a summer Saturday were unique anywhere on BR: pairings of ex-LMS Class 2P 4-4-0s, S&DJR Class '7F' 2-8-0s, Stanier 'Black 5' 4-6-0s, SR 'West Country' and 'Battle of Britain' 4-6-2s, elderly Johnson Class '3F' 0-6-0s, Fowler '4F' 0-6-0s and BR Standard Class '5MT' 4-6-0s were a common sight between Bath Green Park and Evercreech Junction. While the '9Fs' were the first locomotives able to haul heavy passenger trains over the Mendips without assistance, their arrival on the scene came too late to save the line from closure.

◄ Headed by green-liveried and Swindonised BR Standard Class '9F' 2-10-0 No. 92220 'Evening Star', the last down 'Pines Express' climbs out of Bath to Devonshire Tunnel on 8 September 1962. 'Evening Star' was the last steam locomotive to be built for BR, emerging new from Swindon Works in 1960, and was withdrawn from Cardiff East Dock shed in March 1965. After only five years' service this historic loco was preserved and is now part of the National Collection.

THE QUEEN OF SCOTS

LONDON (KING'S CROSS) TO GLASGOW (QUEEN STREET)

Introduced in 1928, this new all-Pullman train operated along the 450 miles between King's Cross and Glasgow (Queen Street) via Leeds, Harrogate, Newcastle and Edinburgh (Waverley). It wasn't a particularly fast service with both the up and down trains taking 9½ hours to complete the journey. This was eventually cut to just under nine hours in 1932. Discontinued during the Second World War, the 'Queen of Scots' was reintroduced with extra coaches in 1948 and continued to operate until 1964 when it was withdrawn. The summer 1961 timetable shows the down train leaving King's Cross at 11.50am and after running non-

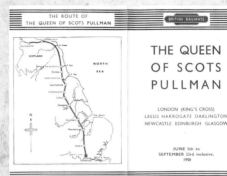

◄ The BR leaflet, route map and timetable for the summer 1950 'The Queen of Scots'.

▲ Stylish luggage labels from 'The Queen of Scots' Pullman train – on the left is the pre-war LNER label while on the right is the early BR version.

stop to Leeds followed by stops at Harrogate, Darlington, Newcastle, Edinburgh (Waverley) and Falkirk (High) it arrived at Glasgow (Queen Street) at 8.55pm. Without the Falkirk stop the up train left Glasgow at 11am and arrived at King's Cross at 8.09pm (8.20pm on Saturdays). In its post-war years 'The Queen of Scots' was normally hauled between London and Leeds by a Leeds (Neville Hill) 'A1' Class

Pacific until these were usurped by English Electric Type 4 and 'Deltic' diesels in the early 1960s. After withdrawal in 1964 the Pullman set used for this train was then transferred to a King's Cross to Harrogate express with the name of 'The White Rose'.

THE QUEEN OF SCOTS
(PULLMAN LIMITED TRAIN)

WEEKDAYS
(Will not run on Monday 7th August)

		SX am pm	SO am pm				SX am pm	SO am pm
LONDON (King's Cross)	.. dep.	11 50	11 50	**GLASGOW** (Queen St.)	.. dep.		11 0	11 0
LEEDS (Central)	.. { arr.	3 20	3 24	EDINBURGH (Waverley)	.. dep.		12 5	12 5
	dep.	3 28	3 32					
HARROGATE	.. { arr.	3 58	4 2	NEWCASTLE	.. { arr.		2 13	2 13
	dep.	4 1	4 5		dep.		2 19	2 19
DARLINGTON	.. { arr.	4 48	4 51	DARLINGTON	.. { arr.		3 4	3 4
	dep.	4 50	4 53		dep.		3 6	3 6
NEWCASTLE	.. { arr.	5 33	5 38	HARROGATE	.. { arr.		3 52	3 52
	dep.	5 39	5 44		dep.		3 55	3 55
EDINBURGH (Waverley)	.. arr.	7 48	7 50	LEEDS (Central)	.. { arr.		4 27	4 27
FALKIRK (High)	.. "	8A32	8A32		dep.		4 38	4 38
GLASGOW (Queen St.)	.. "	8 55	8 55	LONDON (King's Cross)	arr.		8 9	8 20

A—Calls when required to set down passengers from Newcastle and South thereof.
SO—Saturdays only.   SX—Saturdays excepted.

▲ The summer 1961 timetable for 'The Queen of Scots'.

▲ With a banking engine at the rear, the down 'The Queen of Scots' climbs the 1-in-41 Cowlairs Bank behind BR Standard Class '5MT' 4-6-0 No. 73108 on 12 July 1956. This loco was only just over six months old when seen here, having emerged new from Doncaster Works on New Year's Eve 1955. It was withdrawn from Carstairs shed exactly ten years later on the last day of 1966. What a total waste of taxpayers' money when it probably had another 25 years of service ahead of it.

▶ 'Deltic' (Class 55) diesel D9006 crosses the River Ure at Ripon with the down 'The Queen of Scots', circa 1963. The loco emerged new from the Vulcan Foundry of English Electric on 29 June 1961 and was first allocated to Edinburgh Haymarket shed. It was named 'The Fife & Forfar Yeomanry' at Cupar in 1964 and was withdrawn in February 1981.

R

THE ROBIN HOOD

LONDON (ST PANCRAS) TO NOTTINGHAM

By 1959 an unnamed express giving Nottingham businessmen a day in London had been operating between that city and St Pancras for over 60 years. In that year the London Midland Region bestowed the appropriate name of 'The Robin Hood' on this train, which was initially hauled by a 'Royal Scot' 4-6-0 until 'Peak' diesels took over in the early 1960s. Travelling via Manton and Melton Mowbray, the restaurant car express left Nottingham Midland at 8.15am and after stopping at only Manton it arrived at St Pancras at 10.30am. The return service left the capital at 5.25pm but this time stopped at Bedford, Wellingborough, Kettering and Manton before arriving back at Nottingham at 8.04pm (summer 1962 timetable). The introduction of diesel haulage soon saw the schedule of the up train cut to two hours

▲ Kentish Town shed's 'Royal Scot' Class 4-6-0 No. 46133 'The Green Howards' prepares to depart from St Pancras station with the down 'The Robin Hood' in 1961. Originally named 'Vulcan', the loco was built in 1927, rebuilt in 1944 and withdrawn from Newton Heath shed in February 1963.

exactly but the train's name was dropped as early as 1962. The Nottingham to Kettering route via Melton Mowbray was closed to passenger trains on 6 June 1966 but the southern section from Glendon Junction to Wymondham Junction was reopened to passenger traffic in 2009. Part of the route north of Melton Mowbray is now known as the Old Dalby Test Track.

The Robin Hood

Restaurant Car Express

NOTTINGHAM MIDLAND and LONDON ST. PANCRAS

MONDAYS TO FRIDAYS

		am				pm
Nottingham Midland	.. .. dep	8*15	London St. Pancras	.. .. dep		5*25
			Bedford Midland Road	.. .. "		6 25
Manton	.. .. "	8‡53	Wellingborough Midland Road	.. "		6 47
			Kettering	.. .. .. "		7 1
London St. Pancras	.. arr	10 30	Manton	.. .. .. "		7 24
			Nottingham Midland	.. .. arr		8 4

▲ The summer 1962 timetable for the short-lived 'The Robin Hood'.

R

THE RED DRAGON

LONDON (PADDINGTON) TO CARMARTHEN

Compared to the mile-a-minute down 'Pembroke Coast Express', 'The Red Dragon' took a more leisurely journey between London and South Wales. Introduced in 1950, the restaurant car train was soon in the hands of Cardiff Canton's new BR Standard 'Britannia' Pacifics for the journey between Cardiff and London until these were transferred away to the London Midland Region in 1960. They were replaced by 'Castle' and 'King' Class 4-6-0s until the introduction of Hymek and 'Western' diesel hydraulics in the early 1960s. The 1958 summer timetable shows the up train leaving Carmarthen at 7.30am and arriving at Paddington at 1pm, while the down service left London at 5.55pm and arrived in Carmarthen at 11.48pm. Engines were changed at Cardiff while the Carmarthen coaches were attached or detached at Swansea. Strangely, only the down train stopped at Swindon and Badminton, while the up train ran non-stop from Newport to Paddington. The train lost its name in 1965.

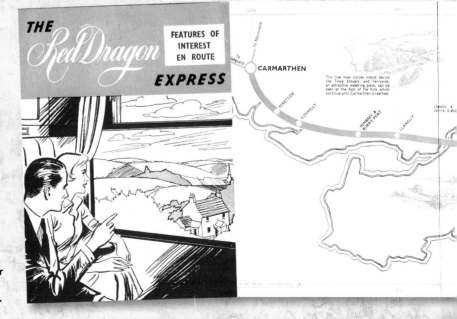

Table 8

THE RED DRAGON
RESTAURANT CAR SERVICE (¶)

LONDON, NEWPORT, CARDIFF, SWANSEA and CARMARTHEN

WEEK DAYS

	pm		am
London (Paddington) .. .. dep	5A55	Carmarthen .. .. dep	7A30
Swindon	7 28	Ferryside	7A42
Badminton	7 58	Kidwelly	7A50
Newport .. .. arr	8 47	Pembrey and Burry Port ..	8A 0
Cardiff (General)	9 7	Llanelly	8A10
Bridgend	9 48	Loughor	8A17
Port Talbot (General)	10 8	Gowerton North	8A22
Neath (General)	10 21	Cockett	8A30
Swansea (High Street)	10 40	Swansea (High Street)	8A45
Gowerton North	10 58	Cardiff (General)	10A 0
Llanelly	11 8	Newport	10A20
Pembrey and Burry Port	11 16		pm
Kidwelly	11 28	London (Paddington) .. .. arr	1 0
Ferryside	11 36		
Carmarthen	11 48		

A—Seats can be reserved in advance on payment of a fee of 2s. 0d. per seat (see page 23).

¶—Restaurant Car available between London (Paddington) and Cardiff (General), in each direction.

▲ The winter 1958/59 timetable for 'The Red Dragon'.

The
Red Dragon Express

TARIFF

◀ The restaurant car tariff for 'The Red Dragon', circa 1955.

THE
Red Dragon
EXPRESS

FEATURES OF INTEREST EN ROUTE

CARMARTHEN

The line now curves inland beside the Towy Estuary, and Ferryside, an attractive watering place, can be seen at the foot of the hills which continue until Carmarthen is reached.

FERRYSIDE

KIDWELLY

PEMBREY & BURRY PORT

LLANELLY

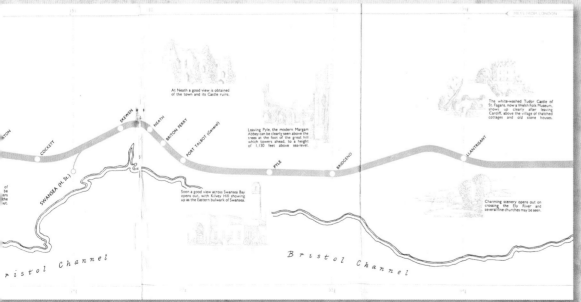

▲ The up 'The Red Dragon' has just arrived from Carmarthen and Swansea at Cardiff General's Platform 2 behind an unidentified 'Hall' Class 4-6-0 in September 1960. Waiting to take the train on to Paddington is 'King' Class 4-6-0 No. 6003 'King George IV'. The loco was built at Swindon in 1927 and withdrawn from Cardiff Canton shed in June 1962.

◄ This early BR leaflet and route guide describes the journey of 'The Red Dragon' through South Wales to Carmarthen.

R

THE RED ROSE

LONDON (EUSTON) TO LIVERPOOL (LIME STREET)

'The Red Rose' was one of three expresses running between Euston and Liverpool that were named in the Festival of Britain year of 1951. The restaurant car train was usually in the capable hands of a 'Princess Royal' Pacific or 'Royal Scot' 4-6-0 from Edge Hill depot until the early 1960s, when English Electric Type 4 diesels took over. The 1962 summer timetable shows the down service leaving Euston at 12.15pm and arriving at Liverpool at 4.10pm (Saturdays 4.20pm) while the up train left Liverpool at 5.30pm and, after stopping at Crewe, arrived at Euston at 9.10pm (9.20pm on Saturdays). The name was dropped following the electrification of the West Coast Main Line in 1966.

The Red Rose
Restaurant Car Express
LONDON EUSTON and LIVERPOOL LIME STREET

WEEKDAYS

London Euston .... dep 12 15 pm		Liverpool Lime Street .... dep 5 30 pm		
Liverpool Lime Street ... ... arr 4†10		Crewe .. .., „ 6 21		
		London Euston .... arr 9‡10		
†—Saturdays arrives 4.20 pm.		‡—Saturdays arrives 9.20 pm.		

▲ The summer 1962 timetable for 'The Red Rose'.

▼ The summer 1951 BR leaflet for the inaugural 'The Red Rose'.

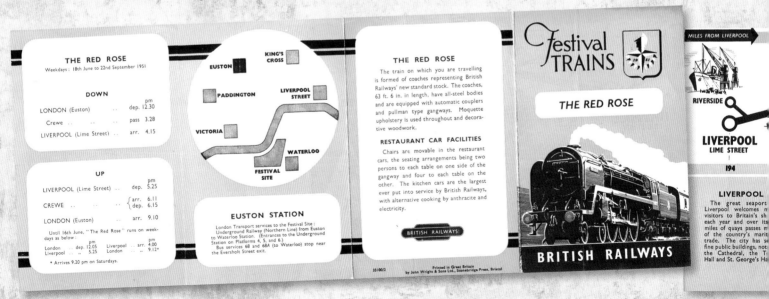

THE RED ROSE
Weekdays : 18th June to 22nd September 1951

DOWN

		pm
LONDON (Euston)	dep.	12.30
Crewe	pass	3.28
LIVERPOOL (Lime Street) ..	arr.	4.15

UP

		pm
LIVERPOOL (Lime Street) ..	dep.	5.25
CREWE	arr. dep.	6.11 6.15
LONDON (Euston)	arr.	9.10

Until 16th June, "The Red Rose" runs on week-days as below :-

	pm			
London ..	dep. 12.05	Liverpool ..	arr.	4.00
Liverpool ..	5.25	London ..		9.12*

* Arrives 9.20 pm on Saturdays.

EUSTON STATION

London Transport services to the Festival Site :
Underground Railway (Northern Line) from Euston to Waterloo Station. (Entrances to the Underground Station on Platforms 4, 5, and 6.)
Bus services 68 and 68A (to Waterloo) stop near the Eversholt Street exit.

THE RED ROSE

The train on which you are travelling is formed of coaches representing British Railways' new standard stock. The coaches, 63 ft. 6 in. in length, have all-steel bodies and are equipped with automatic couplers and pullman type gangways. Moquette upholstery is used throughout and decorative woodwork.

RESTAURANT CAR FACILITIES

Chairs are movable in the restaurant cars, the seating arrangements being two persons to each table on one side of the gangway and four to each table on the other. The kitchen cars are the largest ever put into service by British Railways, with alternative cooking by anthracite and electricity.

BRITISH RAILWAYS

Printed in Great Britain
by John Wright & Sons Ltd., Stonebridge Press, Bristol.

Festival TRAINS

THE RED ROSE

BRITISH RAILWAYS

MILES FROM LIVERPOOL

RIVERSIDE

LIVERPOOL
LIME STREET

194

LIVERPOOL

The great seaport, Liverpool welcomes visitors to Britain's each year and over miles of quays passes of the country's mari trade. The city has fine public buildings, the Cathedral, the Hall and St. George's H

▲ 'Royal Scot' Class 4-6-0 No. 46157 'The Royal Artilleryman' thunders through Lichfield Trent Valley with 'The Red Rose' in April 1957. The loco was built in 1930, rebuilt in 1946 and withdrawn from Carlisle Kingmoor shed in January 1964.

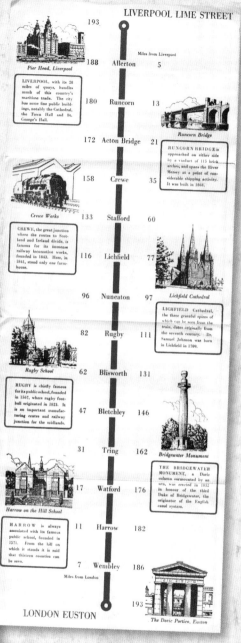

LIVERPOOL LIME STREET

Pier Head, Liverpool

Miles from Liverpool		
193		
188	Allerton	5
180	Runcorn	13
172	Acton Bridge	21
158	Crewe	35
133	Stafford	60
116	Lichfield	77
96	Nuneaton	97
82	Rugby	111
62	Blisworth	131
47	Bletchley	146
31	Tring	162
17	Watford	176
11	Harrow	182
7	Wembley	186
193		

Miles from London

LONDON EUSTON

LIVERPOOL, with its 28 miles of quays, handles much of this country's maritime trade. The city has some fine public buildings, notably the Cathedral, the Town Hall and St. George's Hall.

Crewe Works

CREWE, the great junction where the routes to Scotland and Ireland divide, is famous for its immense railway locomotive works, founded in 1843. Here, in 1841, stood only one farmhouse.

Runcorn Bridge

RUNCORN BRIDGE is approached on either side by a viaduct of 115 brick arches, and spans the River Mersey at a point of considerable shipping activity. It was built in 1868.

Lichfield Cathedral

LICHFIELD Cathedral, the three graceful spires of which can be seen from the train, dates originally from the seventh century. Dr. Samuel Johnson was born in Lichfield in 1709.

Rugby School

RUGBY is chiefly famous for its public school, founded in 1567, where rugby football originated in 1823. It is an important manufacturing centre and railway junction for the midlands.

Bridgewater Monument

THE BRIDGEWATER MONUMENT, a Doric column surmounted by an urn, was erected in 1832 in honour of the third Duke of Bridgewater, the originator of the English canal system.

Harrow on the Hill School

HARROW is always associated with its famous public school, founded in 1571. From the hill on which it stands it is said that thirteen counties can be seen.

The Doric Portico, Euston

▲ This 1955 summer BR leaflet gives details of the journey for 'The Red Rose' between Liverpool and Euston.

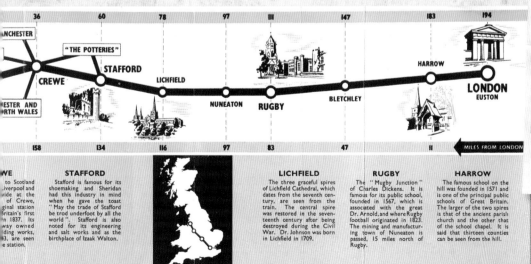

36	60	78	97	111	147	183	194

MANCHESTER — "THE POTTERIES" — STAFFORD — HARROW — LONDON EUSTON

CREWE — LICHFIELD — NUNEATON — RUGBY — BLETCHLEY

MANCHESTER AND NORTH WALES

158	134	116	97	83	47	11

← MILES FROM LONDON

CREWE

...e to Scotland ...iverpool and ...vide at the ...of Crewe, ...Britain's first ...ginal station ...n 1837. Its ...way owned ...ding works, ...3, are seen ...e station.

STAFFORD

Stafford is famous for its shoemaking and Sheridan had this industry in mind when he gave the toast "May the trade of Stafford be trod underfoot by all the world". Stafford is also noted for its engineering and salt works and as the birthplace of Izaak Walton.

LICHFIELD

The three graceful spires of Lichfield Cathedral, which dates from the seventh century, are seen from the train. The central spire was restored in the seventeenth century after being destroyed during the Civil War. Dr. Johnson was born in Lichfield in 1709.

RUGBY

The "Rugby Junction" of Charles Dickens. It is famous for its public school, founded in 1567, which is associated with the great Dr. Arnold, and where Rugby football originated in 1823. The mining and manufacturing town of Nuneaton is passed, 15 miles north of Rugby.

HARROW

The famous school on the hill was founded in 1571 and is one of the principal public schools of Great Britain. The larger of the two spires is that of the ancient parish church and the other that of the school chapel. It is said that thirteen counties can be seen from the hill.

R THE ROYAL DUCHY

LONDON (PADDINGTON) TO KINGSWEAR/PENZANCE

The name 'The Royal Duchy' was bestowed upon the 1.30pm Paddington to Penzance restaurant car train by the Western Region in 1955. The return working left Penzance at 11am – both up and down trains conveyed through coaches for Kingswear (detached or attached at Newton Abbot). Until the advent of diesel hydraulic 'Warship' diesels in the late 1950s, the train was usually hauled between London and Plymouth by a 'Castle' Class 4-6-0 – a pilot engine was added for the journey over the South Devon

Table 5

THE ROYAL DUCHY
RESTAURANT CAR SERVICE
LONDON, EXETER, PLYMOUTH, TRURO and PENZANCE
WEEK DAYS

		pm			pm
London (Paddington) .. .. ..dep	1A30		Penzance .. ..dep	11A 0	
Reading General	2U13		St. Erth	11A13	
Westbury .. ..arr	3 18		Camborne	11A30	
Taunton	4 13		Redruth	11A39	
Exeter (St. David's)	4 53		Chacewater	11A47	
Newton Abbot	5 27			pm	
			Truro	12A 1	
Kingskerswell	5 42		St. Austell	12 27	
Torre..	5 50		Par	12 36	
Torquay	5 53		Lostwithiel	12 48	
Paignton	6 6		Bodmin Road	12 57	
Goodrington Sands Halt	6B10		Liskeard	1 18	
Churston (for Brixham).. ..	6 17		Plymouth	2 0	
Kingswear	6 27				
			Kingswear	1A50	
Plymouth	6 25		Churston (for Brixham).. ..	2A 0	
Liskeard	7 5		Paignton	2A 9	
Bodmin Road	7 21		Torquay	2A18	
Lostwithiel	7 28		Torre..	2 22	
Par	7 38				
St. Austell	7 49		Newton Abbot	2 55	
Truro	8 12		Teignmouth	2 48	
Chacewater	8 27		Dawlish..	2 57	
Redruth	8 38		Exeter (St. David's)	3 30	
Camborne	8 46		Taunton	4 14	
Gwinear Road	8 53		Westbury	5 14	
Hayle	9 1		Newbury .. ..arr	6 2	
St. Erth	9 5		Reading General	6 25	
Penzance	9 20		London (Paddington).. ..	7 15	

A—Seats can be reserved in advance on payment of a fee of 2s. 0d. per seat (see page 23).

B—Commences 4th May, 1959

U—Calls to take up passengers only

▲ The winter 1958/59 timetable for 'The Royal Duchy'.

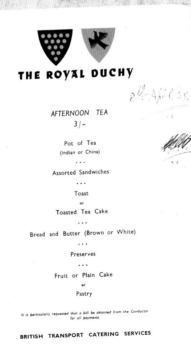

THE ROYAL DUCHY

AFTERNOON TEA
3/-

Pot of Tea
(Indian or China)
· · ·
Assorted Sandwiches
· · ·
Toast
or
Toasted Tea Cake
· · ·
Bread and Butter (Brown or White)
· · ·
Preserves
· · ·
Fruit or Plain Cake
or
Pastry

It is particularly requested that a bill be obtained from the Conductor
for all payments

BRITISH TRANSPORT CATERING SERVICES

W R

THE ROYAL DUCHY
TARIFF

◄ The stylish restaurant car tariff and tea menu (dated 8 April 1959) for 'The Royal Duchy'.

Banks between Newton Abbot and Plymouth. A 'County', 'Hall' or 'Grange' Class 4–6–0 usually hauled the train between Plymouth and Penzance. An express it definitely was not as the summer 1958 timetable clearly shows: the down train left Paddington at 1.30pm and after making 18 intermediate stops it arrived at Penzance at 9.20pm. The up service left Penzance at 11am and after making 19 stops arrived in the capital at 7.15pm. But who could object to this leisurely pace if the loco at the front was a 'Castle'? The train lost its name in 1965.

▲ Plymouth Laira's 'Castle' Class 4-6-0 No. 7022 'Hereford Castle' rolls into Reading General with the down 'The Royal Duchy' in the late 1950s. The loco was built by BR at Swindon in 1949 and withdrawn from Gloucester Horton Road shed in June 1965.

► North British Locomotive Company Type 2 B-B (Class 22) diesel hydraulic D6303 pilots 'Hall' Class 4-6-0 No. 5979 'Cruckton Hall' over the South Devon Banks at Tigley, near Totnes, with 'The Royal Duchy' on 22 July 1961. After being introduced in 1959 the NBL diesels had a short life with withdrawals taking place between 1967 and 1972. The 'Hall' had a much longer life – built at Swindon in 1938, it was withdrawn from Worcester shed in November 1964.

THE ROYAL HIGHLANDER

LONDON (EUSTON) TO INVERNESS

The ancestry of this Anglo-Scottish sleeping car train goes right back to the famous Railway Races to the North of 1897, when the two rival West Coast and East Coast railway companies competed for the fastest journey time between London and Aberdeen. Although the latter trains were lightly loaded and built for speed 'The Royal Highlander', introduced by the London Midland & Scottish Railway in 1927, was a very different animal. Loading up to 13 coaches, the train carried sleeping cars to and from Aberdeen, Inverness and Perth with the train splitting at the latter

city. Such was its popularity during the summer months that up to three trains were run each night. Although the name was dropped during the Second World War the service continued to operate, and the end of hostilities saw a marked improvement in the schedule with LMS 'Coronation' Pacifics in charge for the overnight run between Euston and Perth. By the time the train was renamed in 1957 the Aberdeen portion had been dropped and the advent of English Electric Type 4 diesel power saw further improvements to the schedule – by the summer of 1962 the heavily loaded down train was departing from Euston at 6.40pm (Monday to Friday), 7pm on Sundays and, after stops at Crewe and Perth, arrived at Inverness at 8.39am (Tuesday to Saturday) and 8.46am on Mondays. The up train left Inverness at 5.40pm (Monday to Saturday) and made stops at Perth, Carlisle, Crewe, Nuneaton, Rugby and Bletchley before arriving at Euston at 8.25am (Tuesday to Saturday) and 9am (Sunday). In later years the train also conveyed sleeping cars to and from Fort William, travelling via Glasgow Queen Street. Although the train lost its name in 1985 this service is now provided by the 'Caledonian Sleeper' (see 'ZZZZZZ...').

The Royal Highlander

LONDON EUSTON and INVERNESS

First and second class sleeping accommodation is available between London and Inverness

	Mon. to Fri. nights	Sun. nights		Mon. to Fri. nights	Sat. nights
	pm	pm		pm	pm
London Euston ....dep	6 40	7 0	Inverness ....dep	5†40	5†40
			Perth	9†50	9†50
				am	am
			Carlisle	1 39	1 39
Crewe . . . . ,,	10 13	10 38	Crewe ....arr	4 37	4 41
			Nuneaton	5 51	6 6
	am	am	Rugby Midland .. .. .. ,,	6 20	6 35
Perth ....arr	4 33	4 49	Bletchley		7†40
Inverness . . . . ,,	8 39	8 46	London Euston	8 25	9 0

◄ The summer 1962 timetable for 'The Royal Highlander'.

► Crewe North's 'Coronation' Class 4-6-2 No. 46235 'City of Birmingham' is seen here at its home depot in September 1958. Unusually it is carrying two headboards for 'The Royal Highlander' sleeping car train which it is waiting to take over for the journey up to Scotland. The loco was built with a streamlined casing at Crewe in 1939, de-streamlined in 1946 and withdrawn from Crewe North shed in October 1964. It has since been preserved and can be seen in Birmingham's new ThinkTank Museum.

THE ROYAL SCOT

LONDON (EUSTON) TO GLASGOW (CENTRAL)

One of the most famous long-distance expresses in the world, 'The Royal Scot' was first introduced by the London & North Western Railway and the Caledonian Railway in 1862. Departing at 10am from London Euston the train travelled the length of the West Coast Main Line to Glasgow, a distance of 401¼ miles. Hauled by one of the L&NWR's crack express locomotives such as the 4-4-0 Precursor or the later 4-6-0 Claughton, the train required banking assistance on the climb to Shap before arriving at Carlisle, where a Caledonian Railway loco took over.

▲ The ex-LMS Ivatt 1,600hp diesel twins, Nos. 10000 and 10001, are seen here at Crewe with 'The Royal Scot' on a wet 30 June 1957. Both were built at Derby – No. 10000 in 1947 and No. 10001 by BR in 1948. Both were allocated to Willesden shed, with the former being withdrawn in 1963 and the latter in 1966.

The Royal Scot

It was not until 1927 that *The Royal Scot* received its name, under which it has achieved international renown, but the history of the train goes back over more than a hundred years of railway progress.

The Royal Scot is the lineal descendant of the first train which, in February 1848, linked the Thames with the Clyde, travelling by the West Coast Route, the first all-rail route between London and Glasgow. The pioneer train left Euston at 10.0 a.m. and, apart from a short period before 1862, trains have left from both London and Glasgow at the same time ever since.

Today, *The Royal Scot* still holds a leading place in the list of British named trains. Throughout the years the comfort and amenities of the train have been steadily improved, to culminate in the smooth-riding, all-steel carriages, of the latest British Railways standard design, of which *The Royal Scot* is composed.

The Royal Scot

Wine List

◄ This stylish mid-1950s BR restaurant car wine tariff for 'The Royal Scot' was designed by an artist known only as 'ef'.

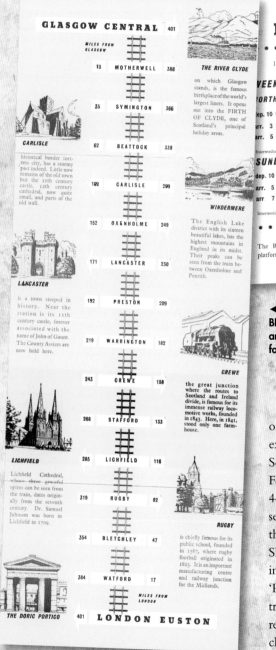

GLASGOW CENTRAL 401

MILES FROM GLASGOW

13	MOTHERWELL	388
35	SYMINGTON	366
62	BEATTOCK	339
102	CARLISLE	299
152	OXENHOLME	249
171	LANCASTER	230
192	PRESTON	209
219	WARRINGTON	182
243	CREWE	158
268	STAFFORD	133
285	LICHFIELD	116
319	RUGBY	82
354	BLETCHLEY	47
384	WATFORD	17
401	**LONDON EUSTON**	

MILES FROM LONDON

THE RIVER CLYDE

on which Glasgow stands, is the famous birthplace of the world's largest liners. It opens out into the FIRTH OF CLYDE, one of Scotland's principal holiday areas.

CARLISLE

historical border fortress city, has a stormy past indeed. Little now remains of the old town but the 11th century castle, 12th century cathedral, now quite small, and parts of the old wall.

WINDERMERE

The English Lake district with its sixteen beautiful lakes, has the highest mountains in England in its midst. Their peaks can be seen from the train between Oxenholme and Penrith.

LANCASTER

is a town steeped in history. Near the station is its 11th century castle, forever associated with the name of John of Gaunt. The County Assizes are now held here.

CREWE

the great junction where the routes to Scotland and Ireland divide, is famous for its immense railway locomotive works, founded in 1843. Here, in 1841, stood only one farmhouse.

LICHFIELD

Lichfield Cathedral, whose three graceful spires can be seen from the train, dates originally from the seventh century. Dr. Samuel Johnson was born in Lichfield in 1709.

RUGBY

is chiefly famous for its public school, founded in 1567, where rugby football originated in 1823. It is an important manufacturing centre and railway junction for the Midlands.

THE DORIC PORTICO

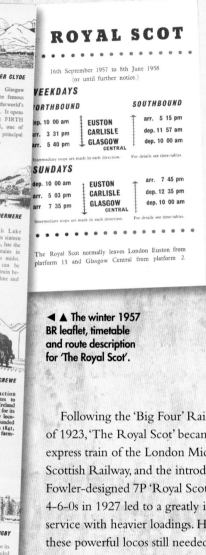

ROYAL SCOT

16th September 1957 to 8th June 1958 (or until further notice.)

WEEKDAYS

NORTHBOUND		SOUTHBOUND
dep. 10 00 am	EUSTON	arr. 5 15 pm
arr. 3 31 pm	CARLISLE	dep. 11 57 am
arr. 5 40 pm	GLASGOW CENTRAL	dep. 10 00 am

Intermediate stops are made in each direction. For details see time-tables.

SUNDAYS

dep. 10 00 am	EUSTON	arr. 7 45 pm
arr. 5 03 pm	CARLISLE	dep. 12 35 pm
arr. 7 35 pm	GLASGOW CENTRAL	dep. 10 00 am

Intermediate stops are made in each direction. For details see time-tables.

The Royal Scot normally leaves London Euston from platform 13 and Glasgow Central from platform 2.

ON A COLD, WINTRY MORNING in February 1848, railway history was made at Euston Station. The time was a few seconds to ten o'clock. Precisely on the hour a guard waved his flag and the first train to Glasgow began its 400 mile journey to the North. On the same day the first train from Glasgow arrived at Euston.

The '10 o'clock', as it was popularly known to the public, swiftly became one of the most famous trains in Great Britain. In 1927 it was officially named 'The Royal Scot'—flag-train of the London Midland & Scottish Railway—the greater part of whose lines are now in the London Midland Region and Scottish Region of British Railways.

Ask an American, or a Canadian for that matter, if he has heard of 'The Royal Scot'. He may surprise you. For in 1933 'The Royal Scot' was exhibited at the Chicago World's Fair. Incidentally she toured the North American continent covering over 11 thousand miles of railway track in five months. Quite an achievement when it is realised that about three million inspected her from wheels to buffers.

If you're wondering what type of locomotive is used on 'The Royal Scot' run, it's either a Diesel locomotive or one of the 'Coronation' Pacific class.

The 'loading' of the train depends on the time of year. For example: the normal Winter weekdays run to Glasgow from London comprises 13 vehicles (455 tons) to Crewe—3 vehicles are then taken off—continuing on to Glasgow with 10 vehicles (345 tons). The opposite run—Glasgow to London—is made up of 10 vehicles (345 tons). During part of the Autumn and Spring periods the train in each direction is increased by one vehicle.

Summer workings, both from London and Glasgow, are uniform—13 vehicles (446 tons). The carriages are the most modern all-steel type with wide observation windows. They are pleasingly furnished and the seats offer armchair comfort.

'The Royal Scot' hits a speed of 90 m.p.h. Speed limits are observed, of course, for permanent way operations, mining subsidences, restrictions over some bridges, and so on. Maximum comfort at maximum speed is harnessed to maximum safety.

Go in comfort — by train

the ROYAL SCO

SEAT RESERVATION

Reserve your seat in advance at Euston and other London terminal stations, Glasgow Central Station or at official railway agents.

FARES

The first class fares between London Euston and Glasgow Central are 100/6d. single and 201/0d. return. The second class fares are 67/0d. single and 134/0d. return. For children 3 years of age and under 14 years, the fare is half those shown.

MEALS

Luncheon and afternoon tea are served in the restaurant car.

Light refreshments and a corridor service are usually provided, but at busy times it may not always be possible.

Published by British Railways (London Midland Region) BR35109/19. Printed in Great Britain by Tinlings, Liverpool.

◄ ▲ The winter 1957 BR leaflet, timetable and route description for 'The Royal Scot'.

► The summer 1962 timetable for 'The Royal Scot'.

Following the 'Big Four' Railway Grouping of 1923, 'The Royal Scot' became the premier express train of the London Midland & Scottish Railway, and the introduction of the Fowler-designed 7P 'Royal Scot' Class 4-6-0s in 1927 led to a greatly improved service with heavier loadings. However, even these powerful locos still needed assistance over Shap – a situation which was only remedied in 1933 with the introduction of Stanier's 8P 'Princess Royal' Class Pacifics. By then the train had officially become non-stop, but in reality it still paused at Carlisle for a crew change. 'Coronation' Class Pacifics took over in

The Royal Scot

Restaurant Car Express

LONDON EUSTON and GLASGOW CENTRAL

WEEKDAYS

	Mons. to Fris.	Sats.		Mons. to Fris.	Sats.
	am	am		am	am
London Euston .... dep.	9 30	9 30	Glasgow Central .... dep.	10 0	10 0
	pm	pm			
Carlisle .... arr.	2 55	3 31	Carlisle	11 51	
				pm	pm
Glasgow Central	4 50	5 30	London Euston .... arr.	5 20	5 45

SUNDAYS

	am			am
London Euston .... dep.	9 30	Glasgow Central .... dep.	10 0
Rugby Midland	11‡26	Motherwell	10§21
		Carstairs	10§58
	pm		pm
Crewe	1§18	Carlisle	12 44
Carlisle .... arr.	4 32	Penrith	1‡21
Beattock	5 39	Crewe .... arr.	4 10
Motherwell	6§55	Rugby Midland	5 49
Glasgow Central	7 20	London Euston	8 20

‡—Stops only to take up passengers.   §—Stops only to set down passengers.

Seats may be reserved in advance for passengers travelling from London and Glasgow and on Sundays only, Carlisle to London on payment of a fee of 2s. 0d. per seat.

A Buffet service is also available on this train.

1937, a duty they were to retain until the end of steam haulage in the early 1960s. By 1962 the departure from Euston had been retimed to 9.30am and with a stop at Carlisle the train reached Glasgow at 4.50pm (Monday to Friday). The Saturday working took 40 minutes longer and on Sundays the train was virtually reduced to stopping-train status, with stops at Rugby, Crewe, Carlisle, Beattock and Motherwell, arriving at Glasgow at 7.20pm.

Following electrification of the WCML to Glasgow in 1974, 'The Royal Scot' continued to run until 2003 when the name was dropped. Today the fastest Pendolino Class 390 trains from Euston to Glasgow take only 4hrs 31min to complete the journey.

▼ Crewe North's maroon-liveried 'Coronation' 4-6-2 No. 46246 'City of Manchester' prepares to leave Euston with the down 'The Royal Scot' on 21 July 1959. The loco was built with streamlined casing at Crewe in 1943, de-streamlined in 1946 and withdrawn from Camden shed in January 1963.

THE ROYAL WESSEX

LONDON (WATERLOO) TO BOURNEMOUTH (WEST)/SWANAGE/WEYMOUTH

Yet another train that received its name during the Festival of Britain year of 1951, 'The Royal Wessex' was the successor to the Southern Railway's pre-war 'Bournemouth Limited' express. With Bulleid's new air-smoothed Pacifics now in charge the heavily loaded train of up to 13 coaches (including portions to and from Swanage and Weymouth) travelled up to London in the morning and returned to Dorset in the afternoon. Such was the demand in the summer months that the Swanage portion was replaced by a separate through

▼ The down 'The Royal Wessex' has just passed Eastleigh station behind 'Merchant Navy' Class 4-6-2 No. 35008 'Orient Line' on 4 August 1962. The loco was built at Eastleigh in 1942, rebuilt in 1957 and withdrawn in July 1967.

◄ No worries about Health & Safety as 'Merchant Navy' Class 4-6-2 No. 35028 'Clan Line' thunders towards Basingstoke with 'The Royal Wessex', circa 1964. The loco was built at Eastleigh in 1948, rebuilt in 1959 and withdrawn in July 1967. It has since been restored and is currently certified for use on the main line.

train between the resort and Waterloo. By the summer Saturdays of 1963 the main up train left Weymouth at 7.37am and after attaching coaches from Bournemouth (West) at Central station it arrived at Waterloo at 10.51am. The down train left Waterloo at 4.35pm and arrived at Weymouth at 7.59pm. The train was withdrawn following completion of the electrification of the Waterloo to Bournemouth route in July 1967.

► The ex-LMS Ivatt 1,600hp diesel No. 10000 is an unusual form of motive power for 'The Royal Wessex' on this 1950s postcard (see 'The Royal Scot' for details of this loco).

S

THE SAINT MUNGO

GLASGOW (BUCHANAN STREET) TO ABERDEEN

In the early twentieth century the Caledonian Railway operated a series of luxurious trains between Glasgow (Buchanan Street) and Aberdeen via Perth and Forfar. Known as 'The Grampian Corridor' (after the new 12-wheeled corridor stock used for the trains and later renamed 'The Grampian') and 'The Granite City' the trains were discontinued on the outbreak of the First World War. Both of these named trains were later revived by the London Midland & Scottish Railway in 1933 and in 1937 the company introduced two more named trains on this route: 'The Saint Mungo' and 'The Bon Accord'. The names for all four of these expresses were dropped during the Second World War but revived in 1949, usually with 'Jubilee' 4-6-0 haulage until 1962 when Gresley 'A4' Pacifics – relocated from their East Coast Main Line duties – were introduced. These superb locomotives performed their swansong on the Glasgow–Aberdeen three hour expresses until 3 September 1966 when diesels took over.

With the 'A4s' in charge of this restaurant car train, the summer timetable of 1964 shows the up 'The Saint Mungo' leaving Aberdeen at 9.30am (Monday to Friday), making 14 intermediate stops and arriving at Buchanan Street at 1.30pm. The down service was a true three-hour train leaving Glasgow at 5.30pm and, after stops at Stirling, Perth, Forfar and Stonehaven, arriving at Aberdeen at 8.30pm.

Glasgow (Buchanan Street) station closed in 1966 and these trains were then diverted to and from Queen Street station. Trains such as 'The Saint Mungo' ceased to operate along this route on 4 September 1967 when the former Caledonian main line between Stanley Junction and Kinnaber Junction via Forfar was closed. They were then diverted via Dundee but with slower timings. The train lost its name in 1968.

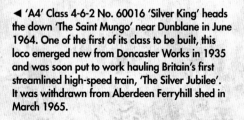

◄ 'A4' Class 4-6-2 No. 60016 'Silver King' heads the down 'The Saint Mungo' near Dunblane in June 1964. One of the first of its class to be built, this loco emerged new from Doncaster Works in 1935 and was soon put to work hauling Britain's first streamlined high-speed train, 'The Silver Jubilee'. It was withdrawn from Aberdeen Ferryhill shed in March 1965.

THE SCARBOROUGH FLYER

LONDON (KING'S CROSS) TO SCARBOROUGH (CENTRAL)

Running during the summer months only, the first through express between London and the resort town of Scarborough was introduced by the London & North Eastern Railway in 1923. It was officially named 'Scarborough Flier' in 1927. Over the following years the train was speeded up until in 1935 the schedule was cut to three hours for the non-stop run between King's Cross and York, making it one of the fastest trains in Britain. Engines were changed at York where a through coach to or from Whitby was detached or attached. Such was the popularity of the train that on summer Saturdays an extra, unnamed, service was laid on. Suspended during the Second World War, the train was reintroduced as 'The Scarborough Flyer' by British Railways in 1950. The new schedule never lived up to the pre-war timings and by the summer of 1961 the down train was scheduled to leave King's Cross at 11.28am (Saturdays only, also Fridays between 21 July and 18 August) and after calling at Grantham arrived at York at 3.11pm (2.58pm on Fridays). Here the Whitby portion was detached and after calling at Malton arrived at Scarborough (Central) at 4.11pm (3.58pm on Fridays). The Whitby portion arrived at its destination after travelling via Malton and Pickering at 5.21pm. The up service was unusual, with a 10.42am departure from Scarborough on Saturdays only, arriving back in the capital with the Whitby portion at 3.42pm; on Sundays there was a 10.35am departure from Scarborough, but this time with no Whitby portion it arrived in London at 3.56pm. The train lost its name at the end of the 1963 summer timetable.

▼ King's Cross shed's 'A4' Class 4-6-2 No. 60014 'Silver Link' roars through New Southgate station with the down 'The Scarborough Flyer' on 8 March 1957. The loco was the first of its class to be built, emerging new from Doncaster Works in 1935 and soon put to work hauling Britain's first streamlined high-speed train, 'The Silver Jubilee'. It was withdrawn from King's Cross shed in December 1962.

THE SCARBOROUGH FLYER
RESTAURANT CAR EXPRESS

LONDON (King's Cross), GRANTHAM, YORK, SCARBOROUGH (Central) and WHITBY (Town)

		A am 11 28 pm	B am 11 28 pm				SO am	SO am	C am
LONDON (King's Cross)	dep.	11 28	11 28	SCARBOROUGH (Central)	dep.		10 42	10 35	
		pm	pm	MALTON	arr.		11	11 1	
GRANTHAM	dep.	1 26	1 34	WHITBY (Town)	dep.		9 33		9F35
	arr.	2 58	3 11	MALTON	arr.		10 43		
YORK	dep.	3 6 3 35	3 19 3 35	MALTON	dep.		10 47		11 6
	arr.	4 3	4 3		arr.		11 20		11 37
MALTON	dep.	4 8	4 8	YORK	dep.		11 44 pm		11 45 pm
WHITBY (Town)	arr.	5 21	5 21				27		29
				GRANTHAM	arr.				
SCARBOROUGH (Central)	arr.	3 58	4 11	LONDON (King's Cross)	arr.		3 42		3 56

A—Fridays only. Runs 21st July to 18th August.

B—Saturdays only. Not after 2nd September.

C—Sundays only. Commences 16th July.

F—Change at Malton.

SO—Saturdays only.

Seats are reservable in advance for passengers travelling from London (King's Cross), Scarborough and Whitby, on payment of a fee of 2s. 0d. per seat.

▲ The summer 1961 timetable for 'The Scarborough Flyer'.

THE SHAMROCK

LONDON (EUSTON) TO LIVERPOOL (LIME STREET)

Introduced by British Railways in 1954, 'The Shamrock' connected with steamers to and from Belfast and Dublin at Liverpool. The heavily loaded restaurant car express was normally in the hands of Edge Hill or Camden 'Princess Royal' Pacifics until these were replaced by English Electric Type 4s around 1960. Connecting with overnight steamers from the 'Emerald Isle', the up train left Liverpool at 8.15am (Monday to Friday) and 8.30am on Saturdays and, after calling at Mossley Hill, Crewe and Bletchley, arrived at Euston at 12.15pm (Monday to Friday) and 12.35pm (Saturday). The down service left Euston at 4.55pm and ran non-stop to Liverpool, arriving at 8.50pm (Monday to Friday). On Saturdays this train left the capital at 4.30pm and, after calling at Rugby and Crewe, arrived at Liverpool at 8.45pm. As with most named trains on the West Coast Main Line, 'The Shamrock' lost its name following completion of electrification in 1966.

The Shamrock
Restaurant Car Express
LIVERPOOL LIME STREET and LONDON EUSTON

WEEKDAYS

	Mons. to Fris.	Sats.			Mons. to Fris.	Sats.
	am	am			pm	pm
Liverpool Lime Street ....dep	8 15	8 30	London Euston ....dep		4 55	4 30
Mossley Hill	8‡23	8‡38	Rugby Midland .. .. ,,			6 18
Crewe............................arr	9 6	9 17				
Bletchley .. .. ,,	11 4	11 23	Crewe .... ,,		8 5	
London Euston .... ,,	12 15	12 35	Liverpool Lime Street ..arr		8 50	8 45

‡—Stops only to take up passengers.

This train connects at Liverpool with the Belfast Steamship and the British & Irish Steam Packet Companies' sailings from and to Belfast and Dublin—for details see Table 4.

▲ The summer 1962 timetable for 'The Shamrock'.

▼ Rugby shed's Stanier 'Black 5' 4-6-0 No. 44866 pilots an unidentified 'Royal Scot' 4-6-0 out of Bletchley with the up 'The Shamrock' on 3 April 1960. Evidence of the building of the flyover can be seen on the left. The 'Black 5' was built at Crewe Works in 1945 and withdrawn from Trafford Park shed in September 1967.

◀ The eye-catching mid-1950s BR restaurant car wine list for 'The Shamrock'.

SHEFFIELD PULLMAN

LONDON (KING'S CROSS) TO SHEFFIELD (VICTORIA/MIDLAND)

The 'Sheffield Pullman' was introduced by the Eastern Region of British Railways in 1958. The train used the same Pullman coaches as the newly diverted 'The Master Cutler', thereby making use of stock that would have otherwise lain idle during the off-peak period. Diesel-hauled from the beginning, the train was upgraded with new Pullman coaches in 1960 by which time the down train was leaving King's Cross at 11.20am. After calling at Peterborough, Grantham and Retford it would arrive at Sheffield (Victoria) at 2.24pm. There then followed a quick turnaround; the up train left at 3.20pm and with the same stops arrived back in the capital at 6.25pm. Using the same stock 'The Master Cutler' departed for Sheffield only 55 minutes later. The service was diverted to and from Sheffield (Midland) station in 1965 and was withdrawn in 1968.

◄ Brush Type 2 (Class 31) diesel D5560 works hard with the six-car up Sheffield Pullman at Stoke in May 1962. The train is a mixture of elderly Pullman coaches and new Metropolitan-Cammell coaches. This long-lived loco entered service from Brush Works at Loughborough in 1959 and was withdrawn from Holbeck depot as No. 31142 in May 2000.

THE SILVER JUBILEE

LONDON (KING'S CROSS) TO NEWCASTLE (CENTRAL)

Named by the London & North Eastern Railway to honour 25 years of King George V's reign, 'The Silver Jubilee' was Britain's first streamlined high-speed train when it went into service on 30 September 1935. Hauled by Gresley's new streamlined 'A4' Pacifics, the train consisted of two pairs of articulated coaches separated by a triplet set (including restaurant car) making seven coaches in all. Engines and coaches were finished in a two-tone silver and grey with stainless steel embellishments. The four 'A4' locos specially built to haul the train were appropriately named 'Silver Link', 'Quicksilver', 'Silver

▼ Featuring 'A4' Class 4-6-2 No. 2509 'Silver Link' and colour-co-ordinated with the train itself, this 1935 LNER booklet for 'The Silver Jubilee' features the seating plan, timetable, speeds and route map for the service.

▲ The colour-co-ordinated luggage label for 'The Silver Jubilee'.

King' and 'Silver Fox'. Setting new standards in speed, luxury and reliability the train was so popular that an extra coach, as part of an articulated triplet set, was later added.

With a two-minute stop at Darlington the total journey time for both up and down trains was exactly four hours, giving an average speed of just over 67mph for the 268-mile journey. The up train left Newcastle at 10am and the down train left King's Cross at 5.30pm. After four years of 100 per cent reliability the onset of the Second World War brought an end to this service. Two of the articulated coaches were later used after the war on the 'Fife Coast Express' in Scotland.

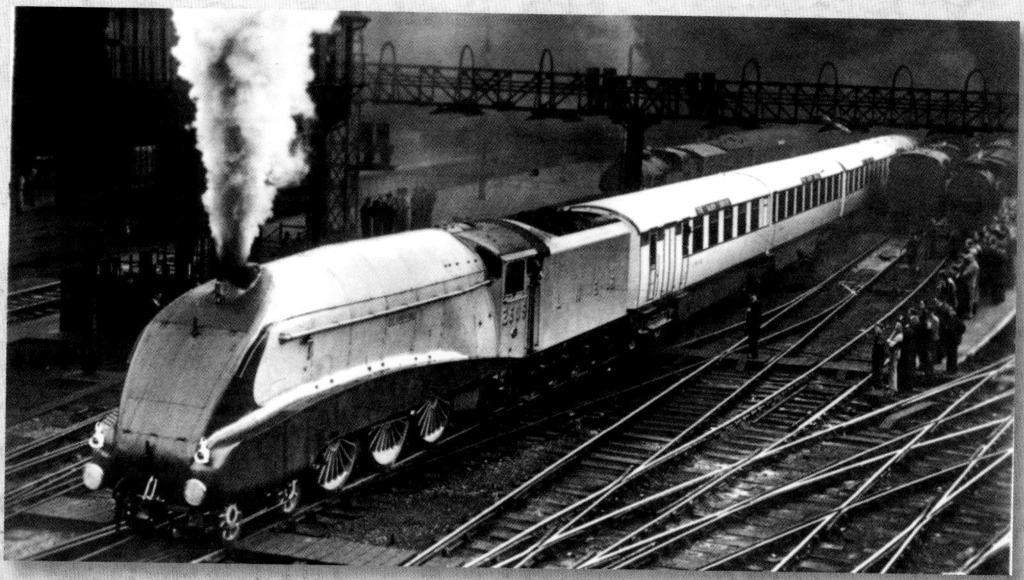

▲ Hauled by 'A4' Class 4-6-2 No. 2509 'Silver Link', the inaugural 'The Silver Jubilee' departs from King's Cross on its run to Newcastle on 30 September 1935.

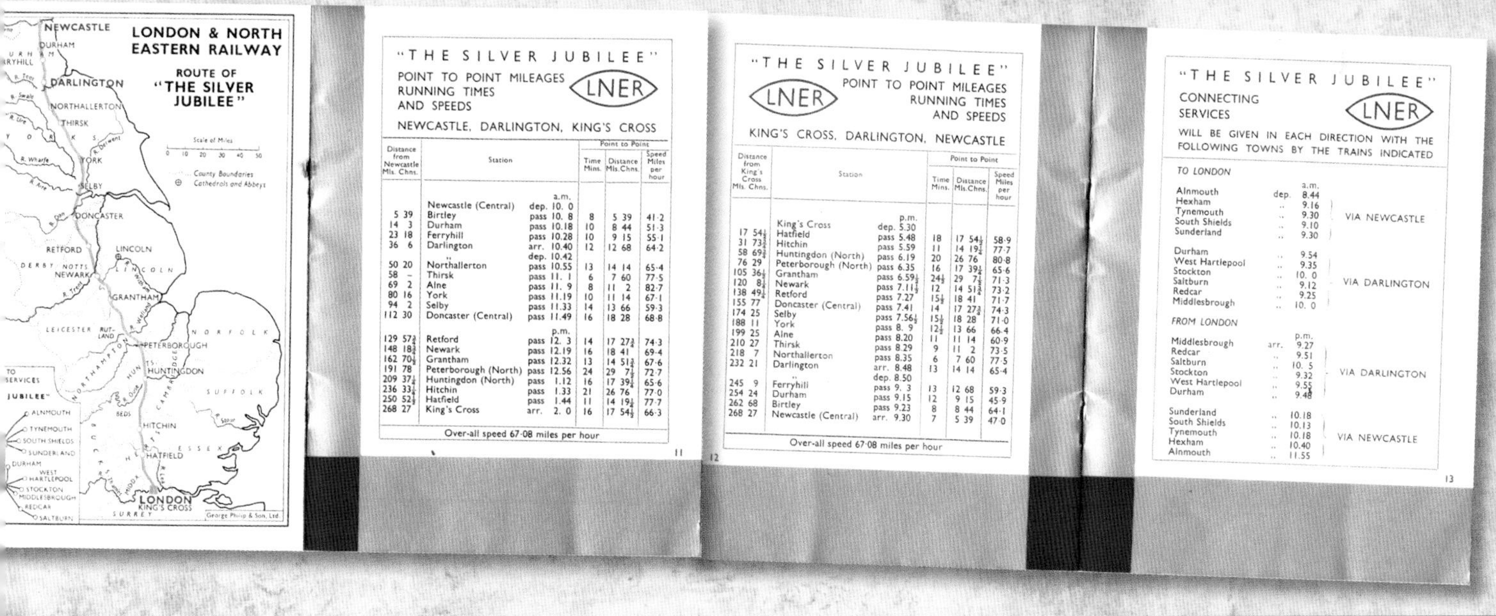

"THE SILVER JUBILEE"

POINT TO POINT MILEAGES RUNNING TIMES AND SPEEDS

LNER

NEWCASTLE, DARLINGTON, KING'S CROSS

Distance from Newcastle Mls. Chns.	Station			Point to Point		
				Time Mins.	Distance Mls. Chns.	Speed Miles per hour
			a.m.			
	Newcastle (Central)	dep.	10. 0			
5 39	Birtley	pass	10. 8	8	5 39	41·2
14 3	Durham	pass	10.18	10	8 44	51·3
23 18	Ferryhill	pass	10.28	10	9 15	55·1
36 6	Darlington	arr.	10.40	12	12 68	64·2
	"	dep.	10.42			
50 20	Northallerton	pass	10.55	13	14 14	65·4
58 –	Thirsk	pass	11. 1	6	7 60	77·5
69 2	Alne	pass	11. 9	8	11 2	82·7
80 16	York	pass	11.19	10	11 14	67·1
94 2	Selby	pass	11.33	14	13 66	59·3
112 30	Doncaster (Central)	pass	11.49	16	18 28	68·8
			p.m.			
129 57¾	Retford	pass	12. 3	14	17 27¾	74·3
148 18¾	Newark	pass	12.19	16	18 41	69·4
162 70½	Grantham	pass	12.32	13	14 51¾	67·6
191 78	Peterborough (North)	pass	12.56	24	29 7½	72·7
209 37¼	Huntingdon (North)	pass	1.12	16	17 39¼	65·6
236 33¼	Hitchin	pass	1.33	21	26 76	77·0
250 52½	Hatfield	pass	1.44	11	14 19¼	77·7
268 27	King's Cross	arr.	2. 0	16	17 54½	66·3

Over-all speed 67·08 miles per hour

11

"THE SILVER JUBILEE"

LNER

POINT TO POINT MILEAGES RUNNING TIMES AND SPEEDS

KING'S CROSS, DARLINGTON, NEWCASTLE

Distance from King's Cross Mls. Chns.	Station			Point to Point		
				Time Mins.	Distance Mls. Chns.	Speed Miles per hour
			p.m.			
	King's Cross	dep.	5.30			
17 54½	Hatfield	pass	5.48	18	17 54½	58·9
31 73¾	Hitchin	pass	5.59	11	14 19¼	77·7
58 69¾	Huntingdon (North)	pass	6.19	20	26 76	80·8
76 29	Peterborough (North)	pass	6.35	16	17 39¼	65·6
105 36½	Grantham	pass	6.59½	24½	29 7½	71·3
120 8¼	Newark	pass	7.11½	12	14 51¾	73·2
138 49¼	Retford	pass	7.27	15½	18 41	71·7
155 77	Doncaster (Central)	pass	7.41	14	17 27¾	74·3
174 25	Selby	pass	7.56½	15½	18 28	71·0
188 11	York	pass	8. 9	12½	13 66	66·4
199 25	Alne	pass	8.20	11	11 14	60·9
210 27	Thirsk	pass	8.29	9	11 2	73·5
218 7	Northallerton	pass	8.35	6	7 60	77·5
232 21	Darlington	arr.	8.48	13	14 14	65·4
	"	dep.	8.50			
245 9	Ferryhill	pass	9. 3	13	12 68	59·3
254 24	Durham	pass	9.15	12	9 15	45·9
262 68	Birtley	pass	9.23	8	8 44	64·1
268 27	Newcastle (Central)	arr.	9.30	7	5 39	47·0

Over-all speed 67·08 miles per hour

12

"THE SILVER JUBILEE"

CONNECTING SERVICES

LNER

WILL BE GIVEN IN EACH DIRECTION WITH THE FOLLOWING TOWNS BY THE TRAINS INDICATED

TO LONDON			
		a.m.	
Alnmouth	dep.	8.44	VIA NEWCASTLE
Hexham	..	9.16	
Tynemouth	..	9.30	
South Shields	..	9.10	
Sunderland	..	9.30	
Durham	..	9.54	VIA DARLINGTON
West Hartlepool	..	9.35	
Stockton	..	10. 0	
Saltburn	..	9.12	
Redcar	..	9.25	
Middlesbrough	..	10. 0	
FROM LONDON			
		p.m.	
Middlesbrough	arr.	9.27	VIA DARLINGTON
Redcar	..	9.51	
Saltburn	..	10. 5	
Stockton	..	9.32	
West Hartlepool	..	9.55	
Durham	..	9.48	
Sunderland	..	10.18	VIA NEWCASTLE
South Shields	..	10.13	
Tynemouth	..	10.18	
Hexham	..	10.40	
Alnmouth	..	11.55	

13

MENU

"THE SILVER JUBILEE"

BRITAIN'S FIRST STREAMLINE TRAIN

TABLE D'HÔ

LUNCHEON 3/6

Oxtail Soup

Curried Eggs
Grilled Herring
Steamed Sole Parsley Sauce

Dressed Cutlets Reforme
Roast Beef, Yorkshire Pudding
Cold Pork and Beetroot
Boiled and Baked Potatoes
Cabbage   Butter Beans

Cabinet Pudding
Apple and Rhubarb Tart

Cheese and Biscuits

LUNCHEON 2/6

Fish or Entrée or Joint with
Two Vegetables

Sweets or Cheese and Biscuits. Butter

Coffee 4d cup extra

14 - 1 - 38   Car 19

For children travelling with half-fare tickets, half price only is charged for lunc
dinner, with a minimum charge of 1s. 9d.

PASSENGERS ARE REQUESTED TO MAKE NO PAYMENT WIT
RECEIVING A BILL WHICH SHOULD BE WRITTEN OUT IN THEIR PRE

Notepaper and envelopes can be obtained on application to the car con

LNER   LNER

▶ Fine dining indeed in 'The Silver Jubilee' restaurant cars, dated 14 January 1938.

À LA CARTE

SOUPS

Clear or Thick	per portion	6d
Cream of Tomato	,,	6d

FISH

Fried or Grilled Dover Sole		2s 6d
Fried or Grilled Fillets of Lemon Sole		1s 9d

GRILLS

"Jubilee" Mixed Grill (Cutlet, Kidney, Sausage, Bacon, Tomato and Mushroom)		3s 6d
Steak, Fillet or Rump and Chips		3s 0d
Mutton Chop and Chips		3s 0d
Mutton or Lamb Cutlets (two) and Chips		3s 0d
Tomatoes		6d

OMELETTES

Plain, Savoury, Ham, Tomato, Sweet		1s 6d

COLD BUFFET

Chicken, Wing Portion with Ham		2s 6d
Chicken, Leg do do		2s 0d
Galantine of Chicken		2s 6d
Roast Beef		1s 9d
Pressed Beef		1s 9d
York Ham		1s 6d
Ox Tongue		1s 6d
Chicken Salad		2s 0d
Egg Salad		1s 3d

VEGETABLES

Peas	per portion	4d
French Beans	,,	4d
Baked Beans	,,	4d
Potatoes Roasted, Boiled or Fried	per portion	3d
Salads (various)	,,	6d

SWEETS

Jam Omelette		1s 6d
Fruit Salad		1s 0d
Banana and Cream		9d
Pears		9d

SAVOURIES

Scotch Woodcock		1s 0d
Sardines on Toast		9d
Welsh Rarebit		9d

SUNDRIES

Tea, Coffee or Cocoa	per pot per person	6d
Tea, Coffee or Cocoa per cup		4d
Milk (hot or cold)	per glass	3d
Malted Milk with added Milk	per glass	6d
Bovril with Biscuits		6d
Bread and Butter	per portion	3d
Buttered Toast		3d
Roll and Butter		2d
Cake or Pastry	per portion	3d
Scotch Shortbread	each	2d
Chocolate Biscuits	each	2d
Eggs	each	
Cream	per portion	3d
Cheese, Biscuits, Butter	,,	6d
Preserves	per portion or pot	3d
Pickles	per portion	3d
Fresh Fruit, Chocolates etc.	from	2d

SANDWICHES

Ham, Beef or Tongue		8d
Sardine		6d
Egg and Cress		6d

ICES

Plain Ices, Vanilla	each	6d
Plain Ices with Cream	each	6d
Neapolitan	each	6d
Banana Split	,,	1s 0d
Peach Melba	,,	1s 0d

WINE LIST

SHERRY		s	d		BRANDIES		
Pale Dry	Per Glass	0	9				Glass
Extra Dry	,,	1	0		Pale Brandy		1 6
Fine Brown	,,	1	0		'Three Star' Brandies		1 6
VERMOUTH, &c					Hine's 1878		2 6
			Glass		**LIQUEURS**		
Vermouth (Fr. or Ital.)			0 8		Bénédictine		1 3
Gin and Vermouth			0 9		Crême de Menthe		1 0
Cocktails (min. botts.)			1 6		Cointreau, ex. dry		1 6
BORDEAUX (White)	half bot	qr bot			Kümmel		1 0
Graves	2 0	1 3			**SCOTCH WHISKY**		
Ch. Rieussec 1925	4 0	—			No. 138 Fine Old		0 10
BURGUNDY (White)					Proprietary Brands		0 10
Chablis	3 6	—			Miniature bottles		1 10
HOCKS & MOSELLE					**MALT LIQUORS**		
Nierstein	2 9	1 6					Bots
Liebfraumilch					Bass & Worthington	0	8½
Auslese 1929	4 6	—			Bass' No. 1 nips 9d		8½
Sparkling Moselle	6 6	—			Newcastle 'Amber' Ale	0	6
BORDEAUX (Red)					Dale's Light Ale	0	6
Medoc	2 0	1 3			Guinness	0	8½
Ch. Palmer Margaux	3 6	—			Graham's Golden Lager (British)	0	8½
BURGUNDY (Red)					Barclay's Lager	,, 0	8½
Macon	3 0	1 9			Red Tower Lager	,, 0	8½
Nuits St. Georges	5 0	2 9			Heineken's (Foreign)	0	10
Spk. Burgundy	6 0	—			Tuborg	0	9
EMPIRE WINES					Hansa	0	10
Hock type, *Australian*	3 0				Urquell Pilsener	1	6
Burgundy type, *South African*	3 0				**CYDER**		
CHAMPAGNES					Gaymer's Cyder	0	6
Bollinger					**MINERAL WATERS &c**		
Special Cuvée	10 6	—			Soda Water	3d &	0 5
Vve. Clicquot dry 1928	11 6	—			Lemonade		0 5
Pol Roger					Dry Ginger Ales		0 5
Cuvée Res. 1926	11 0	—			Tonic Water		0 5
PORT					Ginger Beer		0 5
Light Old, glass 9d.					Grape Fruit Sparkling		0 5
Vintage Character, Old	—	2 6			Apollinaris	4d &	0 6
GIN		Glass			Perrier	4d &	0 6
Dry		0 10			Vichy Water		0 9
					Lime Juice		
					Lemon Squash	4d glass	
					Lemon Barley Water		

Cigars and Cigarettes

THE SOUTH WALES PULLMAN

LONDON (PADDINGTON) TO SWANSEA (HIGH STREET)

Pullman car trains were a rare sight on the Great Western Railway but its nationalised successor, the Western Region, redressed this balance by introducing 'The South Wales Pullman' in 1955. Catering for business travel, the eight-coach set was hauled by a 'Castle' Class 4-6-0 for the 191-mile journey between Paddington and Swansea. The down train left Paddington at 8.50am and ran non-stop to Newport, followed by stops at Cardiff, Bridgend, Port Talbot and Neath, before arriving at Swansea at 1.10pm. The up service left Swansea at 4.30pm and with the same stops arrived back in the capital at 8.45pm (summer 1958 timetable). The train was replaced in September 1961 by the new diesel 'Blue Pullman' train but the original set of locomotive-hauled Pullman coaches were kept as a standby in case of failure of these new trains.

▼ It's 8.50am on Paddington's Platform 1 in the late 1950s – 'Castle' Class 4-6-0 No. 5080 'Defiant' is just about to depart with the down 'The South Wales Pullman' to Cardiff and Swansea. The loco was built at Swindon Works in 1939 and was originally named 'Ogmore Castle' until being renamed in 1941. After spending most of its life allocated to various South Wales sheds it was withdrawn from Llanelli shed in April 1963 and has since been preserved.

Table 6a

THE SOUTH WALES PULLMAN
(LIMITED ACCOMMODATION)

LONDON, NEWPORT, CARDIFF, BRIDGEND, PORT TALBOT, NEATH and SWANSEA

WEEK DAYS
(Mondays to Fridays)

London (Paddington)	dep	am 8 50	Swansea (High Street) ... dep	pm 4 30
Newport	arr	11 21	Neath (General) .... "	4 45
Cardiff (General)	"	11 40	Port Talbot (General) ... "	5 0
Bridgend	"	pm 12 18	Bridgend .... "	5 20
Port Talbot (General)	"	12 38	Cardiff (General) ...... "	6 0
Neath (General)	"	12 50	Newport .... "	6 20
Swansea (High Street)	"	1 10	London (Paddington) ... arr	8 45

MEALS AND REFRESHMENTS SERVED AT EVERY SEAT
Supplementary Fares (for each single journey)
Children under 14 years of age—Half Charges

Between	LONDON (Paddington)		NEWPORT		CARDIFF		BRIDGEND		PORT TALBOT		NEATH		SWANSEA	
	1st	2nd	1st	2nd	1st	2nd	1st	2nd	1st	2nd	1st	2nd	1st	2nd
NEWPORT	7/-	4/-	–	–	1/-	1/-	2/-	1/-	3/-	1/6	3/-	1/6	3/-	1/6
CARDIFF (General)	8/-	4/6	1/-	1/-	–	–	2/-	1/-	2/-	1/-	2/-	1/-	2/-	1/-
BRIDGEND	8/-	4/6	2/-	1/-	2/-	1/-	–	–	1/-	1/-	2/-	1/-	2/-	1/-
PORT TALBOT (General)	10/-	5/-	3/-	1/6	2/-	1/-	1/-	1/-	–	–	1/-	1/-	1/-	1/-
NEATH (General)	10/-	5/-	3/-	1/6	2/-	1/-	2/-	1/-	1/-	1/-	–	–	1/-	1/-
SWANSEA (High Street)	10/-	5/-	3/-	1/6	2/-	1/-	2/-	1/-	1/-	1/-	1/-	1/-	–	–

The Supplementary Charge is payable in addition to the usual First and Second Class Fares applicable to the journey being made.

THE NUMBER OF PASSENGERS CARRIED IS LIMITED TO THE SEATING ACCOMMODATION AVAILABLE.

Seats can be reserved in advance at stations and usual agencies for journeys from and to all the stations shewn above. Subsequent reservations may be effected with the Pullman Car Conductor on the train if accommodation is available.

Pullman Car Tickets will only be issued subject to these conditions.

▲ The winter 1958/59 timetable for 'The South Wales Pullman'.

◀ 'Castle' Class 4-6-0 No. 7035 'Ogmore Castle' speeds the down 'The South Wales Pullman' out of the 4,444 yard-long Chipping Sodbury Tunnel in the late 1950s. The loco was built by BR at Swindon Works in 1950 and withdrawn from Old Oak Common shed in August 1965.

▶ Landore shed's 'Castle' Class 4-6-0 No. 5004 'Llanstephan Castle' speeds along near Wootton Bassett with the down 'The South Wales Pullman' in 1960. The loco was built at nearby Swindon Works in 1927 and withdrawn from Neath shed in April 1962.

S

THE SOUTH YORKSHIREMAN

LONDON (MARYLEBONE) TO BRADFORD (EXCHANGE)

Introduced by the Eastern Region of
British Railways on 31 May 1948, 'The
South Yorkshireman' was one of only
two named trains that operated over the
former Great Central main line out of
Marylebone (see also 'The Master Cutler').
In its first year of service the up train left
Bradford (Exchange) at 10am and after
stops at Huddersfield, Sheffield (Victoria),
Nottingham (Victoria), Loughborough
(Central), Rugby (Central) and Aylesbury
(SO) arrived at Marylebone at 3.15pm
(3.27pm on Saturdays). The down train
left Marylebone at 4.50pm and with the
same stops – except Rugby was omitted

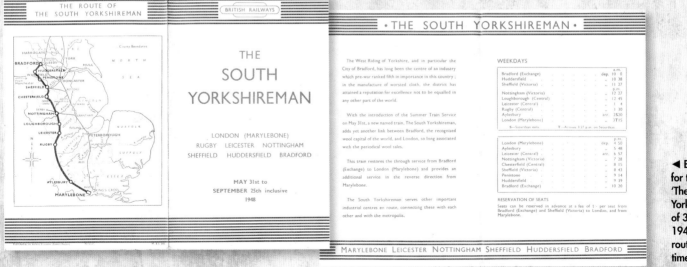

◄ BR's leaflet
for the inaugural
'The South
Yorkshireman'
of 31 May
1948 features a
route map and
timetable.

and a stop at Penistone added – it arrived back at Bradford at 10.20pm. The train was normally hauled by a 'B1' 4-6-0 although the final train on 2 January 1960 was headed by BR Standard Class 5 4-6-0 No. 73066. From this date the Great Central route was handed over to the London Midland Region and was then served by only a few stopping trains between Marylebone and Nottingham until closure in 1966.

◄ The up 'The South Yorkshireman' is seen here at Bradley Junction just to the east of Huddersfield behind 'B1' Class 4-6-0 No. 61020 'Gemsbok' on 26 September 1959. 'Gemsbok' was built at Darlington in 1947 and withdrawn from York North shed in November 1962.

▲ The up 'The South Yorkshireman' climbs the 1-in-50 bank out of Bradford Exchange past Ripley Street en route to Marylebone behind 'B1' Class 4-6-0 No. 61383 on 15 August 1959. The 'B1' was built by the North British Locomotive Company for BR in 1951 and withdrawn from Low Moor shed in January 1963.

◄ Grimy BR Standard Class '5MT' 4-6-0 No. 73066 simmers gently at the bufferstops after arriving at Marylebone with the last up 'The South Yorkshireman' on 2 January 1960. The loco was built at Crewe in 1954 and withdrawn from Bolton shed in April 1967.

THE TALISMAN

LONDON (KING'S CROSS) TO EDINBURGH (WAVERLEY)

Introduced in 1956, 'The Talisman' was the successor to the pre-war streamlined 'The Coronation' express that ran between King's Cross and Edinburgh. Hauled once again by Gresley's 'A4' Pacifics, the restaurant car train included the luxurious first class articulated coaches used by its predecessor, although the beaver tail observation car had gone to pastures new in the Highlands. The new train was a resounding success and the following year British Railways launched an additional morning service in both directions. An experiment to extend this new train (renamed 'The Fair Maid') to Perth in the autumn of 1957 was not a commercial success and it was withdrawn the following year. By the autumn of 1960 the down morning 'The Talisman' was

▶ The Winter 1960/61 timetable for 'The Talisman'..

▼ The colourful restaurant car menu and illustrated route map produced by BR for the new 'The Talisman' service in 1956.

THE TALISMAN
MORNING EXPRESS SERVICE
LONDON (King's Cross)
NEWCASTLE and EDINBURGH (Waverley)

MONDAYS TO FRIDAYS INCLUSIVE
(Except Monday, 26th December 1960; Thursday 30th March Monday, 3rd April, Friday 19th and Monday 22nd May, 1961)

London (King's Cross) .. .. dep	am 8 5	Edinburgh (Waverley) ..dep	am 8 30	
	pm	Berwick-upon-Tweed	9 34	
Darlington .. .. .. { arr	12 5	Newcastle .. .. { arr	10 43	
.. .. dep	12 7	{ dep	10 49	
Newcastle .. .. { arr	12 50	Darlington .. .. { arr	11 33	
{ dep	12 56	{ dep	11 35	
Berwick-upon-Tweed .. .. arr	2 6		pm	
Edinburgh (Waverley) .. .. arr	3 6	London (King's Cross) .. ..arr	3 35	

Restaurant Cars for Table d'Hote meals.

Seats are reservable in advance for passengers travelling from London (King's Cross), Darlington, Newcastle and Edinburgh (Waverley), also from Berwick-upon-Tweed to London (King's Cross) on payment of a fee of 2s. 0d. per seat.

THE TALISMAN
AFTERNOON EXPRESS SERVICE
LONDON (King's Cross)
NEWCASTLE and EDINBURGH (Waverley)

MONDAYS TO FRIDAYS INCLUSIVE
(Except Monday, 26th December 1960; Thursday 30th, Friday 31st March, Monday 3rd April, Friday 19th and Monday 22nd May, 1961)

London (King's Cross) .. ..dep	4 0	Edinburgh (Waverley) .. ..dep	pm 4 0	
Newcastle .. .. .. { arr	8 39	Newcastle .. .. { arr	6 8	
{ dep	8 45	{ dep	6 14	
Edinburgh (Waverley) .. ..arr	10 51	London (King's Cross) .. ..arr	10 49	

Restaurant Cars for Table d'Hote meals

The number of passengers carried is limited to the seating accommodation available

All seats are reservable in advance on payment of a fee of 2s. 0d. per seat.

THE TALISMAN

London
Newcastle
Edinburgh

Edinburgh
Newcastle
London

EDINBURGH

Royal Border Bridge
Berwick
Durham Cathedral
Newcastle
Durham
Darlington
Newcastle, Tyne Bridge
York
Doncaster
Grantham Town Hall
York Minster
Grantham
Peterborough
Peterborough Cathedral

LONDON

Menu

BREAKFAST 7/6

Plain Breakfast 4/-

MORNING COFFEE

A service of Morning Coffee is available
Coffee per cup 9d.   Biscuits per portion 6d.

A light refreshment and corridor service is made available when possible

LUNCHEON 9/6
DINNER 10/6
Coffee 9d.

At Luncheon and Dinner cheese and biscuits may be served in addition to sweet for an extra charge of 1/6

AFTERNOON TEA 3/-

Children travelling at half fares are charged reduced prices for table d'hote meals excepting Afternoon Tea

It is particularly requested that a bill be obtained from the Conductor for all payments. British Transport Catering Services desire to render every possible service to passengers and it will be appreciated if they will report any unusual service or attention to the Regional Catering Superintendent, British Transport Catering Service, Eastern Region, St. Pancras Chambers, London, N.W.1. Complaints, to which the Conductor's attention should be drawn, will be investigated and a remedy sought. In the general interest, passengers are kindly asked to refrain from smoking immediately before or during the service of meals.

Wines

When you are ordering luncheon or dinner on this train, may we draw your attention to the interesting wines now provided at prices as reasonable as any you will find in this country.

SHERRY		Glass
Medium Dry		2/6
Amontillado No. 4, Pale, Dry		2/6
Fino No 7, Pale Dry		2/6
Vilant Brown		2/6

APERITIFS		
Gin and Lime, Orange or Lemon		2/6
Gin and Bitters		2/6
Gin and Vermouth, French or Italian		2/6
Vermouth, French or Italian		1/9
		Baby Bottle
Tomato Juice Cocktail		1/-
Pineapple Juice		1/-

BORDEAUX Red	Bott.	½-Bott.	¼-Bott.
Médoc	13/-	7/-	3/9
Château Talbot 1953	17/6	9/-	—

BORDEAUX White			
Graves	12/-	6/6	3/6
Sauternes	15/-	8/-	—

BURGUNDY Red			
Mâcon	13/-	7/-	3/9
Beaune	17/-	9/-	—

BURGUNDY		
Vin Rosé	13/-	7/-

CHAMPAGNE			
Lanson, 1947	47/6	24/6	
Perrier Jouet, N.V.			8/6
St. Marceaux, N.V.	37/6	19/6	

ALSATIAN		
Sylvaner	16/-	8/6

SPANISH			
Spanish Graves	10/6	5/6	3/-
Spanish Burgundy	10/6	5/6	3/-

SOUTH AFRICAN			
Paarl Amber Hock	10/6	5/6	3/-

AUSTRALIAN			
Emu Burgundy	10/6	5/6	3/-

PORT		Glass
Tawny		2/6
Very Fine Old		3/-

LIQUEURS		Miniature
Van der Hum		4/9
Cointreau		4/3
Bénédictine		3/9

LIQUEURS (contd.)	Miniature
Bolskümmel	3/9
Cherry Heering	3/9
Drambuie	3/9

SPIRITS	Measure
Brandy, Vieux Maison, 30 years old	3/-
Brandy ***	3/-
Gin	2/3
Rum	2/3
Royal Scot Whisky	2/3
Whisky—Proprietary Brands	2/3
	Miniature
Whisky—Proprietary Brands	4/6
Brandy	5/-
Gin	4/6
Rum	4/6

CORDIALS AND FRUIT JUICES	Glass
Lemon Squash	7d
Orange Squash	7d
Grape Fruit Squash	7d
Lime Juice	7d
	Split
Apple Juice	1/-

BEER, STOUT, LAGER, ETC.	Bottle
Bass	1/7
Worthington	1/7
Double Diamond	1/7
Wm. Younger's Monk Export	1/9
Other Proprietary Brands	1/7
Guinness	1/7
Mackeson's Stout	1/4
Whitbread's Pale Ale	1/4
Other Light Ales	1/4
British Lager	1/9
Tuborg Lager	1/9
Carlsberg Lager	1/9

CIDER	Bott's
Cider	10d.
	Repeated Pint
Champagne Cider	3/6

MINERALS	Split
Aerated Waters	Baby 6d. 8½.
Apollinaris	Baby 6d. 9d.
Vichy Célestins	9d.
	Bottle
Ginger Beer	1/-

CIGARS, CIGARETTES, CONFECTIONERY, etc.

departing from King's Cross at 8.05am and, after stops at Darlington, Newcastle and Berwick, arrived at Edinburgh at 3.06pm. The up morning service left Edinburgh at 8.30am and after the same stops arrived at King's Cross at 3.35pm. The afternoon 'The Talisman' was much quicker, with only one stop at Newcastle in both directions; the up train took 6hrs 49min while the down train took two minutes longer. In 1961-1962 steam gave way to the new 'Deltic' diesels and this soon led to an acceleration of the trains. An extension to Glasgow (Queen Street) for morning trains in 1962 bit the dust in fairly short time. The use of older Pullman cars in the make-up of the trains was also a short-lived experiment. Such was the immense power of the 'Deltics' that by 1967 both the up and the down afternoon trains were completing the 393-mile journey in just under six hours. The service was withdrawn in 1968 but reinstated three years later, limited to one train in each direction. HSTs took over from the 'Deltics' in 1978 but the train lost its name in 1991, by which time the East Coast Main Line had been electrified.

▲ The inaugural run of the down morning 'The Talisman' on 17 June 1957, seen here at speed between Greenwood Box and Hadley Wood hauled by King's Cross shed's immaculate 'A4' 4-6-2 No. 60025 'Falcon'. This loco was built at Doncaster in 1937 and withdrawn from New England shed in October 1963.

▼ A pocket timetable for the new, improved 'The Talisman' issued on 15 June 1964.

The Talisman

Details of the new services from 15 June 1964

▲ 'Deltic' (Class 55) diesel D9014 heads 'The Talisman' along the East Coast Main Line at Stoke in the summer of 1962. The loco came into service from the Vulcan Foundry in September 1961 and was named 'The Duke of Wellington's Regiment' at Darlington in October 1963. It was withdrawn in November 1981.

TEES-TYNE PULLMAN

LONDON (KING'S CROSS) TO NEWCASTLE (CENTRAL)

Seen by British Railways as a successor to 'The Silver Jubilee', the all-Pullman 'Tees-Tyne Pullman' entered service in 1948. Sadly, apart from using the same route and calling at Darlington, this new train was a shadow of the pre-war high-speed streamliner, initially taking an hour longer to complete the same journey. Motive power for the nine-coach train was usually an 'A4' Pacific until these were replaced by English Electric Type 4s in the late 1950s. By

▲ The summer 1949 BR leaflet, route map and timetable for the 'Tees-Tyne Pullman'.

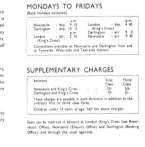

• THE TEES-TYNE PULLMAN •

The Tees-Tyne Pullman links North Eastern England with London. The service provided is especially convenient for those wishing to visit London and return the same day: the round journey is completed, from Newcastle in under 13 hours, from Darlington in 11 hours, with two and a half hours in London.

The train is made up entirely of Pullman Cars, providing the well-known Pullman standard of comfort. A special feature is the Hadrian Bar for the service of refreshments. Meals and refreshments are also served to passengers at their own tables.

The issue of supplementary tickets is limited to the capacity of the train, to ensure a seat for every passenger.

MONDAYS TO FRIDAYS
(Bank Holidays excepted)

	a.m.		p.m.
Newcastle - dep.	9 15	London - dep.	4 50
Darlington - dep.	10 0	(King's Cross)	
		Darlington - arr.	9 0
London - arr.	2 15	Newcastle - arr.	9 45
(King's Cross)			

Connections available at Darlington and Newcastle from and to Tyne-side, Wear-side and Tees-side stations.

SUPPLEMENTARY CHARGES

			First Class	Third Class
between				
Newcastle and King's Cross	-	-	10/-	5/6
Darlington and King's Cross			9/-	5/-

These charges are payable in each direction in addition to the ordinary first or third class fares. Children under 14 years of age, half the above charges.

Seats can be reserved in advance at London (King's Cross) Seat Reservation Office, Newcastle (Enquiry Office) and Darlington (Booking Office), and through the usual agencies.

NEWCASTLE DARLINGTON LONDON (KING'S CROSS)

THE TEES-TYNE PULLMAN
(LIMITED TRAIN)

MONDAYS TO FRIDAYS
(Will not run on Monday 7th August)

			am				pm
NEWCASTLE	... ...	...dep.	9 25	LONDON	... ...	...dep.	4 50
DARLINGTON	... ...	{ arr.	10 9	(King's Cross)			
		{ dep.	10 11	YORK		{ arr.	8 0
LONDON						{ dep.	8 2
(King's Cross)	...	...arr.	pm 2 4	DARLINGTON	...	{ arr.	8 47
						{ dep.	8 49
				NEWCASTLE	... ...	...arr.	9 34

Connections available at York for Scarborough and at Darlington and Newcastle to and from Tees-side and Tyne-side Stations.

MEALS AND REFRESHMENTS SERVED AT EVERY SEAT.

▲ The summer 1961 timetable for the 'Tees-Tyne Pullman'.

1960 timings had improved but were still nowhere near their pre-war levels – however, passengers could while away their time in the popular Hadrian Bar car. In the autumn of that year the up train left Newcastle at 9.25am and after stopping at Darlington reached King's Cross at 2.14pm. The down service left the capital at 4.50pm and after stopping at York and Darlington reached Newcastle at 9.41pm. The introduction of 'Deltic' diesels in the early 1960s saw a marked improvement, with the up train reaching an average speed of just over 80mph between Darlington and York – a first in Britain for a scheduled service. By 1975, 40 years after the introduction of the four-hour 'The Silver Jubilee', the down train was able to reach Newcastle in 3hrs 45min. Despite this the train was withdrawn the following year, although the name was given to a record-breaking HST service in 1985.

▲ 'A4' Class 4-6-2 No. 60019 'Bittern' roars non-stop through Durham with the up 'Tees-Tyne Pullman', circa 1949. Now preserved, this loco was built at Doncaster in 1937 and was withdrawn from Aberdeen Ferryhill shed in September 1966.

Tees Tyne Pullman
Bill of Fare

Prices include 15% VAT, service not included.

Two course meal

This comprises main dish, with sweet, savoury or cheese board. Coffee is included. The price is governed by the choice of main dish. Additional items may be selected from the à la carte list.

Steak "Pullman"   £10·95
Sirloin Steak in a White Wine Sauce
with Tomatoes, Mushrooms and Onions

Fillet of Sole Maître d'Hôtel   £8·95

Smoked Ham and Roast Chicken with Mixed Salad   £7·95

Celery Hearts, Garden Peas
Sauté and Parsley Potatoes

Raspberry Charlotte Russe

Selection of Fresh Fruit

Selection from the Cheese Board with Salad and Biscuits

Sardines on Toast

Coffee Service

If you prefer, select any of the following dishes:—

A la carte

Asparagus Soup with Fresh Cream	95p	Prawn Salad	£3·25
Choice of Chilled Fruit Juices	60p	Raspberry Charlotte Russe	£1·25
Grilled Grapefruit with Honey	£1·15	Selection of Fresh Fruit	£1·00
Avocado Vinaigrette	£1·65	Cheese Board, Salad and Biscuits	£1·20
Avocado with Prawns	£2·35	Sardines on Toast	£1·20
Smoked Salmon Pâté	£1·70	Buttered Toasted Teacake with Preserves or Honey	95p
Ardennes Pâté	£1·35	Fresh Danish Pastry	75p
Sandwich Selection: *Three half rounds chosen from Prawns, Cheese, Ham, Tongue*	£1·60	Biscuits	16p
		Coffee Service	75p
Wholemeal Asparagus Flan with Mixed Salad	£2·95	Pot of Freshly Brewed Tea	75p

TRAVELLERS FARE

PI 7/85

▲ Silver service on board the 'Tees-Tyne Pullman' HST of July 1985.

▲ 'A4' Class 4-6-2 No. 60026 'Miles Beevor' heads the down 'Tees-Tyne Pullman' near New Southgate in July 1961. The majority of the train is made up of brand-new Metropolitan-Cammell Pullman coaches. Built at Doncaster in 1937, this loco was withdrawn in December 1965.

THE THAMES-CLYDE EXPRESS

LONDON (ST PANCRAS) TO GLASGOW (ST ENOCH)

The alternative and more scenic route from London to Glasgow was via the ex-Midland Railway line from St Pancras to Carlisle, via Leeds and the Settle & Carlisle line, and then to Glasgow St Enoch via Dumfries over ex-G&SWR metals. In 1927 the London Scottish & Midland Railway gave the name 'The Thames-Clyde Express' to its 10am departure from St Pancras to Glasgow St Enoch and to the 9.30am departure in the opposite direction. Although serving major population centres in the East Midlands and Yorkshire, the route was much longer and harder to work than the alternative West Coast Mail

▼ Sheffield Millhouses shed's 'Jubilee' Class 4-6-0 No. 45607 'Fiji' storms through Cudworth with the down 'The Thames-Clyde Express' in the late 1950s. Built at Crewe in 1934, this loco was withdrawn from Newton Heath shed in December 1962.

The Thames-Clyde Express

Restaurant Car Express

LONDON ST. PANCRAS and GLASGOW ST. ENOCH

WEEKDAYS

	Mons. to Fris.	Sats.		Mons. to Fris.	Sats.
	am	am		am	am
London St. Pancras ....dep	10 10	10 10	Glasgow St. Enoch ....dep	9 20	9 20
Leicester London Road .. .. ,,	11 59	11 59	Kilmarnock .. .. ,,	9 59	9 59
	pm	pm	Dumfries .. .. ,,	11 14	11 14
Chesterfield Midland......... ,,	1 3	1 5	Annan .. .. ,,	11 35	11 35
Sheffield Midland .. .. .. ,,	1 29	1 29		noon	noon
Leeds City .... ,,	2 44	2 44	Carlisle .... ,,	12 0	12 0
Carlisle .. ..arr	5 3	5 3	Leeds City.. .. ..arr	2 20	2 26
				pm	pm
Annan ....,,	5 33	5 33	Sheffield Midland .... ,,	3 32	3 38
Dumfries .. .. ,,	5 53	5 53	Trent .. .. ,,	4 40	4 43
Kilmarnock .... ,,	7 8	7 8	Leicester London Road .. .. ,,	5 12	5 12
Glasgow St. Enoch .. .. .. ,,	7 50	7 50	Kettering .. .. ,,	5†48	5 50
			London St. Pancras............ ,,	7† 5	7 20

†—Mondays 2nd July to 27th August, also Fridays commencing 6th July arrives Kettering 5.50 pm and London St. Pancras 7.20 pm.

A Buffet service is also available on this train

Seats may be reserved in advance for passengers travelling from London and Glasgow on payment of a fee of 2s. 0d. per seat.

▲ The summer 1962 timetable for 'The Thames-Clyde Express'.

Line, and consequently the journey time was much longer. Suspended during the Second World War, 'The Thames-Clyde Express' was restored in 1949. During this post-war period the train was usually headed by either 'Jubilee' or 'Royal Scot' 4-6-0s until these were replaced by BR Sulzer Type 4 diesels. Journey times remained poor: the summer 1962 timetable showed the train departing St Pancras at 10.10am and, after calling at Leicester, Chesterfield, Sheffield, Leeds, Carlisle, Annan, Dumfries and Kilmarnock, it arrived at St Enoch at 7.50pm – a journey time of 9hrs 40min, and a full 2hrs 20min slower than the rival 'Royal Scot'. This couldn't go on much longer and with the completion of WCML electrification in 1974 the train was withdrawn.

▲ Happy trainspotters at Leeds City station – Holbeck shed's 'A3' Class 4-6-2 No. 60080 'Dick Turpin' waits to depart with the down 'The Thames-Clyde Express' on a wet July day in 1960. Built as a Gresley 'A1' by the North British Locomotive Company in 1924, this loco was rebuilt as an 'A3' in 1942 and withdrawn from Gateshead shed in October 1964.

◄ The down 'The Thames-Clyde Express' passes Wortley Junction about 1½ miles from Leeds City, headed by 'Jubilee' Class 4-6-0 No. 45639 'Raleigh' on 25 September 1960. The loco was built at Crewe in 1934 and withdrawn from Leeds Holbeck shed in November 1963.

TORBAY EXPRESS

LONDON (PADDINGTON) TO KINGSWEAR

Although an express had been run by the Great Western Railway between Paddington and Torbay for many years before the First World War, it was only officially named the 'Torbay Express' in 1923. As was common with GWR practice the train carried coaches that were slipped at Taunton for onward conveyance to Ilfracombe – in the summer months this portion had the distinction of including a restaurant car. By the late 1930s, and with 'King' or 'Castle' 4-6-0s in charge, the train achieved mile-a-minute status between Paddington and Exeter. The Old Oak Common locomotive would begin or end its journey on the heavily graded single-track section between Goodrington Sands and Kingswear (now the Paignton & Dartmouth Steam Railway) – set alongside the picturesque River Dart the latter station possessed a turntable large enough to take the 'King' Class.

► The stylish restaurant car tariff for the 'Torbay Express', circa 1956.

▼ An early 1950s BR route guide for the 'Torbay Express'.

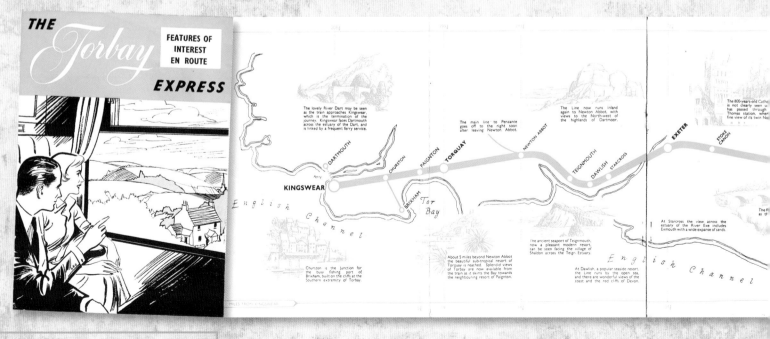

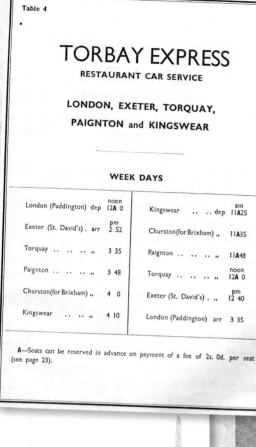

Table 4

TORBAY EXPRESS

RESTAURANT CAR SERVICE

LONDON, EXETER, TORQUAY, PAIGNTON and KINGSWEAR

WEEK DAYS

London (Paddington) dep	noon 12A 0	Kingswear .. .. dep	am 11A25
Exeter (St. David's) . arr	pm 2 52	Churston (for Brixham) ,,	11A35
Torquay .. .. .. ,,	3 35	Paignton .. .. .. ,,	11A48
Paignton .. .. .. ,,	3 48	Torquay .. .. .. ,,	noon 12A 0
Churston (for Brixham) ,,	4 0	Exeter (St. David's) . ,,	pm 12 40
Kingswear .. .. ,,	4 10	London (Paddington) arr	3 35

A—Seats can be reserved in advance on payment of a fee of 2s. 0d. per seat (see page 23).

◄ The winter 1958/59 timetable for the 'Torbay Express'.

The train continued to operate during the Second World War, initially combined with the 'Cornish Riviera Express', but this proved too heavy and the train soon resumed its previous separate (but much slower) identity. Normal running returned after the war and by 1958 the 12 noon departure from Paddington was covering the 173½ miles to Exeter (St David's) in 172 minutes. After stops at Torquay, Paignton and Churston the train arrived at Kingswear at 4.10pm. The up train left Kingswear at 11.25am and with the same stops took 175 minutes from Exeter to Paddington where it arrived at 3.35pm. New 'Warship' diesel hydraulics soon took over from steam but over the following years extra stops were introduced, leading to a longer journey time overall. The train lost its name in 1968 although it has been used in recent years in timetables to describe an HST service to Torquay and Paignton.

Beyond Burlescombe the hills slope upwards towards the wild expanse of Exmoor.

Beyond Taunton splendid views of the Blackdown Hills are obtained, and the Wellington Monument can be seen standing out high above the town of Wellington.

The train now enters the Whiteball Tunnel to emerge in the County of Devon.

▲ Newton Abbot shed's 'Castle' Class 4-6-0 No. 5053 'Earl Cairns' speeds down the relief line in Sonning Cutting with the down 'Torbay Express' on 19 February 1955. This loco was built at Swindon in 1936 and was originally named 'Bishop's Castle'. It was renamed in 1937 and withdrawn from Cardiff Canton shed in July 1962.

TRANS-PENNINE

LIVERPOOL (LIME STREET) TO HULL

Introduced in 1960, the innovative 'Trans-Pennine' series of express trains linking Liverpool and Hull were made up of six sets of diesel multiple units (later Class 124) built at Swindon Works. The stylish six-car trains included a buffet car serving hot meals. With rapid acceleration the lightweight trains made easy going of the former London & Northwestern Railway's heavily graded route across the Pennines, with the majority of the six return services each weekday taking just under three hours for their journey. Two extra services were run on weekdays between Liverpool and Leeds. In their early years the multiple units had the logo 'Trans-Pennine' emblazoned below the wrap-round windows at each end, with the name also carried on roofboards attached to the sides of each coach.

◄ Within a year the distinctive headboards had gone – here one of the 'Trans-Pennine' express diesel multiple units speeds through Copley Hill at Leeds with a Hull to Liverpool service on 3 May 1961.

▼ Headed by unit E51963, a 'Trans-Pennine' train prepares to depart from Leeds City on 25 July 1962. The different coloured roof destination boards and yellow front warning panel contrast with the dull BR green livery.

In 1979 the 'Trans-Pennine' service was reorganised, with locomotive haulage serving the main artery between Liverpool and York. From then onwards the original 'Trans-Pennine' diesel multiple units were combined with reallocated Western Region (Class 123) Inter-City cousins and used for a Leeds to Hull service until they were replaced by locomotive hauled stock in 1984.

◄ An early 'Trans-Pennine' train complete with headboard on the front Swindon-built unit, E51953.

THE ULSTER EXPRESS

LONDON (EUSTON) TO HEYSHAM

A boat train connecting with steamer services to and from Belfast at Heysham was inaugurated by the Midland Railway as early as 1904. Running to and from St Pancras, the unnamed train ran in competition with the London & North Western Railway's boat train that ran between Euston and Fleetwood. Following the Big Four Grouping in 1923, the newly-formed London Midland & Scottish Railway combined these two trains into one service between Euston and Fleetwood. With new 'Royal Scot' 4-6-0s in charge, the name 'The Ulster Express' was bestowed on this service in 1927. The following year the train was diverted to run to and from Heysham

The Ulster Express

The Ulster Express

Quite early in railway history, services were established between London and Belfast and over fifty years ago the former Midland Railway, to improve and shorten the journey, constructed a magnificent harbour at Heysham. In 1927 when the regular daily route between London Euston and Belfast via Heysham was inaugurated it was decided to name the train *The Ulster Express*. What more suitable title could be conceived to denote the link between the Capital and Northern Ireland?

Many will agree that a meal in a comfortable restaurant car with views of the countryside unfolding through the wide observation windows is a pleasant interlude on a journey. Overleaf is the menu, which combines quality and, within the limitations of this type of service, a range of choice which will satisfy. It may perhaps, be difficult to please everyone, but this is the objective of the experienced restaurant car staff on this train.

There is also an interesting wine list overleaf with prices as reasonable as any to be found in the country.

The Red Hand appearing on the front of this menu is included in the Coat of Arms of Northern Ireland and Ulster. It is the badge of the O'Neills, a powerful family, whose head was King of Ulster from time immemorial to about 400 years ago. A popular legend attempts to explain its origin by telling of a boat race between two chieftains, to decide the ownership of disputed territory. O'Neill was losing and cut off his hand, flinging it on to the shore.

Printed by Leonard Ripley & Co., Ltd., London.

London   Belfast

Belfast   London

▲ This early BR restaurant car menu for 'The Ulster Express' features the Red Hand of the powerful O'Neill family of Ulster.

Table 2

The Ulster Express
EXPRESS SERVICES
LONDON, MANCHESTER, LEEDS
to
BELFAST
Via HEYSHAM
TO BELFAST

Monday to Friday nights

	A FX pm 5*40	A FO pm 5*45	pm	pm	pm 4b25
London Euston .. dep					
Birmingham New Street ..					6 20
Crewe ..	8*56	9*3	8*55		8 7
Manchester Victoria ..			9 17		
Bolton Trinity Street ..			9 36		
Chorley ..			9 57		
Preston ..					9 20
Leeds City .. dep				9 25	
Bradford Forster Square ..				9c10	
Keighley ..				9 52	
Skipton ..				10 10	
Heysham .. arr	11 5	11 12	10 50	11 35	10 10
Belfast Donegall Quay .. arr	11 55 pm / 7 0 am				

Saturday nights / Sunday nights Commencing 8th july

	pm 6 20	pm	pm	A pm 6*40	A pm 3*55	pm
London Euston .. dep						
Birmingham New Street ..	8 9				7 42	
Crewe ..				9 57		
Manchester Victoria ..		9 27				9 29
Bolton Trinity Street ..		9 46				9 49
Chorley ..						10 13
Preston ..	9 23	10 6	11 13			
Leeds City .. dep			9 25			
Bradford Forster Square ..			9c10		8c50	
Keighley ..			9 52		9 28	
Skipton ..			10 10		9 45	
Heysham .. arr	10 20	11 0	12 0	11 0	10 57	11 10
Belfast Donegall Quay .. arr	12 40 am (Sun.) / 8 0 am (Sun.)		11 55 pm (Sun.) / 7 0 am (Mon.)			

*—Seats may be reserved in advance on payment of a fee of 2s. 0d. per seat.
‡—Stops only to take up passengers.
A—The Ulster Express.
FO—Fridays only.

FX—Fridays excepted
RB—Bu &c Car.
RC—Restaurant Car.
TC—Through Carriages.
b—Change at Crewe.
c—Change at Skipton.

For details of Cabins and Berth Charges and addresses to which applications should be made for accommodation on the vessels—see page 69.

For details of Sailing Tickets and general arrangements—see separate folder, to be obtained at Stations and Agencies.

▲ The summer 1962 timetable for 'The Ulster Express'.

---

and by the outbreak of the Second World War had been considerably accelerated. The name was dropped for the duration of the war but reinstated in 1949, by which time 'Princess Royal' Pacifics were sharing duties with the 'Royal Scots'.

By the summer of 1962 steam haulage had been replaced by English Electric Type 4s; the down train was departing from Euston at 5.40pm (Monday to Thursday, 5.45pm on Friday) and after stopping at Crewe arrived at Heysham at 11.05pm (11.12pm on Fridays) to connect with the overnight steamer to Donegal Quay in Belfast. On Saturdays the train left Euston at 6.40pm and after calling at Crewe and Preston it rrived at Heysham at midnight. There was also much slower service on Sunday nights. The p train left Heysham at 6.55am seven days week with an arrival at Euston at 11.50am 1pm on Sundays). Both the up and down ervices conveyed restaurant and buffet cars.

Following electrification of the West Coast Main Line, 'The Ulster Express' continued to operate until the Heysham to Belfast steamer ervice was withdrawn in 1975. The Heysham branch was closed on 4 October 1975 but eopened in 1987 to connect with sailings to nd from the Isle of Man.

Prior to hauling the down 'The Ulster Express' rom Euston, 'Royal Scot' Class 4-6-0 No. 46147 'The Northamptonshire Regiment' is seen here under the oaling tower at its home shed of Camden, circa 1957. he loco was built by the North British Locomotive Company in 1927 and withdrawn from Willesden shed n December 1962.

▼ 'The Ulster Express' was photographed at two different locations north of London on 5 July 1960. The picture on the left was taken at Watford Junction while that on the right is at Bushey Troughs where there appear to be a few 'Health & Safety' issues! The train engine is maroon-liveried 'Princess Royal' 4-6-2 No. 46207 'Princess Arthur of Connaught', which was built at Crewe in 1935 and withdrawn from Willesden shed in November 1961.

THE WAVERLEY

LONDON (ST PANCRAS) TO EDINBURGH (WAVERLEY)

Opening throughout in 1862, the North British Railway's Waverley Route between Edinburgh and Carlisle only came into its own as a third Anglo-Scottish route after the Midland Railway's Settle & Carlisle line had opened fourteen years later. The opening of the latter enabled through running of trains between London (St Pancras)

▲ Carlisle Kingmoor's unkempt 'Jubilee' Class 4-6-0 No. 45730 'Ocean' prepares to leave Leeds City station with the down 'The Waverley' on 28 May 1960. The loco was built at Crewe in 1936 and was withdrawn from Warrington (Dallam) shed in October 1963.

and Scotland – trains to Glasgow (St Enoch) travelled via the Glasgow & South Western Railway's line through Dumfries and Kilmarnock (see 'The Thames-Clyde Express'). Prior to the First World War the Midland Railway and the North British Railway were operating overnight sleeper trains via the Waverley Route with through coaches between St Pancras and Aberdeen, Perth, Inverness and Fort William.

Following the Big Four Grouping of 1923, the newly formed London & North Eastern Railway and London Midland & Scottish Railway gave the name 'The Thames-Forth Express' to a daytime restaurant train running between Edinburgh and St Pancras. The train

The Waverley

Restaurant Car Express

LONDON ST PANCRAS and EDINBURGH WAVERLEY

WEEKDAYS

	Mons. to Fris. am	Sats. am		Mons. to Fris. am	Sats. am
London St Pancras ......dep	9*10	9*10	Edinburgh Waverley ......dep	10* 5	10* 5
Nottingham Midland	11 21	11 29	Galashiels	11* 1	11* 1
	pm	pm	Melrose	11* 8	11* 8
Chesterfield Midland	12 9	12 17	St. Boswells	11*19	11*19
Sheffield Midland	12 33	12 42	Hawick	11*37	11*37
Leeds City	1 47	1 56		pm	pm
Skipton	2 24	2 34	Newcastleton	12 15	12 15
Hellifield	2 40	2 51	Carlisle	12 58	12 58
Settle......................	2 48	3 1	Appleby West	1 37	1 42
Appleby West	3 41	3 55	Settle......................	2 24	2 35
Carlisle ....arr	4 14	4 29	Hellifield ....arr	2 33	2 43
Newcastleton	4 56	5 13	Skipton	2 48	2 57
Hawick	5 30	5 47	Leeds City	3 25	3 34
St. Boswells	5 49	6 8	Rotherham Masborough	4 32	4 45
Melrose	5 58	6 18	Sheffield Midland	4 43	4 56
Galashiels	6 4	6 24	Chesterfield Midland	5 11	5 23
Edinburgh Waverley	6 55	7 17	Nottingham Midland	5 58	6 10
			London St. Pancras	8 10	8 30

*—Seats may be reserved in advance on payment of a fee of 2s. 0d. per seat.

◄ The summer 1962 timetable for 'The Waverley'.

was discontinued during the Second World War but was reinstated minus its name in 1945. The year 1957 saw an acceleration of this service which was renamed as 'The Waverley'. Haulage between London and Leeds (where there was an engine change) and Leeds and Carlisle was usually provided by a 'Jubilee' or 'Royal Scot' 4-6-0, and between Carlisle and Edinburgh by an 'A3' Pacific. The latter locos also put in an appearance on the Settle & Carlisle section for a few years before 'Peak' diesels took over in the early 1960s – by then the train had been reduced to a summer-only working.

The summer 1962 timetable shows the down train leaving St Pancras at 9.10am (Monday to Saturday) and arriving at Edinburgh at 6.55pm (7.17pm on Saturdays). The up train left Edinburgh at 10.05am (Monday to Saturday) and arrived at St Pancras at 8.10pm (8.30pm on Saturdays). With 14 intermediate stops for the down train and 15 for the up train this was hardly an express and could not compete with the much faster journey times on the West Coast and East Coast Main Lines. With dwindling patronage and the closure of the Waverley route imminent, the train was withdrawn in 1968. The Waverley Route closed on 6 January 1969.

◄ 'A3' Class 4-6-2 No. 60068 'Sir Visto' calls at Carlisle Citadel with the down 'The Waverley' in June 1961. Built as a Gresley 'A1' by the North British Locomotive Company in 1924, this loco was rebuilt as an 'A3' in 1948 and withdrawn from Carlisle Canal shed in August 1962.

THE WELSHMAN

LONDON (EUSTON) TO LLANDUDNO/PORTMADOC/PWLLHELI

Introduced by the London Midland & Scottish Railway in 1927, 'The Welshman' was a summer-only restaurant car express that linked London with the seaside resorts of North Wales. Suspended during the Second World War it reappeared again in 1950 with through coaches to and from Llandudno, Portmadoc and Pwllheli. The summer 1962 timetable shows the Monday to Friday down service leaving Euston at 11.20am and, after calling at Rugby and Crewe, arriving in Chester at 3.26pm where the train was divided. The Llandudno portion called at resorts along the North Wales coast before arriving at its destination at 5.03pm. The second portion continued non-stop to Penmaenmawr, and then called at Llanfairfechan and Bangor where engines were changed – a Fairburn 2-6-4 tank from Bangor shed taking over for the rest of the journey. From Bangor the train headed south to Caernarvon and then along the single track line to Afonwen on the Cambrian Coast line where the Pwllheli coaches were detached. Portmadoc was reached at 6.33pm. The up train left Portmadoc at 11am (Monday to Friday) and Llandudno at 1.05pm, reaching Euston at 6.35pm – some journey! On Saturdays the Llandudno portion ran as a separate buffet car train in both directions.

The Welshman

Through Restaurant Car Express

between

LONDON

and

NORTH WALES

WEEKDAYS ONLY

	am 11 20 pm 1 14 3 0 3 26 3 35	RC & RB London to Bangor (Mon–Fri, 2nd July to 31st August)	RC & RB London to Bangor (Saturdays only)	am 11 10 pm 1 2	RC & RB London to Chester (Saturdays only)	am 11 15 pm 1 9 3 22 3 30
London Euston .... dep	11 20			11 10		11 15
Rugby Midland .... „	1 14			1 2		1 9
Crewe .... „	3 0					
Chester General arr	3 26					3 22
Chester General dep	3 35	3 40				3 30
Prestatyn ...... arr		4 10				4 1
Rhyl .... „		4 17				4 8
Abergele & Pensarn „		4 28				4 20
Colwyn Bay ...... „		4 41				4 33
Llandudno Junction „		4 50				4 42
Deganwy .... arr		4 58				4 51
Llandudno ...... „		5 3				4 56
Penmaenmawr .... arr		4 32	4 32			
Llanfairfechan .... „		4 41	4 41			
Bangor .... „		4 52	4 52			
Caernarvon ...... „		5 14	5 14			
Groeslon .... „		5 33	5 33			
Penygroes .... „		5 42	5 42			
Brynkir .... „		5 54	5 54			
Chwilog .... „		6 5	6 5			
Afonwen .... „		6 9	6 9			
Pwllheli .... arr		6 26	6 26			
Criccieth .... arr		6 25	6 25			
Portmadoc .... „		6 33	6 33			

	am 11 0 11 9 11 0	RC and RB Bangor to London	am 10 0 10 9 10 0	RC and RB Bangor to London (Saturdays only)	MB Llandudno to London
Portmadoc .... dep	11 0		10 0		
Criccieth .... „	11 9		10 9		
Pwllheli .... dep	11 0		10 0		
Afonwen .... dep	11 27		10 25		
Chwilog .... „	11 31		10 29		
Brynkir .... „	11 44		10 42		
Penygroes ...... „	11 55		10 53		
Groeslon .... „	12 0		10 58		
			pm		
Caernarvon ...... „	12 15				
Menai Bridge .... „	12 31		11 30		
Bangor .... „	12 50		11 45		
Llanfairfechan .... „	1 1		11 57		pm
Penmaenmawr .... „	1 8		12 5		
Llandudno ...... dep				1 5	12 20
Deganwy .... „				1 10	12 25
Llandudno Junction dep	1 28				12 35
Colwyn Bay ...... „	1 36			12 40	12 46
Rhyl .... „	1 52				1 5
Prestatyn .... „	1 59			12 40	
Chester General .... „	2 40			1‡15	1‡50
Crewe .... arr	3 12				
Stafford .... „	3 44				
Nuneaton Trent Valley „	4 24				
Rugby .... „	4 46				
Bletchley .... „	5 25				
London Euston .... „	6 35			5 5	5 34

Through Carriages between London and Llandudno, Bangor, Pwllheli, Portmadoc.

‡—Stops only to take up passengers
MB—Miniature Buffet Car
RB—Buffet Car
RC—Restaurant Car

Seats on these trains may be reserved in advance for passengers travelling from London, Portmadoc, Criccieth, Pwllheli and Llandudno on payment of a fee of 2s. 0d. per seat.

▶ The summer 1962 timetable for 'The Welshman'.

It is 5.15pm and Bangor shed's Fairburn 2-6-4T No. 42075 has just arrived at Caernarvon with the Portmadoc/Pwllheli portions of the own 'The Welshman' in July 1963. Built by BR at Brighton in 1950, this versatile locomotive was withdrawn from Bangor shed in May 1965.

THE WEST RIDING

LONDON (KING'S CROSS) TO LEEDS (CENTRAL)/BRADFORD (EXCHANGE)

Introduced by British Railways in 1949, 'The West Riding' was the successor to the London & North Eastern Railway's pre-war streamlined high-speed 'The West Riding Limited' (1937–39) which was suspended, never to return, on the outbreak of the Second World War. Some of the luxurious coaches from the pre-war train were incorporated in this new restaurant car service which had Pacific haulage between King's Cross and Leeds. Between Leeds and Bradford the 'express' was ignominiously hauled by two ex-LNER 'N2' 0-6-2 tank engines in its early years! By the autumn of 1960 the routine had changed with the down train leaving King's Cross at 7.45am and after calling at Hitchin, Retford, Doncaster and Wakefield (where the Bradford portion was detached for its journey via Morley Top) it arrived at Leeds at 11.38am. The up train left Leeds at 7.30am (Bradford 7.05am) and arrived in King's Cross at 11.15am. Brand new 'Deltic' diesels took over a year later but the train lost its name in 1967.

▲ The BR leaflet, route map and timetable for the inaugural 'The West Riding', 23 May 1948.

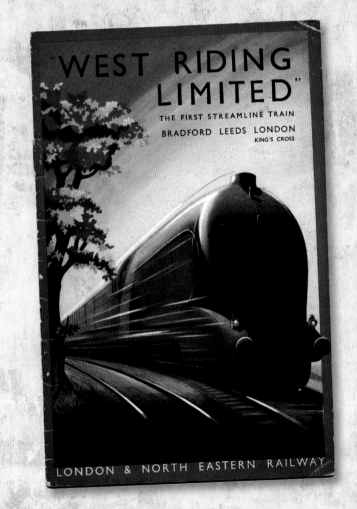

▲ Dated 27 September 1937, the stylish leaflet, timetable and point-to-point speeds for the newly inaugurated 'West Riding Limited'.

THE WEST RIDING
LONDON (King's Cross), LEEDS (Central)
and
BRADFORD (Exchange)

WEEKDAYS

		am				am
London (King's Cross) .. .. ..dep		7 45	Leeds (Central).. .. ..dep		"	7 30
Hitchin .. .. "		8 25	Bradford (Exchange)		"	7 5
Retford .. .. "		10 16	Morley Top		"	7 27
Doncaster .. ..arr		10 39	Wakefield (Westgate)		"	7 53
Wakefield (Westgate) .. .. .. "		11 9	Doncaster		"	8 26
Bradford (Exchange) .. .. .. "		11 56	London (King's Cross) .. .. ..arr			11 15
Leeds (Central) .. .. "		11 38				

Restaurant Cars for Table d'Hote meals

Seats are reservable in advance for passengers travelling from London (King's Cross), Hitchin (except for journeys to Bradford (Exchange)), Leeds (Central) and Bradford (Exchange) on payment of a fee of 2s. 0d. per seat.

◄ The winter 1960/61 timetable for 'The West Riding'.

▼ The down 'The West Riding' passes Copley Hill, Leeds, nearly at the end of its journey from King's Cross behind an as yet unnamed 'Deltic' (Class 55) diesel D9006 on 12 April 1962. Built at the English Electric's Vulcan Foundry, the loco entered service on 29 June 1961 and received the name 'The Fife & Forfar Yeomanry' at Cupar in 1964. It was withdrawn in February 1981.

THE WHITE ROSE

LONDON (KING'S CROSS) TO LEEDS (CENTRAL)/BRADFORD (EXCHANGE)

Introduced by British Railways on 23 May 1949, 'The White Rose' was the post-war successor to an unnamed express service that had operated between the West Riding and London since the early twentieth century. The new train conveyed through carriages to and from Bradford and was in the capable hands of 'A4' or 'A1' Pacifics between Leeds and London until 'Deltic' diesels appeared at the end of 1961. The winter 1960/61 timetable shows the down train leaving King's Cross at 9.20am and after calling at Doncaster and Wakefield (where the Bradford portion was detached) arriving in Leeds (Central) at 1.16pm. The up train left Leeds at 3.02pm and after calling at Wakefield and Doncaster arrived at King's Cross at 7.32pm. The up Saturday service had more stops and was 26 minutes slower.

▼ The winter 1960/61 timetable for 'The White Rose'.

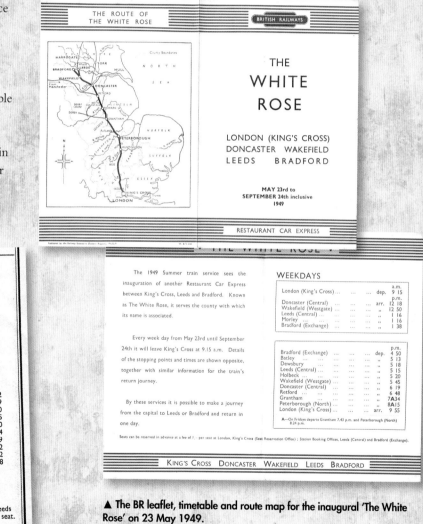

THE WHITE ROSE
LONDON (King's Cross), LEEDS (Central)
and
BRADFORD (Exchange)

WEEKDAYS

			E pm	S pm
London (King's Cross) ... ...dep	9 20 am	Leeds (Central) ... ...dep	3 32	3 32
	pm	Bradford (Exchange) ... ,,	3 12	
Doncaster ... ...arr	12 15	Morley Top ... ... ,,		3 30
Wakefield (Westgate) ... ... ,,	12 47	Wakefield (Westgate) ... ,,	3 55	3 55
Morley Top ... ... ,,	1S 16	Doncaster ... ... ,,	4 30	4 30
Bradford (Exchange) ... ... ,,	1A 35	Retford ... ... ,,		4 54
Leeds (Central) ... ... ,,	1 16	Newark (North Gate) ... ,,		5 19
		Grantham ... ... ,,		5 42
		Peterborough (North) ... ,,		6 22
		London (King's Cross) ...arr	7 32	7 58

A On Saturdays arrives Bradford 1 41 p.m.
E Except Saturdays.   **S** Saturdays only.
Restaurant Cars for Table d'Hote meals
Seats are reservable in advance for passengers travelling from London (King's Cross), Leeds (Central), Bradford (Exchange) and Wakefield (Westgate) on payment of a fee of 2s. 0d. per seat.

THE ROUTE OF
THE WHITE ROSE

BRITISH RAILWAYS

THE
WHITE
ROSE

LONDON (KING'S CROSS)
DONCASTER WAKEFIELD
LEEDS   BRADFORD

MAY 23rd to
SEPTEMBER 24th inclusive
1949

RESTAURANT CAR EXPRESS

The 1949 Summer train service sees the inauguration of another Restaurant Car Express between King's Cross, Leeds and Bradford. Known as The White Rose, it serves the county with which its name is associated.

Every week day from May 23rd until September 24th it will leave King's Cross at 9.15 a.m. Details of the stopping points and times are shown opposite, together with similar information for the train's return journey.

By these services it is possible to make a journey from the capital to Leeds or Bradford and return in one day.

Seats can be reserved in advance at a fee of 1/- per seat at London, King's Cross (Seat Reservation Office); Station Booking Offices, Leeds (Central) and Bradford (Exchange).

WEEKDAYS

		a.m.
London (King's Cross) ... ... dep		9 15
Doncaster (Central) ... ... arr		12 18
Wakefield (Westgate) ... ... ,,		12 50
Leeds (Central) ... ... ,,		1 16
Morley ... ... ,,		1 16
Bradford (Exchange) ... ... ,,		1 38

		p.m.
Bradford (Exchange) ... ... dep		4 50
Batley ... ... ,,		5 13
Dewsbury ... ... ,,		5 18
Leeds (Central) ... ... ,,		5 15
Holbeck ... ... ,,		5 20
Wakefield (Westgate) ... ... ,,		5 45
Doncaster (Central) ... ... ,,		6 19
Retford ... ... ,,		6 48
Grantham ... ... ,,		7A34
Peterborough (North) ... ... ,,		8A15
London (King's Cross) ... ... arr		9 55

A—On Fridays departs Grantham 7.43 p.m. and Peterborough (North) 8.24 p.m.

KING'S CROSS DONCASTER WAKEFIELD LEEDS BRADFORD

▲ The BR leaflet, timetable and route map for the inaugural 'The White Rose' on 23 May 1949.

Gradually replacing steam from the autumn of 1961, the new 'Deltics' at the front of the train soon brought a rapid acceleration to its schedule. However when 'The Queen of Scots' all-Pullman' train was withdrawn in 1964 the coaches from that train were transferred to 'The White Rose' service, which was then extended to run to and from Harrogate. The train was withdrawn in 1967.

▲ Doncaster shed's 'A3' Class 4-6-2 No. 60046 'Diamond Jubilee' heads out of Leeds with the up 'The White Rose' in the early 1950s. Built at Doncaster in 1934, this loco was withdrawn from Grantham shed in June 1963.

◄ All polished up at King's Cross shed and ready to haul the down 'The White Rose' in March 1958 – 'A1' Class 4-6-2 No. 60122 'Curlew' is flanked on the left by 'V2' Class 2-6-2 No. 60983 and on the right by fellow classmate No. 60139 'Sea Eagle'. 'Curlew' was built by BR at Doncaster in 1948 and withdrawn from Doncaster shed in December 1962.

THE YORKSHIRE PULLMAN

LONDON (KING'S CROSS) TO HULLLEEDSBRADFORDHARROGATE

Running between King's Cross and Leeds, with portions for Bradford, Halifax, Harrogate and Newcastle, the 'West Riding Pullman' was introduced by the London & North Eastern Railway in 1927 and by 1935 the train was also conveying through Pullman coaches to and from Hull. In that year the train was renamed 'The Yorkshire Pullman' although the Newcastle portion no longer ran north of Harrogate. Timings were altered following the introduction of the streamlined 'West Riding Limited' in 1937 (see 'The West Riding') and the train continued to run until the outbreak of the Second World War.

Reinstated in 1946, the heavy eleven-coach express with portions to and from Bradford and Hull was usually hauled between King's Cross and Leeds by an 'A3' Pacific until the new Peppercorn 'A1' Pacifics entered service in 1948-49. By the winter of 1960/61, less than twelve months

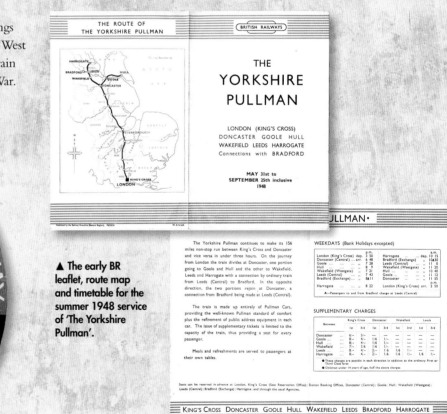

▲ The early BR leaflet, route map and timetable for the summer 1948 service of 'The Yorkshire Pullman'.

◄ The LNER's stylish luggage label for the pre-war 'The Yorkshire Pullman'.

...efore the arrival of 'Deltic' diesels, the ...team-hauled up train was leaving Harrogate ...t 10.07am and, after collecting the Bradford ...ortion at Leeds and the Hull portion at ...Doncaster, arrived at King's Cross at 2.45pm. ...The down train left King's Cross at 5.20pm ...nd arrived at Harrogate at 10.02pm.

The arrival of the 'Deltics' and new ...Metropolitan-Cammell Pullman cars in the ...utumn of 1961 saw a rapid acceleration ...o the down train, with 38 minutes being ...lashed off the King's Cross-Leeds schedule. ...The up train saw a similar acceleration a year ...ater. The Hull portion became ...he separate 'Hull Pullman' in ...967 and consequently the ...top at Doncaster was omitted, ...esulting in the down train taking ...only 181 minutes between King's ...Cross and Leeds. The train was ...withdrawn in 1978.

◄ The summer 1961 timetable for 'The Yorkshire Pullman'.

THE YORKSHIRE PULLMAN
(LIMITED TRAIN)

WEEKDAYS
(Will not run on Monday 7th August)

		SX pm	SO pm				SX am	SO am
LONDON (King's Cross)	.. dep	5 20	5 8	HARROGATE	.. dep		10 7	10 37
DONCASTER	.. arr	8 15	8 3	BRADFORD (Exchange)	.. ,,		10 15	10 47
Goole	.. ,,	8 49	8 37	LEEDS (Central) ..	.. ,,		10 45	11 17
Brough	.. ,,	9 9	8 57	WAKEFIELD (Westgate)	.. ,,		11 5	11 37
HULL	.. ,,	9 27	9 15	HULL	.. ,,		10 33	11 0
WAKEFIELD (Westgate)	.. ,,	8 47	8 37	Goole	.. ,,		11 3	11 30
LEEDS (Central) ..	.. ,,	9 13	9 5				pm	pm
BRADFORD (Exchange)	.. ,,	9 39	9 31	DONCASTER	.. ,,		11 45	12 17
HARROGATE	.. ,,	9 53	9 45	LONDON (King's Cross)	.. arr		2 41	3 22

SO—Saturdays only.   SX—Saturdays excepted.

MEALS AND REFRESHMENTS SERVED AT EVERY SEAT

Dig those cars man! World famous ...resley 'A3' 4-6-2 No. 60103 'Flying ...cotsman' heads the down 'The ...orkshire Pullman' through Brookmans ...ark in July 1959. Built at Doncaster ...s an 'A1' Class loco in 1923, this ...elebrity loco was rebuilt as an 'A3' ...n 1947, withdrawn from King's Cross ...hed in January 1963 and, after a ...hequered life in private hands, has ...ince been preserved as part of the ...lational Collection.

ZZZZZZ...

SLEEPING ALONG THE LINE

The first sleeping car in Britain was introduced by the North British Railway on 2 April 1873 between London King's Cross and Glasgow Queen Street. Soon other companies were following suit by using Pullman cars with convertible seating. However, all sleeping arrangements on trains were communal until the Great Western Railway introduced a sleeping car with double berth cabins, similar to those still used today, in 1890.

By the turn of the twentieth century sleeping car trains were running from London to Scotland, the West Country, North Wales and Northern England. These services remained relatively intact until the 1960s, by which time British Rail was running around 40 trains on most nights.

The London Midland Region summer timetable for 1962 shows the following destinations served by sleeping car trains from London:

◄ Running very late and hauled by Class 57 diesel No. 57602, the 'Night Riviera' from Paddington to Penzance passes along the sea wall at Dawlish in the early hours of 3 February 2007. This is the sole remaining sleeping car service in the south of England.

▲ The Inverness portion of the down 'Highland Caledonian Sleeper' is seen here at Moy behind EWS Class 67 diesel No. 67001 on 10 May 2006.

Barrow-in-Furness, Carlisle, Corkickle, Edinburgh Waverley, Galashiels, Glasgow Central, Glasgow St Enoch, Holyhead, Inverness, Leeds City, Liverpool Lime Street, Manchester Piccadilly, Motherwell, Oban, Perth, Preston and Stranraer Harbour. In addition there were services between Birmingham and Glasgow, Newcastle and Bristol. Edinburgh Princes Street and Birmingham, Glasgow and Liverpool, Glasgow and Manchester, Manchester and Plymouth. The only named sleeper trains of this period were 'The Royal Highlander' between Euston and Inverness, 'The Northern Irishman' between Euston and Stranraer, and 'The Irish Mail' between Euston and Holyhead.

The 1960/61 winter timetable for the Eastern, North Eastern and Scottish Regions shows the following destinations served from London: Aberdeen, Arbroath, Dundee, Edinburgh Waverley, Fort William, Montrose and Newcastle. The only named sleeper trains of this period were 'The Tynesider' between King's Cross and Newcastle, 'The Aberdonian' between King's Cross and Aberdeen, and 'The Night Scotsman' between King's Cross and Edinburgh.

Apart from the cross-Channel services to Paris and Brussels on 'The Night Ferry' there were no sleeping car trains on the Southern Region. The Western Region ran services from Paddington to Birkenhead Woodside, Carmarthen, Penzance, Plymouth and between Plymouth and Manchester. None of these were named trains.

With the advent of cheaper domestic air travel and high-speed motorways BR's network of sleeping car trains has shrunk considerably since the heady days of the 1960s. Now only two routes remain in operation, the 'Caledonian Sleeper' and the 'Night Riviera', whose futures have recently been secured. Operating six nights each week, these trains are among the last locomotive-hauled passenger trains in the UK.

The 'Caledonian Sleeper' is effectively two trains. The Lowland Caledonian Sleeper carries two portions between London Euston and Glasgow/Edinburgh. The Highland Caledonian Sleeper carries three portions between Euston and Aberdeen/Inverness/Fort William. The 'Night Riviera' operates between London Paddington and Penzance.

Note: Page numbers in **bold** refer to captions.

PICTURE CREDITS

t = top; b = bottom; r = right; l = left; m = middle

The publisher has endeavoured to contact all contributors of pictures for permission to reproduce. If there are any errors or omissions please notify the publisher in writing.

All images and ephemera are from the author's private collection apart from the following:

John Ashman: 27br; 29b; 37br; 38bl; 51bl; 95br; 143tr; 159tl; 173tr

Ben Ashworth: 51tm

I S Carr: 128tr

Henry Casserley: 57br; 58b

C R L Coles: 70br

Colour-Rail: 6tr (T B Owen); 8bl (T B Owen); 12l (A Gray); 14br; 15bl (Michael Mensing); 16br; 17bl (A E R Cope); 23b; 24tr; 24bm; 25br; 26br (P M Alexander); 31br (K C H Fairey); 33tl (P H Wells); 33tr (Bruce Nathan); 34bl (E Oldham); 35b (K Oldham); 37tl (P S); 39tl (Malcolm Thompson); 40bl (T B Owen); 43br (C R Gordon Stuart); 45b; 49t (T B Owen); 60bl (R H N Hardy); 60br (J Harrison); 61br; 62br (J G Wallace); 63tl (P M Alexander); 63br (T B Owen); 65br (G W Powell); 66br (E Alger); 69br (J T Inglis); 71m (J G Dewing); 73tr; 75; 86bl; 87bl (A E R Cope); 88bl (J B McCann); 89b (D Preston); 91tr (C J B Sanderson); 93b; 97br (The Historical Model Railway Society); 100bl; 103tr (Tony Cooke); 103br (D C Ovenden); 106bl (T B Owen); 107bl; 110br; 112bl (B J Swain); 117tr (M J Reade); 120tr; 121bl (R Shenton); 123tr (T B Owen); 124b (C J B Sanderson); 126bl (M Covey-Crump); 129br (P J Hughes); 131br (G D King); 132br (J Aylard); 133bl (W Potter); 134bl (J B Snell); 136br; 137tr (A Drake); 141tl (D Preston); 143tl (T B Owen); 143br (T B Owen); 144br (Alan Chandler MBE); 145tr; 149tl (P J Hughes); 150bl (A E R Cope); 151br (M J Reade); 153b (N F Ingram); 159br (P M Alexander); 163; 165br (A C Sterndale); 170b; 171br; 173bl; 173br (T B Owen); 175b (J M Chamney); 177 (Tony Cooke); 181bl (Bruce Chapman Collection); 183br (T B Owen); 184bl (Roger Siviter); 185t (Nigel Birkin)

Stanley Creer: 152br

Mike Esau: 11tr; 12bl; 19tl; 21tr; 25tr; 25bl; 41br; 69tl; 83br; 84bl; 84br; 85bl; 98br; 161bl

Kenneth Field: 81tr; 124t; 131tl; 158bl; 166bl

J A Fleming: 120br; 130br

John Gilks: 13b

G F Heiron: 8br; 27br; 112tr

R W Hinton: 105tr; 110tl; 128bl

Colin Hogg: 20; 114; 167tr

Alan Jarvis: 139t

Locomotive & General Railway Publishing: 48br

Milepost 92½: 42br; 44br; 76b; 99bl; 127bl; 165tr

Gavin Morrison: 18bl; 21bl; 31tr; 33br; 41tl; 51tl; 68br; 77bl; 80br; 81bl; 91br; 92b; 101t; 104b; 116t; 125br; 136tr; 147br; 148b; 160tr; 161tr; 167bl; 171tl; 174tr; 179b

J Scrace: 123br

T E Williams: 115br; 169br

A DAVID & CHARLES BOOK

© F&W Media International, Ltd 2013

David & Charles is an imprint of F&W Media International, Ltd
Brunel House, Forde Close, Newton
Abbot, TQ12 4PU, UK

F&W Media International, Ltd is a subsidiary of
F+W Media, Inc
10151 Carver Road, Suite #200, Blue Ash, OH 45242, USA

First published in the UK in 2013

Text copyright © Julian Holland 2013
Photographs copyright © see page 191

A catalogue record for this book is
available from the British Library.

ISBN-13: 978-1-4463-0295-8
ISBN-10: 1-4463-0295-4

Printed in China by R.R. Donnelley for
F&W Media International,
Brunel House, Newton Abbot, Devon

Junior Acquisitions Editor Verity Graves-Morris
Art Editor Jodie Lystor
Production Manager Beverley Richardson

F+W Media publish high quality books on a wide range
of subjects.
For more great book titles visit:
www.fwmedia.co.uk